Study Guide

for

Introduction to Criminal Justice

Tenth Edition

Larry J. Siegel
University of Massachusetts, Lowell

Joseph J. Senna
Northeastern University

THOMSON
™
WADSWORTH

Australia • Canada • Mexico • Singapore • Spain • United Kingdom • United States

Printed in the United States of America
1 2 3 4 5 6 7   07 06 05 04

Printer: West Group

ISBN: 0-534-62950-4

For more information about our products,
contact us at:
Thomson Learning Academic Resource Center
1-800-423-0563

For permission to use material from this text,
contact us by:
Phone: 1-800-730-2214
Fax: 1-800-730-2215
Web: http://www.thomsonrights.com

Thomson Wadsworth
10 Davis Drive
Belmont, CA 94002-3098
USA

Asia
Thomson Learning
5 Shenton Way #01-01
UIC Building
Singapore 068808

Australia/New Zealand
Thomson Learning
102 Dodds Street
Southbank, Victoria 3006
Australia

Canada
Nelson
1120 Birchmount Road
Toronto, Ontario M1K 5G4
Canada

Europe/Middle East/South Africa
Thomson Learning
High Holborn House
50/51 Bedford Row
London WC1R 4LR
United Kingdom

Latin America
Thomson Learning
Seneca, 53
Colonia Polanco
11560 Mexico D.F.
Mexico

Spain/Portugal
Paraninfo
Calle/Magallanes, 25
28015 Madrid, Spain

TABLE OF CONTENTS

Student Introduction

This study guide was designed and written to introduce students to the field of criminal justice by helping them master the important concepts and principles presented in Senna and Siegel's *Introduction to Criminal Justice*, 10th edition, and to further stimulate their interest in defining the problems and solutions that confront America's criminal justice system. The following is a brief description of how you can make the best use of this study guide in assimilating the materials in the text and in preparing yourself for your examinations.

It is suggested that you follow several steps to achieve maximum benefits from this study guide. First, read the **Learning Objectives** to familiarize yourself with the key issues that will be addressed in the chapter. Second, review and study the **Key Terms and Concepts** to assist you in understanding the important terms and concepts as they appear in the chapter. Third, read the **Chapter Outline** and the **Chapter Summary** to obtain an overview of the chapter's contents. Fourth, carefully read the chapter itself, highlighting the significant points in the text.

The last step is to attempt to complete the **Fill-in-the-Blank**, **True/False**, and **Multiple Choice Questions** without using the text for reference. If you have problems completing some of the questions, you should review the text until you can complete most of the answers. To assist you in locating the correct responses, the textbook is annotated to indicate the sections from which the questions came. In addition, all questions are listed in sequential order with the material in the text. After you have answered all the questions, you can evaluate your accuracy by turning to the **Answer Key** at the end of the chapter. If you do not do as well on the sample questions as anticipated, you may wish to intensify your study of the textbook and conduct a further review of the study guide.

After you have studied the chapter material, you should complete the **Essay Questions** as though you were actually taking an examination. Although most examinations in introductory courses tend to be primarily multiple choice in nature, the essay questions in this section will help you assess your overall knowledge of the materials and increase your understanding of the major issues in each chapter. If you do take an examination that contains essay questions, this review should prepare you very well.

Good luck and enjoy the materials.

Chapter 1

Crime and Criminal Justice

Learning Objectives

1. Discuss the history of crime and violence in the United States.

2. Discuss the concept of criminal justice and how it has evolved since the 18th century.

3. Describe the role and history of the federal government's involvement in criminal justice.

4. Discuss the three main types of agencies of the criminal justice system.

5. Describe the formal criminal justice process. Identify each of the 15 steps in the process and the actions taken in each step.

6. Comprehend the role that the major criminal justice agencies play in each of the 15 steps of the formal criminal justice process.

7. Describe the operation of the informal criminal justice process.

8. Describe the four layers of the criminal justice wedding cake model and connections to the informal criminal justice process.

9. Describe the various perspectives of contemporary criminal justice.

10. Analyze how the various perspectives of criminal justice shape the policies of the war on drugs.

Keywords and Definitions

Criminal Justice System: The composite of the police, court, and corrections agencies that seek to prevent and respond to crime in society.

London Metropolitan Police: The first formal police agency, developed in 1829 by Sir Robert Peel to keep the peace and identify criminal suspects on the streets of England's capitol city.

Wickersham Commission: A national study group appointed by President Hoover, the National Commission of Law Observance and Enforcement analyzed the American justice systems and uncovered the complex rules and regulations that govern the system and exposed how difficult it was for justice personnel to keep track of its legal and administrative capability.

The Crime Commission: Refers to the President's Commission on Law Enforcement and the Administration of Justice, appointed by President Johnson in the tumultuous 1960s, created a comprehensive view of the criminal justice process and offered recommendations for its reform.

Law Enforcement Assistance Administration (LEAA): Started with a provision in the Safe Streets and Crime Control Act of 1968, this federal initiative provided hundreds of millions of dollars in aid to local and state justice agencies to fund crime control efforts. The program came to an end in 1982.

Social Control: Functions of the criminal justice system that seek to control or outlaw behaviors that are considered dangerous to society, includes formalized efforts of agencies and informal efforts of private entities.

Legislature: Branch of government that defines the law by determining what conduct is prohibited and establishes criminal penalties for those who violate the law.

Judiciary: Branch of government that interprets the existing law and determines whether it meets constitutional requirements. Also presides over the trial and appeals process for accused criminals.

Executive Branch: Branch of government that plans programs, appoints personnel and exercises administrative responsibility for criminal justice agencies.

Formal Criminal Justice Process: The 15-step process that takes an offender through a series of decision points beginning with initial contact with law enforcement officials and concluding with reentry into society.

Initial Contact: The first step in the formal criminal justice process, occurs the moment that a suspected law violator comes to the attention of law enforcement officials. This can include an officer observing a crime, receiving a report from a victim, or being directed to the situation by a private citizen or government official.

Arrest: The moment a person is taken into custody and consequently believes he or she has lost his or her liberty. An action used to restrain the accused until he/she can be held accountable via court proceedings.

Arrest Warrant: A court order that empowers any police officer to arrest a suspect and bring that named individual before the court.

Probable Cause: A legal standard that exists when a police officer believes there is sufficient evidence that a crime is being or has been committed and that the suspect is the person who committed it.

In-Presence Requirement: The requirement that a police officer must have witnessed a misdemeanor crime personally in order to make an arrest.

Custody: The moment after arrest is made. Once in custody, police may wish to a lawful search, interrogate or gather personal information from the accused.

Charging: Step in the formal criminal justice process in which the accused is turned over to the prosecutor who then formally alleges violation of specific criminal statutes.

Nolle Prosequi: A decision on the part of the prosecutor to dismiss a case and take no further action against the accused.

Preliminary Hearing (Probable Cause Hearing): Alternative to the grand jury. The defendant and defense attorney appear before a magistrate or judge to dispute the prosecutor's charges. Suspect will stand trial if the magistrate or judge accepts the prosecutor's evidence as factual. It must be held within 48 hours of arrest.

Information: A charging document filed before a lower trial court at the preliminary hearing that details the merits of the state's case against the accused.

Grand Jury: A group of private citizens brought together to consider the merits of a case as presented by the prosecutor in order to determine if there is probable cause that the accused committed the crime with which he or she is charged.

Bill of Indictment: A document issued by the grand jury that specifies the charges on which the accused will stand trial if it considers evidence as sufficient to warrant a trial.

Arraignment: The court hearing in which the formal charges are read, the defendant is advised of his or her constitutional rights, the initial plea is entered, a trial date is set, and bail is considered.

Bail: A money bond levied to insure the return of a criminal defendant for trial while allowing the person pretrial freedom to prepare a defense to the charges.

Plea Bargaining: The exchange of a guilty plea for a reduction or dropping of some of the charges or for a more lenient sentence. Determined in consultation between the prosecutor and defense and approved by a judge or magistrate.

Trial/Adjudication: A court preceding held before a judge or jury to decide whether the prosecution evidence against the defendant is sufficient beyond a reasonable doubt to prove guilt.

Sentence/Disposition: Formal sanctions handed down by the court against a person convicted of a crime.

Appeal/Postconviction Remedies: Formal actions taken by a defendant who seeks to challenge some aspect of his or her guilty verdict.

Appellate Courts: Those courts in which defendants appeal when they believe they did not receive fair treatment or that their constitutional rights were violated.

Correctional Treatment: Postconviction programs or actions taken on the part of justice authorities to aid in the successful readjustment to society.

Release: Point in the formal criminal justice process when the convicted individual is determined to have paid his or her debt to society and is now free to resume their life in the community.

Postrelease: Period in which a person who has been recently released from a correctional facility is subject to programs that seek to reintegrate him or her back into free society.

Criminal Justice Assembly Line: Term used to describe the endless stream of cases that are subject to sequential decision points of the formal criminal justice process.

Criminal Justice Funnel: Term used to describe the screening out effect that occurs as cases are processed through the formal criminal justice process.

Courtroom Workgroup: Group made up of the prosecutor, defense attorney, judge, and other court personnel that cooperate to enhance the efficiency of the adjudication process through the use of plea bargains and other alternatives.

Wedding Cake Model of Justice: Samuel Walker's dramatic way of describing the informal criminal justice process by comparing it to a four-layer wedding cake.

Crime Control Perspective: A model of criminal justice that maintains that the proper role of the criminal justice system is to prevent crime through the judicious use of criminal sanctions.

Profiling: Practice on the part of law enforcement officers that seeks use behavioral or demographic markers to more efficiently identify persons who are thought to engage in improper behavior.

Rehabilitation Perspective: A model of criminal justice that sees crime as an expression of frustration against social inequality and seeks to use treatment approaches to help people who cannot manage for themselves.

Due Process Perspective: A model of justice that emphasizes individual rights and constitutional safeguards aimed at making the system run in an efficient and fair manner against those accused of crime.

Nonintervention Perspective: A model of justice that favors limited involvement on the part of formal agencies against criminal defendants.

Stigma: Enduring label that taints a person's identity or changes him or her in the eyes of others.

Decriminalization: The reduction of penalties and/or the legalization of specific criminal offenses.

Pretrial Diversion: Informal, community-based treatment programs used to minimize formal contact with the criminal justice system, specifically incarceration.

Widening the Net: Assertion that new laws and justice programs serve to unnecessarily stigmatize individuals and broaden the scope of criminal justice involvement in citizen's lives.

Justice Perspective: A model of criminal justice maintaining that all people should receive the same treatment under the law.

Truth-in-Sentencing Laws: Legislative mandates that specify the portion a incarceration sentence that must be satisfied before an individual is eligible for early release.

Restorative Justice Perspective: A model of justice asserting that the true purpose of the criminal justice system should be to promote a peaceful and just society through mutual aid and mediation and not punishment.

Source Control: Crime control policy initiative that seeks to cut off supplies of drugs by destroying crops and arresting members of drug cartels in drug-producing countries.

Border Control: Crime control policy initiative that uses border patrols and military personnel to interdict drug supplies as they enter a country.

Police Crackdowns: Crime control policy initiative that utilizes local, state, and federal law enforcement agencies to combat large-scale drug rings or the street-level drug deals.

Mandatory Minimum Sentence: Legislative mandate that restricts judicial discretion by specifying a minimum sentence that a judge must hand down to anyone convicted of a specific criminal charge.

Drug Abuse Resistance Education (DARE): Elementary school course designed to give students the skills for resisting peer pressure to experiment with tobacco, drugs, and alcohol.

Methadone Program: Drug treatment program in which controlled dispensing of a synthetic narcotic is substituted for heroin as a way of accomplishing abstinence.

Legalization: Noninterventionist initiative calling for the removal of all criminal penalties from a previously outlawed act.

Chapter Outline

I. Introduction
    A. Crime in America
        1. Pensacola abortion clinic shooting
        2. Taking the law into one's own hands
        3. Formal response criminals such as Paul Hill
    B. The case of the lovers lane bandit
        1. Solving "cold cases"
        2. The role of technology in contemporary crime fighting
        3. Determining what is fair and consistent justice
    C. Introduction to the criminal justice system
        1. Various roles the criminal justice system plays
        2. Employs more than 2 million people
        3. Costs more than $150 billion per year
        4. Organization of Chapter 1

II. Analyzing Criminal Justice Issues and Policies
    A. Is crime a recent development?
        1. Crime in the old west
        2. Crime in early American cities

3. Gangs of New York
B. Milestones in criminal justice
   1. Casare Beccaria, the Italian social philosopher
   2. London Metropolitan Police
   3. Chicago Crime Commission
   4. American Bar Foundation project
   5. President's Commission on Law Enforcement and Administration of Justice
   6. Safe Streets and Crime Control Act of 1968 - LEAA
C. The criminal justice system today
   1. Instrument of social control
   2. Three main components of the system-Law Enforcement, Courts, Corrections
   3. Three branches of government
      a. Legislature
         i. Defines criminal behavior and establishes criminal penalties
         ii. Passes laws governing criminal procedure
         iii. Provides funding for crime-control programs
      b. Judiciary
         i. Interprets existing law
         ii. Provides legal oversight on criminal justice practices
      c. Executive
         i. Plans justice programs
         ii. Appoints agency personnel
         iii. Exercises administrative responsibilities over agencies
D. Scope of the system
   1. Overall size
      a. 55,000 agencies
      b. $150 billion per year
   2. Capital costs
      a. $70,000 per cell to build a prison
      b. $22,000 per year to house an adult inmate
      c. $33,000 per year to house a juvenile resident
   3. Persons processed annually
      a. 2 million adult felony arrests
      b. 1.5 million juveniles processed
      c. 1 million adult felony convictions
   4. People under correctional supervision
      a. 6.5 million people under control of correctional system
         i. 2 million behind bars
         ii. 4.5 million on probation or parole
      b. Prison population has doubled since 1990

III. The Formal Criminal Justice Process
   A. Discretionary points of the criminal justice system that process the offender from initial contact through reentry into society
   B. There are 15 stages in the process wherein a criminal justice official must make a determination to pass the case on to the next stage or to discharge it at that point
   C. Discretion of the decision-makers determines whether to discharge or pass on a case
      1. Legal factors such as seriousness of charge, available evidence, and criminal history shape decision making
      2. Extra-legal factors such as race, gender, class & age may also shape decisions

D. The stages in the formal criminal justice process
   1. Initial contact
   2. Investigation
   3. Arrest
   4. Custody
   5. Charging
   6. Preliminary hearing/grand jury
   7. Arraignment
   8. Bail/detention
   9. Plea bargaining
   10. Trial/adjudication
   11. Sentencing/disposition
   12. Appeal/post conviction remedies
   13. Correctional treatment
   14. Release
   15. Post-release
E. Criminal justice assembly line
   1. Moving a never-ending stream of cases through the 15 stages of the system
   2. The system as a screening process -- the criminal justice funnel

IV. The Informal Justice System
   A. Factors beyond the stated formal processes that impact decision making
   B. The courtroom work group and its role in moving cases along quickly
   C. The "Wedding Cake" model of justice
      1. Samuel Walker's model to describe the informal justice process
      2. Four layers of the wedding cake
         a. Celebrated case layer
         b. Serious felony layer
         c. Less serious felony layer
         d. Misdemeanor layer

V. Perspectives on Justice
   A. Areas of debate in the field
      1. The meaning of the term "criminal justice"
      2. A lack of consensus on numerous specific topics
      3. Six dominant views have emerged
   B. Crime control perspective
      1. James Q. Wilson and "Thinking About Crime"
         a. Wicked people exist
         b. Criminal motivation
      2. Crime control as the central role of the justice system
         a. Apprehend, try, and punish known offenders
         b. Prevent future crimes through sanctions - deterrence
      3. Focus on the victims
         a. Focus of justice should be on the victim not the criminal
         b. Effective police protection, tough sentences, and more prisons
         c. Reduce technicalities and profile potential offenders
         d. Skeptical about potential for rehabilitation

C. Rehabilitation perspective
　　1. Justice system to treat and care for offenders who can not manage themselves
　　　　a. Help people improve life-style through conventional endeavors
　　　　b. Society must seek to combat larger social problems to reduce crime
　　2. Alternatives to crime
　　　　a. Provide people with legitimate employment and community ties
　　　　b. Punishment does not solve problem of blocked opportunities
D. Due process perspective
　　1. Criminal justice system should provide fair equitable treatment
　　　　a. Consequences of the adversary system of justice
　　　　b. A need for strict monitoring of discretion
　　　　c. Reduce the miscarriages of justice
　　2. Balancing the rights of the accused with the rights of the victim and society
　　　　a. Greatest concern must be for fair & equitable treatment of accused
　　　　b. Preserving democratic ideals takes precedent over punishing guilty
　　3. Due process law in review – drug testing in Pottawatomie County schools
E. Nonintervention perspective
　　1. Want to limit involvement of the criminal justice agencies with defendants
　　　　a. Long-term effects of agency involvement are harmful
　　　　b. Stigma and labeling processes impact one's behavior and psyche
　　2. Key non-interventionist concepts
　　　　a. Decriminalization
　　　　b. Legalization of victimless crimes
　　　　c. Deinstitutionalization of first-time offenders
　　　　d. Pretrial diversion to community-based treatment programs
　　　　e. Net widening effect
F. Justice perspective
　　1. All people should be treated fairly under the law
　　　　a. Seek to reduce discretion & unequal treatment in the justice system
　　　　b. Evaluate offenders on the basis of their current not past behavior
　　　　c. Sentences should be equitably administered & based on just deserts
　　2. Advocate sentencing reforms
　　　　a. Mandatory minimum sentences
　　　　b. Truth-in-sentencing laws
G. Restorative justice perspective
　　1. Purpose of criminal justice systems is to promote a peaceful and just society
　　　　a. Inspired by religious and philosophical teachings
　　　　b. Condemn violent punishing acts of the state
　　2. Principles of restoration
　　　　a. Community "ownership" of conflict (including crime)
　　　　b. Material and symbolic reparation for crime victims
　　　　c. Social reintegration of the offender
　　　　d. Mutual aid to replace coercive punishment
　　3. Policy initiatives
　　　　a. Mediatory role of police officers essential to community policing
　　　　b. Financial and community service restitution programs

VI. Perspectives in action: Controlling the drug trade
　A. Crime control approaches
　　1. Source control

        a.   Destroy overseas crops
        b.   Arrest drug cartel members
  2.   Border control
        a.   Interdict drug supplies as they enter the country
        b.   Increase the use of military personnel and equipment
  3.   Police crackdowns
        a.   Focus efforts on large-scale drug rings
            i.   Thwart gang involvement in drug dealing
            ii.   Still, huge profit margins encourage entrepreneurs
        b.   Problems of street-level enforcement of dealers and users
            i.   Makes drug use a hassle though street sweeps
            ii.   Clogs the courts and correctional facilities
           iii.   Drains police resources
           iv.   May result in a displacement effect

B.   Justice model
  1.   Enacting sentencing reforms
        a.   Advocates lobby for standardized punishment for drug offenders
        b.   Federal Anti-Drug Abuse Act 1988
        c.   Court backlogs and prison overcrowding can result
  2.   Use of mandatory minimum sentences and truth-in-sentencing laws

C.   Rehabilitation strategies
  1.   Drug prevention to reduce the demand of users
        a.   Reduce public's desire to use drugs
        b.   DARE program to stem youth desire to start using drugs
  2.   Offender treatment
        a.   Rehabilitate known users
            i.   Drug testing of arrestees and drug testing in the workplace
            ii.   Increase self-esteem and self-reliance among users
            ii.   Group therapy and Alcoholics Anonymous approach
           iv.   Residential programs and methadone
            v.   Psychological treatments
        b.   Little evidence of effectiveness

D.   Restorative justice strategies
  1.   Advocate integrative treatment of offenders
  2.   Drug courts and the immediate referral to multiphased outpatient treatment

E.   Non-intervention strategies
  1.   Legalization of drugs
        a.   Governmental control of price and distribution
        b.   Tax the sale of drugs and dealer income
        c.   Break drug cartels and reduce drug-related crime
  2.   Analyzing the prospects of legalization
        a.   Potential benefits
            i.   Racial disparities
            ii.   Environmental benefits
           iii.   Tax revenue
           iv.   Restore civil liberties
        b.   Potential harms
            i.   New networks of manufacturers and distributors
            ii.   Increase in drug users and drug use
           iii.   Health and social damage

     iv. Drug-related DUI fatalities
  F. Due process strategies
    1. Civil rights violations of the war on drugs
     a. Wrongful suspicion, arrest, and conviction
     b. Privacy violations of forced drug testing
    2. Racial outcomes of the war on drugs
     a. Racial disparities in sentencing
     b. Powered cocaine vs. crack cocaine sentencing disparities
  G. Perspectives in perspective
    1. Multiple perspectives have an impact on justice policy
    2. Crime control perspective has flourished lately
     a. Tougher laws
     b. Increased incarceration
     c. Use of the death penalty
    3. Reduced reliance on rehabilitation programs
    4. Due process for accused criminals remains intact
    5. No single perspective is right

Chapter Summary

The modern era of criminal justice study was ushered in during the late 1960's with the **Crime Commission** study of America's crime problem and the passage of the **Safe Streets and Crime Control Act** which funded the Law Enforcement Assistance Administration (LEAA). The term **Criminal Justice** refers to both a system and a process. As a **system**, it functions cooperatively among several primary agencies: police, courts, and corrections. As a **process**, criminal justice consists of a series discretionary decision point steps that the offender follows from the initial contact with the police through trial, sentencing, and appeal.

The term **criminal justice** refers to an area of knowledge devoted to controlling crime through the operation and administration of police, court, and correctional agencies. The **police** maintain order, enforce the laws, provide traffic and emergency services, and create a sense of community safety. The **courts** determine the responsibility of criminal defendants. However, the courts also seek truth, obtain justice, and most importantly maintain the integrity of the rule of law. **Correctional agencies** provide post-adjudication care, community supervision, and incarceration facilities for those convicted of crimes. The correctional system is also responsible for adult and juvenile parole.

Each branch of government is involved in the criminal justice system. The **legislature** defines what is prohibited by law and prescribes penalties as well as providing financial support for criminal justice programs. The **judiciary** is responsible for judicial review, ensuring that the law meets constitutional standards. The **executive branch** has the power of appointment of figures such as judges and heads of administrative agencies such as police chiefs. Executives also play a major leadership role in criminal justice matters and maintain both the power to develop programs and veto legislation.

The **formal criminal justice process** has several steps that must be followed. **Initial contact** as a result of police action leads to an **investigation** that will gather evidence to identify a suspect and support a legal arrest. Once an arrest is made, the individual is taken into **custody** for searching, processing, interrogation, etc. The case is then turned over to the prosecutor for **charging**, either by the filing of a complaint in a misdemeanor, or in the case of a felony, either by a **preliminary hearing** or by the **grand jury** issuing a **bill of indictment**. Once charged, the offender is brought before the judge for **arraignment** for the formal notification of charges, reading of constitutional rights, entering of a plea, setting a trial date, and the determination of **bail**. Without bail, the offender remains in **detention**. Often the prosecutor and the defense attorney will **plea bargain** where the offender receives a lenient sentence in exchange for a guilty plea. If this does not occur, the **trial** takes place and the verdict is determined. If found guilty, the offender will be **sentenced** to pay a fine, probation, incarceration, or in some cases, be given the death penalty. Of course the offender can **appeal**, if he or she believes his or her constitutional rights were violated or that there was no fair trial. With supervision under the correctional system, the offender may undergo **correctional treatment**. Ultimately, all offenders are **released** back into society. Some however, may be under continuing supervision during **post release**.

This informal justice process has been compared by Samuel Walker to a four-layer cake, known as the **"Wedding Cake"** Model of Justice. Cases in the first layer of the cake are usually **celebrated cases** receiving the full array of criminal justice procedures. In the second layer are the **serious felonies**: rapes, robberies and burglaries. Level three of the wedding cake consists of either **less serious felonies**, committed by young or first-time offenders, and/or involving people who knew each other or were otherwise related. Level three crimes typically results in a probationary sentence or intermediate sanction. The fourth layer of the cake is made up of the many types of **misdemeanors**, handled by lower criminal courts in assembly-line fashion. Few defendants insist on exercising their constitutional rights because the delay would cost them valuable time and money.

There are several perspectives or philosophies on the role of the criminal justice system in society and how it should function. The **crime control perspective** is a conservative philosophy that believes the proper role of the criminal justice system society is to prevent crime by the judicious use of criminal sanction. The **rehabilitation perspective** sees the criminal justice system as caring for and treating people who cannot manage themselves because they are the victims of social, economic, or other conditions beyond their control. Some of these are poor education, poor health care and broken down neighborhoods. The **due process perspective** falls in between the previous two and posits that regardless of its aims, the justice system must be made to run efficiently and fairly, and it must provide fair and equitable treatment to all those accused of crime. The **nonintervention perspective** argues that criminal justice agencies should limit their involvement with criminal defendants regardless of whether intervention is designed to punish or treat because such intervention produces undesirable long term effects. The **justice perspective** believes that all persons should receive the same treatment under the law, otherwise there will be a sense of unfairness about the system. Criminal justice agencies can achieve this goal only if they limit discretion and reduce unfair treatment. The **restorative justice perspective** sees the purpose of the criminal justice system as promoting a peaceful and just society, not the imposition of punishment. Therefore, resolution of conflict between the offender and the victim can take place only in the community when the offender appreciates the damage caused, makes amends, and becomes reintegrated into society.

Fill-in-the-Blank

1. _____ _____ was an 18th century Italian social philosopher who wrote the book "On Crime and Punishment" that argued against the use of torture and capital punishment and in favor deterrence principles.

2. The Safe Streets and Crime Control Act of 1968 provided federal funding for the _____ _____ _____ _____ which granted hundreds of millions of dollars annually in aid to local and state justice agencies from 1968 until 1982.

3. The three components of the criminal justice system in the United States are the _____, the _____, and _____ .

4. The three branches of the American system of government are the _____, the _____, and the _____ branches.

5. The _____ branch of government defines the law by determining what conduct is prohibited and establishes criminal penalties for those who violate the law.

6. The purpose of the investigation stage of justice is to gather sufficient _____ to identify a _____ and support a legal _____ .

7. An _____ occurs when a person is taken into custody and consequently believes he or she has lost his or her liberty.

8. The _____ _____ means an officer must personally witness a misdemeanor offense before the officer can arrest the offender.

9. Once a suspect is in _____, the police may wish to _____ the suspect for weapons, and _____ him or her to gain more information.

10. A preliminary hearing is sometimes referred to as a _____ _____ hearing.

11. _____ courts review such issues as whether evidence was used properly, if there was fair treatment, and if _____ rights were violated.

12. _____ is the final stage in the formal criminal justice process, wherein after termination of correctional treatment, the offender may be asked to spend some time in a community correctional facility to aid with his or her reintegration into society.

13. Many suspects are released before trial because of a procedural error, evidence problems, or other reasons that result in a dropped prosecution or _____ _____ .

14. The courtroom work group consists of the _____, _____, _____, and other court personnel.

15. The _____ _____ perspective on criminal justice endorses the use of restitution and mediation in place punishment as a means of combating crime.

16. The _____ _____ perspective agrees that the U.S. government should make a major effort to cut off the supply of drugs by destroying crops and arresting members of drug cartels in drug producing countries.

True/False Questions

T F 1.   The executive branch interprets the existing law and determines whether it meets constitutional requirements.

T F 2.   The justice system today consists of over 55,000 public agencies.

T F 3.   Though the crime rate has declined, we are now punishing criminals more harshly and forcing them to spend more of their sentence behind bars than ever before.

T F 4.   It is lawful for a police officer to make a misdemeanor arrest without first obtaining an arrest warrant.

T F 5.   Initial contact with the criminal justice system usually takes place as a result of action by the prosecutor or district attorney.

T F 6.   The arraignment stage in the formal criminal justice process comes after the preliminary hearing stage.

T F 7.   In a misdemeanor offense, the police officer must have witnessed the crime in order to arrest the suspect.

T F 8.   A preliminary hearing is held before a judge and jury.

T F 9.   An information is a charging document filed in a lower court, which then conducts an open hearing on the case.

T F 10. The defendant may appear at a preliminary hearing, but defense counsel cannot attend.

T F 11. Plea bargains can include bringing a case to a conclusion without a trial.

T F 12. All convicted felons are automatically eligible to have their cases heard by an appellate court.

T F 13. The court has primary jurisdiction over the sentencing/disposition stage of the formal criminal justice process.

T F 14. Today, most inmates serve the full term of their sentence.

T F 15.   Incarceration is a form of disposition.

T F 16.   Release is the final stage in the formal criminal justice process.

T F 17.   Many cases are settled in an informed pattern of cooperation between the major actors in the justice process.

T F 18.   Stigma and labeling are central concerns of advocates of the noninterventionist perspective on justice.

T F 19.   Level III crimes in Samuel Walker's "Wedding Cake" model of justice includes the serious felonies which have become all too routine in U.S. society.

T F 20.   The crime control perspective views the proper role of the justice system as preventing crime through the judicious use of criminal sanctions.

T F 21.   The rehabilitation perspective argues that the greatest concern of the justice system should be providing fair and equitable treatment to those accused of crime.

T F 22.   The justice perspective holds that there should be mandatory minimum sentences for drug crimes.

Multiple Choice Questions

1.   In 1931, President Herbert Hoover appointed the _____ commission to make a detailed analysis of the U.S. justice system.
    a.   Wickersham
    b.   Hoover
    c.   Walker
    d.   Chicago

2.   The branch of government that plans programs, appoints personnel, and exercises administrative responsibility for criminal justice agencies is the_____ branch.
    a.   executive
    b.   legislative
    c.   judicial
    d.   U.S. Department of Justice

3.   When an offender is sentenced by the court to a period of confinement, responsibility for custody and rehabilitation lies with the _____.
    a.   court
    b.   correction agency
    c.   district attorney
    d.   all of the above

4. The _____ was funded as a result of the safe Streets and Crime control Act of 1968.
   a. Chicago Crime Commission
   b. Alcoholics Annonymous
   c. Law Enforcement Assistance Administration
   d. Federal Anti-Drug Abuse Act

5. During the _____ stage, the police may conduct a line-up, take personal information from the suspect, or search the suspect's home and office.
   a. investigatory
   b. charging
   c. initial contact
   d. custody

6. The decision to _____ the suspect with a specific criminal act involves many factors including evidence sufficiency, crime seriousness, case pressure, and political issues and personal factors.
   a. arrest
   b. charge
   c. take into custody
   d. indict

7. The stage of the formal criminal justice process where formal charges are read, the defendant is informed of his or her rights, the defendant enters an initial plea and bail is considered is called the
   a. preliminary hearing.
   b. arraignment.
   c. trial.
   d. charging.

8. Roughly what percent of all criminal cases end in a plea bargain, instead of a trial?
   a. 25
   b. 50
   c. 75
   d. 90

9. Which of the following would be unlikely to happen at an arraignment?
   a. The defendant would be informed of his/her constitutional rights
   b. The prosecutors would demonstrate that a trial was warranted
   c. The formal charges would be read to the defendant
   d. Both a and c are correct

10. Most inmates do not serve the full term of their sentence, but are freed via an early-release mechanism, such as _____.
    a. parole
    b. pardon
    c. probation
    d. all of the above

11. According to Herbert Packer, each of the fifteen stages in the criminal justice process acts like a _____ through which cases flow.
    a. wedding cake
    b. step
    c. funnel
    d. sieve

12. The _____ perspective is popular among political conservatives because it focuses on the rights of the victim and seeks to punish the offender.
    a. restorative justice
    b. nonintervention
    c. crime control
    d. justice

13. The _____ perspective advocates that government programs can help reduce crime on both a macro (societal) and micro (individual) level.
    a. crime control
    b. rehabilitation
    c. due process
    d. justice

14. Increasing economic opportunities, family counseling, educational services, and crisis intervention are programs offered by the _____ perspective.
    a. rehabilitation
    b. justice
    c. nonintervention
    d. restorative justice

15. The _____ perspective argues that legal technicalities should not help the guilty go free.
    a. crime control
    b. rehabilitation
    c. due process
    d. justice

16. The perspective that falls between the extremes of the crime control and rehabilitation perspectives is the _____ perspective.
    a. restorative justice
    b. justice
    c. nonintervention
    d. due process

17. The perspective that has major concerns about an all-powerful state overwhelming a solitary individual accused of a crime is the _____ perspective.
    a. rehabilitation
    b. due process
    c. justice
    d. restorative justice

18. The perspective that is concerned with offenders suffering the harmful effects of stigma and labels is the _____ perspective.
    a. nonintervention
    b. rehabilitation
    c. justice
    d. restorative justice

19. Those who call for decriminalization and/or legalization of non-serious victimless crimes usually talk about removing penalties from
    a. possession of small amounts of marijuana.
    b. public drunkenness.
    c. vagrancy.
    d. all of the above.

20. The _____ perspective has fought the implementation of community notification laws which require convicted sex offenders to register with state law enforcement officials and allows the officials to make it publicly known when a registrant moves into the community.
    a. nonintervention
    b. due process
    c. justice
    d. restorative justice

21. The _____ perspective believes that all people should receive the same treatment under the law with no differentiation between criminal offenders.
    a. crime control
    b. due process
    c. justice
    d. restorative justice

22. Advocates of the _____ perspective have had considerable influence in molding the nation's sentencing policy and reducing discretion and guaranteeing that every offender convicted of a crime receives the same punishment.
    a. crime control
    b. due process
    c. justice
    d. restorative justice

23. The _____ perspective believes that the true purpose of the criminal justice system is to promoted a peaceful and just society.
    a. crime control
    b. due process
    c. justice
    d. restorative justice

24. According to the _____ perspective, resolution of the conflict between criminal and victim should take place in the community from which it originated and not in some far off prison.
    a. crime control
    b. due process
    c. justice
    d. restorative justice

Essay Questions

1. Briefly discuss the effect of the Law Enforcement Assistance Administration on the modern era of justice.

2. List and briefly discuss the functions of the major component parts of the criminal justice system.

3. Explain the role of the three branches of government in criminal justice.

4.   Describe the scope of the criminal justice system.

5.   Explain the formal criminal justice process.

6.   Describe what is meant by the criminal justice assembly line.

7. Describe Walker's "wedding cake" model, and give an example of a crime at each of the four levels and the expected disposition.

8. Explain the six major perspectives on justice.

9. Provide a drug control policy initiative for each of the six major perspectives on justice.

10. Provide an anti-terrorism policy initiative for each of the six major perspectives on justice.

CHAPTER 1 ANSWER KEY

FILL-IN THE BLANKS ANSWERS

1. Cesare Beccaria
2. Law Enforcement Assistance Administration (LEAA)
3. police, courts, corrections
4. legislature, judiciary, and executive
5. legislature
6. evidence, suspect, arrest
7. arrest
8. in-presence requirement
9. custody, search, interrogate
10. probable cause
11. appellate, constitutional
12. postrelease
13. nolle prosequi
14. prosecutor, defense attorney, judge
15. restorative justice
16. crime control

TRUE/FALSE ANSWERS

1.	F	12.	F
2.	T	13.	T
3.	T	14.	F
4.	T	15.	T
5.	F	16.	F
6.	F	17.	T
7.	T	18.	T
8.	F	19.	F
9.	T	20.	T
10.	F	21.	F
11.	T	22.	T

MULTIPLE CHOICE ANSWERS

1.	A	13.	B
2.	A	14.	A
3.	B	15.	C
4.	C	16.	D
5.	D	17.	B
6.	B	18.	A
7.	B	19.	D
8.	D	20.	A
9.	B	21	C
10	D	22.	C
11	A	23.	D
12.	C	24.	D

Chapter 2

The Nature and Extent of Crime

Learning Objectives

At the conclusion of this chapter, the student should have the ability to achieve the following learning objectives:

1.   Name the three major sources of crime data.

2.   Know the similarities and differences between the Uniform Crime Reports, National Crime Victimization Survey, and self-report data.

3.   Recognize the problems associated with the three major sources of crime data

4.   Describe the factors that explain the rise and fall of crime rates in America.

5.   Describe crime trends around the world

6.   Recognize the stable patterns in crime rates and offending in America

7.   Understand and describe the ecological patterns in crime

8.   Discuss the social, gender, age, and racial differences in crime rates.

9.   Argue the pro and con positions on gun control.

10. Appreciate the concept of chronic or career criminals.

11. Explain how chronic offending influences crime policy.

12. Provide a number of explanations for modern crime trends.

Keywords and Definitions

Official Records: Source of crime data gathered from the records of a variety of sources including schools, courts, police departments, social service centers, and correctional agencies.

Uniform Crime Report (UCR): The best known and most widely cited source of aggregate statistics compiled by the Federal Bureau of Investigation from information provided by over 17,000 police departments.

Part I Crimes (Index Crimes): Those crimes included in the UCR data collection effort. Criminal homicide, forcible rape, robbery, aggravated assault, burglary, larceny/theft, motor vehicle theft, and arson are included. Know offenses and arrests are reported.

Part II Crimes: All other crimes included in the UCR, except traffic violations. Arrest data only are reported.

Criminal Homicide: Part I crime category that includes all acts of murder and non-negligent manslaughter as well as manslaughter by negligence. Acts of manslaughter are excluded from the crime index.

Murder: The willful killing of another. It excludes negligent killings, attempts to kill, suicides, accidents, and justifiable homicides.

Manslaughter: Part I crime category that involves the killing of another through gross negligence. Traffic fatalities are excluded.

Forcible Rape: Part I crime category that involves the carnal knowledge of a female against her will.

Robbery: Part I crime category that involves the taking or attempted taking of anything of value from the care, custody, or control of another by force, threat of force, or by putting the person in fear.

Aggravated Assault: Part I crime category that involves the unlawful attack of another for the purpose of inflicting severe or aggravated bodily injury. Act is usually accompanied by the use of a weapon. Simple assaults are excluded.

Burglary: Part I crime category that involves the unlawful entry of a structure to commit a felony or theft. Attempted forcible entry is included.

Larceny/Theft: Part I crime category that involves the unlawful taking, carrying, leading, or riding away of property from the possession or constructive possession of another. Deceptive theft act such as embezzlement, con games, forgery, worthless checks are excluded.

Motor Vehicle Theft: Part I crime category that involves the theft or attempted theft of a self-propelled motor vehicle that runs on a surface and not on rails. Motorboats, construction equipment, airplanes, and farming equipment are excluded.

Arson: Part I crime category that involves any willful or malicious act of burning or attempted burning, with or without intent to defraud, of a dwelling, house, public building, motor vehicle, aircraft, or personal property of another.

National Incident-Based Reporting System (NIBRS): A new form of crime data collection created by the FBI requiring police agencies to provide incident-level data on the event, victim, and offender, and arrest outcomes for 22 different types of crime.

Victim Surveys: A source of crime data that involves asking crime victims about their encounters with criminals.

National Crime Victimization Survey (NCVS): A large, carefully drawn sample of citizens used to estimate the total number of criminal incidents that occur each year in the United States. It is conducted by the Bureau of Census in cooperation with the Bureau of Justice Statistics and is the most well known form of victim survey.

Self-Report Surveys: A source of crime data that involves questionnaires administered to groups of subjects designed to reveal information about their law violations.

Brady Bill: The Brady Handgun Violence Prevention Act enacted into law on November 30, 1993 that imposed a waiting period of 5 days before a licensed importer, manufacturer, or dealer may sell, deliver, or transfer a handgun to an unlicensed individual.

Instrumental Crimes: Crimes perpetrated to obtain desired goods and services.

Expressive Crimes: Crimes committed by those living in poverty as a means of expressing rage.

Masculinity Hypothesis: The view that women who commit crime do so because they have biological or psychological traits similar to those of men.

Chivalry Hypothesis: Assertion that female offenders and defendants receive more lenient treatment from the criminal justice system due to society's paternalistic or protective attitudes toward women.

Liberal Feminist Theory: An ideology that contends that women suffer oppression, discrimination, and disadvantage as a result of their sex. Calls for gender equality in society.

Career Criminals: The small group of offenders that accounts for a majority of all offenses.

Chronic Offender: Discovered by Wolfgang and his associates, the group of boys arrested five times or more who were involved in almost 52 percent of the crime committed by the cohort.

Three Strikes Laws: Justice perspective sentencing codes that require that an offender receive a life sentence after being convicted on a third felony.

Chapter Outline

I.   Introduction
    A.   America's image as an extremely violent nation
        1.   Eric Rudolph case
            a.   abortion clinic bomber
            b.   1996 Olympic bomber
            c.   extreme political views
        2.   shocking reminders of the damage one person can do
    B.   American violent crime rates are dropping while rates abroad increase

II. How crime is measured
   A. Official data
      1. official records from schools, courts, police departments, social service centres and correctional agencies
      2. Uniform Crime Reports (UCR)
         a. best known and most widely cited source of official crime statistics
         b. compiled annually by the FBI
         c. annual crime data from 17,000 local and state police departments
         d. offense and arrest data on 8 index or part I crimes
            i.. criminal homicide
            ii.. forcible rape
            iii. robbery
            iv. aggravated assault
            v. burglary
            vi. larceny/theft
            vii. motor vehicle theft
            viii.. arson
         e. arrest data on other part II crimes
         f. cleared crimes
         g. characteristics of offenders
         h. characteristics of offenses
         i. provides raw numbers of crimes plus crime rates per 100,000 people
         j. shows changes over time
      3. limited accuracy of the UCR
         a. reporting practices
         b. law enforcement practices
         c. methodological issues
      4. future of the UCR
         a. shift to individual criminal incidents to provide more detailed data
         b. National Incident-Based Reporting System (NIBRS)
            i.. brief account of each criminal incident
            ii. broadened list of 22 crimes
            iii. includes federal crimes and hate crimes
      5. Problems with the UCR
         a. no federal crimes
         b. reports are voluntary and vary in accuracy
         c. not all departments comply
         d. FBI uses estimates
         e. only most serious offense is recorded
         f. incomplete acts are lumped with completed acts
         g. FBI definitions of offenses differ from jurisdictional ones
   B. Victim Surveys
      1. National Crime Victimization Survey (NCVS)
         a. ask victims about their encounters with crime
         b. method of getting at unreported crime
         c. annual national survey of housing units
            i. multistaged sampling technique
            ii. interviews with people 12 years or older
         d. shows that many crimes go unreported to police
         e. problems with the NCVS

          i.   over reporting due to victim misinterpretation
          ii.   under reporting due to embarrassment
          iii.   cannot record criminality of the interviewee
          iv.   sampling errors
          v.   inadequate questions

C. Self report surveys:
1. question large groups of subjects about their behaviour
2. most focus on juvenile crime
3. reveal limits of using official data
4. reveal offender attitudes, values, personal characteristics and behaviors

D. Are self reports accurate?
1. lying a problem
2. exaggeration
3. comparisons between groups are highly misleading
4. missing cases and refusal rates
5. reliable measures of drugs, but crime is questionable

E. Evaluating Crime Data
1. each measure has its strengths and weaknesses
2. UCR is carefully tallied
3. NCVS contains unreported crimes
4. self reports provide important background information.

III. Crime trends

A. Some crime trends in the last hundred years
1. gradual increase in crime, especially violent crime, from 1830 to 1860
2. crime generally declined from 1880 until the Depression in about 1930
3. crime gradually increased from the 1930s until the 1960s
4. crime dramatically increased during the 1960s and 1970s
5. the number of index crimes peaked in 1981 and then began a decline until 1984
6. crime began to increase from 1985 to 1991 but has declined since then

B. Why do crime rates change?
1. age, crime rates follow young male proportion of the population
2. economy, crime rates rise during prolonged periods of economic weakness
3. social malaise, increased social problems may lead to increased crime rates
4. abortion, John Donohue and Steven Levitt show evidence that crime rate drops connected to availability of legalized abortion
5. gun availability puts weapons in young people's hands
6. gangs, growth of gangs in the 1980s may have contributed to crime rate increase.
7. drug use, well-armed gangs fighting over the drug market in large cities
8. violent themes in the media
9. medical technology increases assault rates and decreases murder rates
10. justice policy and aggressive police action
11. market conditions shape criminal opportunities

C. Violent crime trends
1. violent crimes include murder, rape, assault, and robbery
2. murder statistics are most accurate part of UCR
3. violence decreased in the 1990's

D. Property crime trends
1. property crimes include robbery, larceny, motor vehicle theft, and arson
2. property crimes rates decreased in 1990s

E. Trends in Self Report and Victimization
   1. self reports more stable than UCR
   2. according to the NCVS there are more than 23 victimizations in 2002
   3. lowest number since 1973
   4. crime drop may be stabilizing
F. Self-report findings
   1. almost everybody breaks the law in some way
   2. depict a mixed bag of crime and deviance
   3. Monitoring the Future annual survey of 2,500 high school seniors

IV. What the future holds
   A. James Fox's prediction of age-driven crime wave on the horizon
   B. Importance of technological advances
   C. Crime is deceasing in U.S. but increasing abroad
      1. homicide is highest in countries in social and political turmoil
      2. U.S. still has high rape rates
      3. U.S. robbery rate is now comparable to many others
      4. U.S. burglary rate is now comparable to many others
      5. Europe is gaining in gun ownership
      6. modernization view
      7. globalization view
      8. not all countries fit the modernization pattern
      9. other social factors are important

V. Crime Patterns
   A. Ecology and crime
      1. crime is not spread equally across time and space
      2. most crimes occur in July and August
      3. murders and robberies also peak during December and January
      4. large urban areas have higher crime rates than do rural and suburban areas
      5. western and southern regions of the country have the highest crime rates
   B. Use of firearms
      1. proliferation of handguns single most significant factor separating the crime problem in the US from the rest of the develop world
      2. gun control debate
         a. 50 million illegal guns in U.S.
         b. handguns linked to violent crimes
         c. Federal Gun Control Act of 1986
         d. Brady law and instant background checks at purchase point
         e. Bartlett-Fax law on mandatory prison term for gun crimes
         f. California's 10-20-life law
         g. outlawing guns
         h. Gary Kleck argues guns may prevent violence
         i. defensive gun use
   C. Social class patterns
      1. instrumental crimes are committed to obtain desired goods and services
      2. expressive crimes reflect feelings of rage and frustration with society
      3. higher arrest rates and incarceration rates for lower class
      4. self-reports show a less clear distinction
      5. class-crime controversy continues

D. Age and crime
  1. age is inversely related to crime
  2. young people between 13 and 17 account for 30 percent of index crimes
  3. the peak age for property crime is 16 and 18 for violence
  4. natural cycle of life -maturity and desistance
E. Gender and crime
  1. males commit 80% of violent crimes
  2. males commit more serious crimes – 5:1 violent crimes, 8:1 murders
  3. female arrest rates are increasing
  4. Lombroso's masculinity hypothesis
  5. chivalry hypothesis claims female crimes hidden by benevolent system
  6. boys are socialized differently
  7. feminist focus on social and economic roles of women
  8. prospect of future convergence
F. Race and crime
  1. African-Americans comprise 12% of population but 40% of violent arrests
  2. comparison of UCR with other data sources may demonstrate a differential selection policy for arrest
  3. racial profiling
  4. not all disparity explained away by racism or arrest, plight of some inner cities
  5. little difference in self report crime rates of minorities
  6. racism and discrimination
  7. institutional racism's role
  8. economic and social disparities
  9. family dissolusion and single, female-headed households
  10. prospects for racial convergence
G. Criminal careers and chronic offenders
  1. persistent offenders are referred to as career criminals or chronic offenders
  2. Philadelphia birth cohort study
    a. Marvin Wolfgang, Robert Figlio and Thorsten Sellin
    b. boys born in Philadelphia in 1945
    c. 627 out of 9,945 responsible for 51.9 percent of all offenses
    d. referred to as the chronic 6 percent
  3. new sentencing policies (3 strikes laws) target career criminals

Chapter Summary

The **Uniform Crime Report** (UCR), prepared by the Federal Bureau of Investigation, is the best known and most widely cited source of aggregate criminal statistics. The FBI receives and compiles reports from over 17,000 police departments so the UCR is based on crimes reported to the police. **Index crimes**, also know as **Part I** offenses include criminal homicide, forcible rape, robbery, aggravated assault, burglary, larceny, arson, and auto theft and are the major unit of analysis in the UCR. All other crimes (excluding traffic violations) constitute **part II** offenses are also recorded in the UCR. The UCR provides the number of crimes reported to the police, the number of arrests made, the **clearance rate**, the crime rate for the offenses per 100,000 people, and the change in the number and rate of crime over time. The **National Incident-Based Reporting System** is a new dimension to the FBIs data collection efforts, one that request incident-level police data on the events, victims, offenders, and arrests for an expanded list of 22 crime types.

The UCR does not provide the complete story about crime, since the UCR provides only information on those crimes reported to the police. Therefore, researchers also utilize the **National Crime Victimization Survey** (NCVS) which is conducted by the U.S. Bureau of the Census in cooperation with the Bureau of Justice Statistics of the U.S. Department of Justice. The NCVS annually surveys a sample of roughly 45,000 households that includes approximately 94,000 persons over the age of 12 to determine the estimate of victimizations within the United States. Although a valid estimate of victimizations, the NCVS suffers from over-reporting, under-reporting, sampling errors, and the inability to record the personal criminal activity of those interviewed.

Self-report surveys, usually administered by questionnaires, ask people to reveal information about their law violations. Most self-report surveys focus on delinquency and youth crime because the school setting makes testing convenient and universal school attendance provides a cross-section of the community. Self-reports have found that the amount of crime is greater than official data indicate, delinquents do not specialize in one type of crime, and the young report a great deal of crime. The accuracy of self-reports is a concern. It may be unreasonable to expect candid admissions of illegal acts, but it may also be that some respondents exaggerate, forget, or become confused. While they may not be totally valid or accurate, they are considered reliable and do serve as a measure of pattern and trends.

While many crime victims do not report criminal incidents to the police, evidence indicates that the crimes reported tend to be more serious. Consequently, UCR and NCVS data may be more similar than some critics believe. These data indicate some distinct patterns of crime: it occurs more often in large urban areas, during the summer, and on the first day of the month.

Crime is usually thought to be something committed by the lower socioeconomic class because crime rates are higher in the inner-city, high-poverty areas. This point of view is not supported by self-reports because they indicate there is no relationship between **social class** and crime. However, most self-report studies deal with trivial offenses, and when comparing serious crimes, it has been found that members of the the lower-class are more delinquent.

Age is inversely related to crime meaning that people commit less crime as they mature. This phenomenon is known as the aging out process. The explanation for this occurrence is that the young tend to discount the future and are unwilling or unable to defer gratification. As the young mature, they develop a long-term view and resist the need for immediate gratification.

The relationship between **gender** and crime is pronounced; there are 3.5 UCR male arrests for each female arrest, but for violent crimes, there are 5 male arrests for each female arrest. Self-report studies support the pattern, but the ratios are smaller. The current situation is that although male arrests are still higher, female rates are rising at a faster pace.

When it comes to **race** and crime, minority members are involved in a disproportionate share of criminal activity. Self-report studies report few interracial differences, so it may suggest other factors. Some explanations are **racial profiling**, racism, and discrimination. However, even racism cannot explain away the significant differences in arrest rates. There is the possibility of convergence of the crime rates as economic conditions for minorities continue to improve and residential integration may have a substantial impact.

29

Most offenders commit a single criminal act and others commit a few serious crimes. However, there is a small group that accounts for a majority of all criminal offenders and this group is known as **chronic offenders**. The studies by Wolfgang and his colleagues found that arrest and court experience do not deter this group, and traditional theories of crime cannot explain why this happens. New theories must be developed to explain the **persistence** of some offenders in crime and the **desistance** of others.

Fill-in-the-Blank Questions

1. The source of record data is the analysis of _____ _____.

2. The _____ _____ _____are compiled by the FBI and are the best known and most widely cited source of criminal statistics.

3. Index crimes include criminal homicide, _____ _____, robbery, _____ _____, burglary, _____, motor vehicle theft, and _____.

4. According to the FBI, _____ _____is defined as an unlawful attack of another for the purpose of inflicting severe bodily harm.

5. A crime is considered _____ when at least one person is arrested, charged, and turned over to the court for prosecution.

6. The _____ _____-_____ _____ _____ is a new data collection initiative by the FBI that seeks to collect incident-level data on the events, victims, offenders, and arrests associated with 22 types of crimes.

7. The number of crimes accounted for by the NCVS is considerably _____ than the number of crimes reported to the FBI through the UCR program.

8. There is a concern that victims _____ crimes out of a sense of embarrassment of reporting the incident to interviews who they don't know, out of fear of getting in trouble, or because the simply forgot the incident.

9. Areas with rural and suburban populations are more likely to have much _____ crime rates than large _____ areas.

10. While there are most reported crimes during the _____ months, the crimes of_____ and _____ occur most frequently in December and January.

11. Lombroso's _____ _____ states that a few " _____ " females were responsible for the handful of crimes women commit.

12. UCR data consistently shows that males have a _____ crime rate than females. However, the female crime rate has recently _____ at a faster rate than males.

13. _____ crime data indicate that minority group members are involved in a _____ share of criminal activity.

14. Criminal acts such as robbery that are intended to improve the financial or social position of the criminal are known as _____ crimes.

15. _____ offenders was a term that was derived from the Philadelphia Birth Cohort study to describe delinquents who were arrested at least 5 times prior to their 18th birthday.

True/False Questions

T F 1.   The Uniform Crime Reports are an example of a self-report survey.

T F 2.   Arson is a Part II crime.

T F 3.   Simple assault is an index crime.

T F 4.   Force, the threat of force, or the presence of fear is required for a robbery to occur.

T F 5.   An arrest must occur for a crime to be considered cleared.

T F 6.   No federal law violations are included in the Uniform Crime Reports data.

T F 7.   In the UCR, the number of crimes reported to the police and arrests made are reported as raw numbers.

T F 8.   Attempted criminal acts are not included in the Uniform Crime Reports.

T F 9.   The National Crime Victimization Survey (NCVS) is conducted by the FBI.

T F 10. The NCVS data are considered a relatively biased estimate of all victimizations for the target crimes included in the survey.

T F 11. The personal criminal activity of those interviewed for the NCVS are not included in the results.

T F 12. The most common offenses involving juveniles are truancy, alcohol abuse, and using a false ID.

T F 13. Young people do not self-report a great deal of crime.

T F 14. Self-report surveys are a good way to accurately measure serious forms of crime.

T F 15. Property crime rates have dropped in recent years, but not as dramatically as the violent crime rate.

T F 16. There has been a significant reduction in self-reported criminality.

T F 17. Criminologist James A. Fox predicts a significant decrease in teen violence if the current age-driven trends persist.

T F 18. According to international criminologists, the proliferation of handguns and the high rate of lethal violence they cause are the most significant factor separating the crime problem in the United States and the rest of the developed world.

T F 19. Expressive crimes are those committed by those unable to obtain desired goods and services through conventional means.

T F 20. Age is inversely related to criminality.

Multiple Choice Questions

1. _____ is typically gathered from subjects who are asked to fill out instruments or questionnaires which contain questions about their behavior, attitudes, beliefs, and abilities.
    a. Survey data
    b. Official data
    c. Cohort data
    d. Interview data

2. Which of the following is not an index crime?
    a. robbery
    b. forgery
    c. arson
    d. burglary

3. Which of the following is not a Part II crime?
    a. simple assault
    b. vandalism
    c. prostitution
    d. motor vehicle theft

4. Of the following, _____ is (are) problems with the Uniform Crime Report (UCR).
    a. not all crime is reported
    b. errors
    c. non-standard definitions of crime
    d. all of the above

5. The crime rates in the UCR are expressed in terms of the number of offenses per _____ population:
    a. 1,000
    b. 10,000
    c. 100,000
    d. 1,000,000

6. Which type of crime is most likely to be reported to the police?
    a. violent crime
    b. household theft
    c. personal theft
    d. all of the above

7. Which of the following is **not** a problem associated with the NCVS?
    a. overreporting of crime incidents
    b. underreporting of crime incidents
    c. no federal crimes are included
    d. inadequate question format

8. Which of the following is **not** a common usage for self-report data
    a. testing theories of crime
    b. measuring attitudes toward crime
    c. computing the association between crime and important social variables
    d. monitoring arrest practices

9. The Monitoring the Future study is an example of which type of data collection effort?
    a. victims reports
    b. official data
    c. observational data
    d. self-report data

10. Which is **not** a reason why most self-report studies have focused on youth crime?
    a. they are the most reliable of subjects
    b. the school setting makes it convenient
    c. school attendance is universal
    d. juveniles have the highest crime rates

11. Which of the following findings is true concerning self-report studies?
    a. the number of people who break the law is far greater than the number projected by the UCR
    b. delinquents specialize in one type of crime
    c. most common offenses include larceny over $50
    d. the findings are inconsistent

12. Which of the following is **not** true concerning the accuracy of self-reports?
    a. some surveys contain an overabundance of trivial offenses
    b. some people may exaggerate their criminal acts
    c. it is reasonable to expect people to candidly admit illegal acts
    d. some respondents may be confused about what is being asked

13. Which of the following is true concerning crime?
    a. crime may be lower on the first of the month
    b. domestic assault increases as the temperature rises
    c. rural areas have higher crime rates than large, urban areas
    d. most crimes occur in the spring

14. Which of the following is an accurate statement about violent crime trends in the United States?
    a. the violence rate has increased more than 20 percent
    b. murder has increased dramatically since 1900
    c. both a and b are correct
    d. violence has decreased significantly during the past decade

15. Crimes committed by those unable to attain desired goods and services through conventional means are called:
    a. expressive crimes
    b. instrumental crimes
    c. index crimes
    d. Part II crimes

16. Which of the following is **not** true concerning social class and crime?
    a. crime rates are higher in high-poverty areas
    b. prison inmates were usually unemployed in the years before incarceration
    c. police devote more resources to poor areas
    d. self-reports cannot test the class-crime relationship

17. The aging out effect in crime occurs because:
    a. young people discount the future
    b. young people are impatient
    c. as they mature, young people develop a long-term life view
    d. all of the above are correct

18. Which of the following is **not** true about gender and crime?
    a. murder arrests are 8:1 male
    b. the overall arrest ratio is 3.5:1 male
    c. self-reports indicate the ratio is 1:1 male
    d. for serious violent crime, the ratio is 5:1 male

19. While comprising approximately 12 percent of the U.S. population, African-Americans account for what percent of violent crime arrests.
    a. 15
    b. 20
    c. 25
    d. 41

20. Self-report studies seem to indicate that the criminal behavior rates of black teenagers are _____ those of white teenagers.
    a. significantly lower
    b. significantly higher
    c. generally similar
    d. almost equal to

21. The concept of the chronic offender is most closely associated with the research efforts of:
    a. Robert Merton
    b. Marvin Wolfgang
    c. Emile Durkheim
    d. Ronald Akers

22. The Philadelphia Birth Cohort study found that the "chronic 6%" offenders accounted for roughly ____ of all crimes committed by the sample.
    a. 25%
    b. 50%
    c. 75%
    d. 6%

23. Persistent repeat offenders who organize their lifestyle around criminality are known as:
    a. chronic offenders
    b. career criminals
    c. the chronic 6%
    d. habitual criminals

24. Which new sentencing initiative is specifically directed toward career criminals?
    a. three strikes laws
    b. mandatory minimum sentences
    c. truth-in-sentencing laws
    d. indeterminate sentences

Essay Questions

1. Explain the three significant methods used to measure crime.

2. Compare and contrast the Uniform Crime Report (UCR) and the National Crime Victimization Survey (NCVS); list the advantages and weaknesses of each.

3. Compare and contrast the trends in violent and property crime.

4. Describe the main social, economic, personal, and demographic factors that have been forwarded by experts to account for the recent crime drop in the United States.

5. Explain the relationship between crime and class; explain what the weight of evidence says about the relationship.

6. Describe the relationship between gender and crime giving three possible reasons for the relationship.

7. Discuss the evidence and policy initiatives on both sides of the gun control debate.

8. Explain the concept of chronic offenders.

9. Discuss the Philadelphia birth cohort study and how its findings have shaped justice policy.

10. Discuss the three strikes laws and how they relate to the chronic offender concept.

CHAPTER 2 ANSWER KEY

FILL-IN THE BLANK QUESTIONS

1. official records
2. Uniform Crime Reports (UCR)
3. forcible rape, aggravated assault, larceny, arson
4. aggravated assault
5. cleared
6. National Incident-Based Reporting System
7. larger
8. underreport
9. lower, urban
10. summer, murder, robberies
11. masculinity hypothesis, masculine
12. higher, risen
13. Official, disproportionate
14. instrumental
15. chronic

TRUE/FALSE QUESTIONS

1.	F	11.	T
2.	F	12.	T
3.	F	13.	F
4.	T	14.	F
5.	F	15.	T
6.	T	16.	F
7.	T	17.	F
8.	F	18.	T
9.	F	19.	F
10.	F	20.	T

MULTIPLE CHOICE QUESTIONS

1.	A	13.	B
2.	B	14.	D
3.	D	15.	B
4.	D	16.	D
5.	C	17.	D
6.	A	18.	C
7.	C	19.	D
8.	D	20.	C
9.	D	21.	B
10.	A	22.	B
11.	A	23.	A
12.	C	24.	A

Chapter 3

Understanding Crime and Victimization

Learning Objectives

At the conclusion of this chapter, the student should have the ability to achieve the following learning objectives:

1. Describe the problems of violent and economic crimes and substance abuse.

2. Know the reasons that crime seems rational.

3. Recognize the difference between general and specific deterrence.

4. Understand the concept of situational crime prevention.

5. Discuss the biological factors linked to crime.

6. Discuss the psychological factors linked to crime.

7. Describe the relationship between crime and the media.

8. Discuss why social and economic factors influence crime.

9. Discuss the sociocultural factors related to crime.

10. Explain how social conflict leads to crime.

11. Understand the concept of human development and crime.

12. Discuss the behavioral patterns that increase the chances of becoming a crime victim.

Keywords and Definitions

Spree Killer: A serial killer who constrains their murderous outburst to a few days or weeks.

White-Collar crime: Those crimes committed by people or institutions during the course of business operation for the purpose of profit or self interest.

Criminology: The scientific study of the nature, extent, and cause of crime.

Deterrent: Preventing crime before it occurs through the threat of criminal sanctions.

General Deterrence: A crime control policy that uses the imposition of criminal penalties against an offender as a means of invoking fear and compliance from others.

Specific Deterrence: A crime control policy that uses the pain of criminal sanctions to stop a convicted criminal from re-offending.

Situational Crime Prevention: The view that crime prevention is best achieved by reducing specific opportunities for people to commit crime.

Atavistic Anomalies: Primitive, animalistic physical qualities thought to be traits of the born criminal.

Neurotransmitters: Nerve endings that transmit chemical substances such as dopamine and serotonin from one nerve cell to another. Abnormalities are thought to be associated with a propensity for violence.

Social Learning Theory: The view that adolescents are taught the attitudes, values, and behaviors that support criminal involvement.

Moral Development Theory: A cognitive theory that traces adult criminal involvement to poor socialization about right and wrong during early childhood development.

Psychopath: An offender, who, from early childhood, demonstrates bizarre behavior, enjoys killing, is immune to his/her victim's suffering, and basks in the limelight when caught.

Disinhibition: A learning experience that takes place in youth when violence is viewed as being rewarded or socially acceptable among adults.

Anomie: The absence or weakening of rules and social norms in any person or group that leads an individual to lose the ability to distinguish between right and wrong.

Social Structure: The stratifications, classes, institutions, and groups that serve as the foundation for a social system.

Culture of Poverty: Subculture marked by apathy, cynicism, and helplessness that is brought about by long term exposure to urban poverty.

Focal Concerns: The core values and goals of the lower-class that include trouble, toughness, smartness, excitement, fate, and autonomy.

Strain: Status frustration occurring when the legitimate means for achieving desired goals are blocked.

Negative Affect States: States of emotional discomfort that result from experiencing strain. These forms of frustration can lead to antisocial behavior.

Differential Association Theory: View that people learn the attitudes and beliefs that cause crime in close and intimate relationships with significant others.

Social Control Theory: View that crime results from a weakening or absence of social bonds causes crime.

Labeling Theory: View that society produces criminals by stigmatizing certain individuals, thus leading to a deviant self-identity. Emphasize the process of making and enforcing the law.

Degradation Ceremonies: Degrading social or physical restraints that leave a lasting negative impression on the accused.

Conflict Theory: View that the economic and political forces operating in a society are the fundamental causes of criminality.

Left Realists: Conflict criminologists who attempt to reconcile the views of critical criminology with the social realities of crime and its impact on the lower-class.

Radical Feminism: A branch of conflict theory that attributes female criminality and victimization to capitalist male dominance.

Peacemaking Criminology: A branch of conflict theory that stresses humanism, mediation, and conflict resolution in place of punishment as a means to respond to crime.

Developmental Theories: Share the view that people experience events or stages on their way through the life course that shape their criminality.

Latent Trait Theory: A branch of developmental theory that attributes criminality to a master trait that is developed early in life or present at birth.

Self-Control Theory: View that adult criminality results from low levels of self-control that are formed through early childhood development processes. When presented with opportunities, persons with low self-control are likely to produce deviant outcomes.

Life Course Theory: A branch of developmental theory that views criminality as a dynamic process that is influenced by individual characteristics, traits, and social experiences.

Social Capital: Positive relations with individuals and institutions that are life sustaining.

Victim Precipitation: The role of the victim in provoking or encouraging criminal behavior in another.

Routine Activities Theory: Views crime as a function of the interaction of motivated offenders, suitable targets, and a lack of capable guardians.

Chapter Outline

I.   Introduction
        A.   Crime as a major social problem
            1.   predatory criminals
            2.   intimate violence

B.   Chante Mallard hit and run case

II.   Crime in the United States
   A.   Violent crime
      1.   media images and the resulting fear of certain types of crime
      2.   gang violence
         a.   motivated by drug profits & power rather than loyalty or geography
         b.   use handguns and automatic weapons
         c.   secrecy is replacing traditional "colors"
         d.   middle-class and female gang members are increasing
         e.   gangs are no longer restricted to urban areas
         f.   Youth gangs have more than 750,000 members
      3.   serial and mass murder
         a.   serial killers
            i.   no single explanation
            ii.   they may operate in different locales (Ted Bundy) or terrorize a single city (Jeffrey Dahmer)
         b.   mass murderers kill many victims in a single violent outburst (Columbine)
         c.   spree killers spread their murderous outburst over days or weeks
         d.   possible causes
            i.   mental illness
            ii.   sexual frustration
            iii. neurological damage
            iv.   child abuse and neglect
            v.   smothering maternal relationships
            vi.   childhood anxiety
      4.   terrorism
         a.   Oklahoma City bombing made Americans aware of domestic terrorism
         b.   September 11th attacks made Americans aware of international terrorism
         c.   types of modern terrorism
            i.   revolutionary terrorism (e.g., Egyptian Islamic Jihad)
            ii.   political terrorism (white supremacist groups)
            iii. nationalist terrorism (Palestinian groups)
            iv.   cause-based terrorism Osama Bin Laden)
            v.   environmental terrorism (ELF)
            vi.   state-sponsored terrorism Peruvian death squads)
            vii. criminal terrorism (organized crime groups)
      5.   intimate violence
         a.   greatest danger comes from people in close and intimate contact
         b.   child physical, emotional, sexual abuse or neglect
            i.   estimated that over 1.5 million US kids abused annually
            ii.   1/3 of women experience sexual abuse by the age of 18
         c.   spouse abuse
            i.   usually defined as the assault of a wife by a husband
            ii.   national survey found that 16% of families experienced it
   B.   Substance abuse
      1.   U.S. at "war on drugs"
      2.   most commonly abused substance is alcohol
         a.   suspected in 1/2 of all U.S. murders, suicides and accidental deaths
         b.   strong links between alcohol abuse and violent crime & deviance
      3.   drugs and crime relationship

        a.   Arrestee Drug Abuse Monitoring program (ADAM)

        b.   almost 2/3 of all arrestees test positively for drugs

   C.   Economic crimes

      1.   millions of property and theft-related crime occur annually in U.S.

        a.   occasional criminals (situational inducement)

        b.   professional criminals

      2.   white-collar crime

        a.   criminal activities of people or institutions through illegal business transactions

        b.   some of the most costly and damaging economic crime

        c.   perceived as less harmful and dangerous than theft and violence

        d.   role of technology

      3.   organized crime

        a.   the criminal activity of people and organizations whose acknowledged purpose is economic gain through illegal enterprise

        b.   fill the public's demand for outlawed goods and services

        c.   ethnic membership

        d.   law enforcement efforts to wipe out organized crime

III.   The cause of crime

   A.   Criminology is the scientific study of the nature, extent, and causes of crime

   B.   Criminologists find few answers

   C.   Numerous theoretical examinations of crime

IV.   Because they want to: Choice theory

   A.   People weigh the potential benefits and consequences of crimes

      1.   crimes are committed if benefits outweigh the potential risks

      2.   core principles

        a.   free will to choose

        b.   crime is attractive for some

        c.   refrain from crime if punishment is greater than the potential gain

        d.   punishment deters crime

      3.   punishment factors

        a.   severity

        b.   certainty

        c.   speed

   B.   Rational criminals

      1.   crime is a matter of personal choice in the moment

      2.   offenders weigh factors

        a.   personal needs

        b.   situational factors

        c.   fear of apprehension

      3.   life circumstances and social standing influence the individual's decisions

   C.   Rational crimes

      1.   all crimes are planned events

      2.   target selection

   D.   Make 'em afraid I: The concept of general deterrence

      1.   reduce the benefits of crime through swift, sure and severe punishment

      2.   fear of criminal penalties makes onlookers reconsider criminal decisions

      3.   why has general deterrence failed?

        a.   lack of efficiency reduces perceived certainty of punishment

        b.   overcrowded and understaffed system reduces severity via pleas

        c.   criminals may not be rational

E.   Make 'em afraid II: Specific deterrence
1. must convince past offenders never to repeat their criminal acts
2. why has specific deterrence failed?
    a.   impulsive criminals lack rationality
    b.   current practices lack swiftness and certainty of punishment
    c.   severe physical punishment does little to help troubled offender

F.   Make it difficult: Situational crime prevention
1. reduce crime opportunities
2. Oscar Newman and the defensible space idea
3. Ronald Clarke's four tactics to prevent specific crimes through specific acts
    a..   increase effort
    b.   increase risk
    c.   reduce the rewards
    d.   induce shame or guilt
4. target hardening tactics
5. change the environment, not the criminal

V.   Because they're different: Biological theories
A.   Crime may be inherited or due to uncontrollable biological or psychological traits
B.   Origins of scientific criminology
1. Cesare Lombroso
    a.   scientific study of prison inmates and Italian soldiers
    b.   atavistic anomalies
2. Lombroso discredited in 20th century
C.   Modern biological theory
1. each person has a unique biochemical, neurological and genetic makeup
2. biocriminologists attempt to link physical traits with violent tendencies
D.   It's in the blood: Biochemical factors
1. vitamins, mineral deficiencies, improper diet, environment and allergies
2. sugar and caffeine levels
3. hormone levels
E.   The abnormal brain: Neurological problems
1. EEG abnormalities
2. neurotransmitters
3. attention deficit disorder (ADHD)
F.   The bad seed: Genetic factors
1. twin research
    a.   monozygotic v. dizygotic twins
    b.   genetic makeup as a predictor of criminality
2. adopted children research

VI.   In their heads: Psychological theories
A.   The disturbed mind: Psychoanalytic theory
1. Sigmund Freud's psychodynamic theory
    a..   neurotics, psychotics, and schizophrenics
    b.   early damage to the ego and superego
2. mental illness and crime
    a.   violence as a symptom of mental illness
    b.   Belfrage's Swedish study

            c.   no clear link has been identified
    B.   Learning to commit crime: Behavioral theory
        1.   criminal behavior learned through interactions with others
            a.   behavior that is rewarded becomes habitual
            b.   behavior that is punished becomes extinguished
        2.   social learning theory
            a.   influence of peers
            b.   influence of media violence
            c.   disinhibition through the media
            d.   Emerge program for domestic abusers
    C.   Developing criminal ideas: Cognitive theory
        1.   focus on how people engage in information processing
        2.   moral development and its link to criminal judgment
    D.   Personality and crime: The psychopath
        1.   crime results from faulty personality also known as antisocial or sociopathic
        2.   lack emotional depth and empathy, persistent substance abusers
        3.   linked to improper socialization or autonomic nervous system
    E.   IQ and crime
        1.   link crime to intelligence
        2.   contradictory findings
        3.   focus on IQ tests

VII.   Blame society: Sociological theories
    A.   Social patterns in crime rates
    B.   Emile Durkheim
        1.   anomie and the division of labor
        2.   crime is functional to society
    C.   Sociological criminology
        1.   emphasizes environmental conditions
        2.   produced a shift from punishment to rehabilitation
    D.   Because they're poor: Social structure theory
        1.   focus on stratified society and the unequal distribution of wealth and status as causes of crime
        2.   culture of poverty and crime
            a.   poverty contributes to crime through apathy, cynicism, mistrust
            b.   truly disadvanteged
        3.   the disorganized neighborhood
            a.   physical deterioration, conflicting values and social system
            b.   Shaw and McKay research on disorganized urban neighborhoods
        4.   race, gender and ethnicity in criminal justice
            a.   William Julius Wilson's Truly Disadvantaged
            b.   permanent underclass
        5.   deviant values and cultures
            a.   Walter Miller's lower class focal concerns
                i..   trouble
                ii.   toughness
                iii.   smartness
                iv.   excitement
                v.   fate
                vi.   autonomy
            b.   cultural transmission of values from one generation to the next

6. strain theory
    a. status frustration because of the inability to achieve social success
    b. Robert Merton's anomie theory
        i. normlessness from gap between goals and means
        ii. modes of adaptation (innovation, retreatism, rebellion)
    c. Robert Agnew's general strain theory
        i. four sources of strain
        ii. negative affect states
        iii. resulting antisocial behavior
E. Socialized to crime: Social process theories
    1. crime results from socialization in family life, the educational experience, and institutions in society
        a. interpersonal relationships influence behavior
        b. quality of family life shape's adolescent development
        c. educational experiences shape choices
        d. deviant peers exert influence
    2. students of crime: learning theories
        a. we are taught attitudes, values and behaviors to support crime
        b. Sutherland's differential association theory
    3. out of control: control theories
        a.. people would commit crime without tie to conventional bonds
        b. Travis Hirschi's social control theory and the elements of the bond
            i. attachment
            ii.. commitment
            iii. involvement
            iv. belief
        c. weak bonds result in crime
    4. the outsider: labeling theory
        a. criminals are created when social control agencies define and stigmatize with a deviant label
            i. degradation ceremonies
            ii. stereotypes
            iii. adoption of new identity
            iv. secret or primary deviance
            v. secondary deviance
        b. racial, gender and economic discrimination in labeling process

VIII. Conflict theory
    A. Crime is caused by economic and political forces in society
        1. criminal justice system serves the rich and powerful and controls the poor
        2. crimes are defined and enforced in a way that meets the needs of the rich
    B. Variations of conflict theory
        1. conflict criminology
        2. critical, radical or Marxist criminology
        3. left realists
        4. radical feminists
        5. constitutive criminology
        6. peacemaking criminology

IX.   The path to crime: Developmental theories
      A.   Seek to identify, describe, understand the trajectory of criminal careers
            1.   onset issues
            2.   escalation issues
            3.   desistence issues
            4.   types of offenders and pathways of offending
      B.   Latent trait theories
            1.   a master personal characteristic controls the propensity to offend
            2   traits are identifiable early in life and remain stable through adulthood
            3.   offending rates fluctuate because of changing criminal opportunities
            4.   Gottfredson and Hirschi's general theory of crime (self-control theory)
                  a.   low self-control
                  b.   criminal opportunity
      C.   Life course theory
            1.   criminal career is a developmental process
            2.   changing perceptions and experiences over the life course shape
                  criminality
      D.   Age-graded theory
            1.   Sampson & Laub argue that turning points produce knifing off of crime
                  a.   building social capital
                  b.   building strong social bonds
            2.   stability in life keeps people away from crime

X.   It's how you live: Theories of victimization
      A.   Shifting focus to the victim's genesis of crime
      B.   Victim precipitation
            1.   victims may initiate the criminal event
                  a.   Wolfgang's 1958 homicide study of criminal homicide
                  b.   active precipitation
                  c.   passive precipitation
            2.   criminal as predator but victim as willing prey
      C.   Life-style theories
            1.   victims share many personal characteristics with criminals
            2.   proximity hypothesis where victims and offenders share social space
      D.   Routine activities theory
            1.   crime is related to normal patterns of human behavior
            2.   Cohen and Felson's 3 factors that shape criminal events
                  a.   supply of motivated offenders
                  b.   presence of suitable targets
                  c.   absence of effective guardians

Chapter Summary

There are many crime patterns occurring across the United States that concern most citizens. Among these are violent acts such as gang violence, serial and mass murder, terrorism, intimate violence, drugs, and economic crimes including white-collar crime and organized crime.

Several theoretical perspectives have attempted to explain why people engage in criminal behavior in hopes of creating effective crime reduction programs. **Choice theory** believes that offenders are rational criminals who weigh the potential costs and benefits of their criminal activity. Criminologists holding this view believe that society can deter crime by the imposition of swift, certain and severe punishments. When punishment is applied in this manner, society achieves the two goals of **general deterrence** (preventing others in society from engaging in crime) and **specific deterrence** (preventing the offender from repeating criminal behavior). Other choice theorists prefer **situation crime prevention** measures aimed at reducing or displacing criminal opportunities.

Biological theories attempt to link criminality to biochemical factors, neurological problems and genetic factors, while **psychological theories** point to personality disorders, the social learning process, cognitive deficiencies, and psychopathic personality, and low IQ as the cause of criminality.

Since research indicates that there are patterns in crime rates, **sociological theories** equate crime with a variety of social factors. The **social structure theories** argue that crime is a function of the manner in which society is organized, emphasizing the influence of factors such as race and poverty. **Disorganized neighborhood theory** argues that the breakdown in neighborhoods with the concomitant failure of the social institutions to function is what brings about crime. **Deviant values and cultures** contends that the lower-class creates a subculture that has a set of focal concerns or value system different from the rest of society and those values lead members of the subculture to engage in crime. **Strain theory** proposes that the United States is a stratified society with blocked access to desired goals that brings about strain or status frustration, models of adaptation, and eventually deviance. The **social process theories** point to the socialization process as the key to understanding the onset of criminality. Branches of the social process theory include learning theory, social control theory and labeling theory.

The **conflict theories** view the economic and political forces operating in society are fundamental causes of crime. They also argue that the criminal justice system is a vehicle to control poor numbers of society. The two branches of conflict theory are conflict criminology, which contends that crime is the product of class conflict that can exist in any society, and critical criminology, which has developed into several branches including **left realists**, **radical feminists**, and **peacemaking criminology**.

Developmental theories stress the changes that occur over the life course and how they cshape criminality. **Latent trait theory** is a developmental theory contending that certain people maintain a personal characteristic that controls their propensity to offend. One major latent trait theory is **general theory of crime** that argues that a low of self-control and criminal opportunities cause crime. **Life course theory** states that a criminal career is an evolutionary process and that age-graded life events such as marriage and career moves influence the behavior of people.

There are three **theories of victimization**. The **victim precipitation theory** holds that many victims actually provoke the attacks which led to their injury or death. **Lifestyle theory** contends that the lifestyle choices such as going out to public places at night, and living in an urban area increase one's probability of victimization. The **routine activities theory** holds that the incidence of criminal activity is related to the nature of everyday behavioral patterns. Three factors can explain crime – the supply of motivated offenders, the supply of suitable targets, and the absence of effective guardians of protection.

Fill-in-the-blank Questions

1. The Aryan Nation and other white supremacist organizations are considered examples of _____ terrorist groups that use violence and fear to suppress or destroy those people or groups that they define as a threat to the white race.

2. Most experts view serial killers as _____ who from early childhood demonstrated bizarre behavior, enjoy killing, are immune to their victims' suffering, and bask in the media limelight when caught.

3. There are strong links between the controlled substance _____ and violent crime and other antisocial behaviors.

4. Some organized crime elements prey upon the public and also upon other criminals through _____, _____, and _____.

5. Choice theory contends that people choose to commit crime after weighing the potential _____ and _____ of the criminal act.

6. Only by reducing the benefits of crime through _____, _____, and _____ punishment can society deter criminal behavior.

7. _____ _____ asserts that actual punishment at the hands of the justice system should convince arrested offenders from reoffending.

8. Ronald Clarke's four main types of situational crime prevention tactics include increasing the _____ needed to commit the crime, increasing the _____ of committing the crime, reducing the _____ for committing the crime, and inducing _____ or shame.

9. Psychoanalysts believe that law violators may have suffered damage to their _____ or _____ early in their development that renders them powerless to control their impulses and urges.

10. Social learning theory states that behavior that is _____ becomes habitual and that behavior that is _____ becomes extinguished.

11. _____ is described as the absence of rules, norms, or guidelines regarding what is socially or morally acceptable.

12. According to _____ _____ theories, high crime rates result from institutional inequities such as race and class biases.

13. Walter Miller argued that trouble, toughness, smartness, _____, _____, and _____ are the core focal concerns of lower class culture.

14. Travis Hirshi's _____ _____ theory stresses the importance of the social bond as a means of controlling youth behavior.

15. Differential association theory states that criminal behavior is _____ just like any other behavior whereby the individual internalizes the relevant _____ and _____ by watching others.

True/False Questions

T F 1.   It is uncommon for drug cliques to form within gangs.

T F 2.   Child abuse is a form of intimate violence.

T F 3.   Osama bin Laden is an example of a cause-based terrorist.

T F 4.   The white-collar crimes of the upper-class are more costly and damaging than are the violent acts of inner-city gang youths or deranged serial killers.

T F 5.   Organized criminals infiltrate legitimate organizations, such as unions, for money laundering purposes.

T F 6.   According to choice theory, property crimes are usually rational but violent crimes are usually irrational.

T F 7.   Choice theorist believe that violent crime cannot be deterred.

T F 8.   At their core, biological theories assume that variation in human physical traits can explain behavior.

T F 9.   Biological theories assume that all persons are born equal.

T F 10.   Hormonal imbalance has not been scientifically linked to aggressive behavior.

T F 11.   Attention-deficit-hyperactive-disorder (ADHD) is considered a biochemical theory of crime.

T F 12.   Genetic theorist predict that the behavior of dizygotic (DZ) twins should be more similar than that of monzygotic (MZ) twins.

T F 13.   Cognitive psychologists are concerned with the way people perceive and mentally represent the world in which they live.

T F 14.   Psychopaths are believed to be aggressive, antisocial individuals who act in a callous manner, but they are not believed to be dangerous.

T F 15.   The concept of anomie was first introduced by Emile Durkheim.

T F 16.   According to the social structure approach, a significant majority of people who commit violent crimes and serious theft offenses live in the lower-class culture, and a majority of all serious crimes occur in the inner-city areas.

T F 17.   In lower-class communities, people are evaluated by their actual or potential involvement in making trouble.

T F 18. Positive parental relationships cannot insulate children from criminogenic influences in the environment.

T F 19. An impulsive personality is said to be an indicator of the low self-control trait.

T F 20. Life course theory is a branch of the developmental theories.

T F 21. Abused children grow up to become abusers themselves.

T F 22. "Primary deviants" are those who have committed undetected antisocial acts.

T F 23. In time, the stigmatized person may believe that the deviant label is valid, but the person will never assume it as a personal identity.

T F 24. Getting married is a key way to build social capital according to age-graded theory.

Multiple Choice Questions

1. Palestinian terrorist groups such as Hezbollah are accused of engaging in the form of terrorism known as:
    a. revolutionary terrorism
    b. nationalist terrorism
    c. criminal terrorism
    d. state-sponsored terrorism

2. _____ means that most property crimes occur when there is an immediate opportunity to commit crime.
    a. situational inducement
    b. strain theory
    c. economic crime
    d. white-collar crime

3. The principle that onlookers will not choose crime if they fear legal punishment is called:
    a. situational crime prevention
    b. total deterrence
    c. specific deterrence
    d. general deterrence

4. According to choice theorists, the reason punishments may not work as a specific deterrent is that:
    a. some offenders may have impulsive personalities
    b. they are encouraged to commit crime once released
    c. they are heavy substance abusers
    d. all of the above

5. Crime prevention by reducing the opportunities people have to commit particular crimes is a process or technique known as:
   a. rational choice
   b. deterrence
   c. situational crime prevention
   d. general deterrence

6. The origin of scientific criminology is usually traced to the research of:
   a. Cesare Lombroso
   b. Travis Hirschi
   c. Ronald Clarke
   d. Edwin Sutherland

7. Which of the following is **not** a biological theory?
   a. biochemical factors
   b. cognitive theory
   c. neurological problems
   d. genetic factors

8. According to behavior theory, if one wants a behavior extinguished, that must be:
   a. rewarded
   b. understood
   c. punished
   d. accepted

9. Which of the following is **not** a factor contributing to the development of the psychopathic personality?
   a. genes
   b. psychopathic parent
   c. lack of love
   d. parental rejection

10. The culture of poverty concept is most closely associated with which of the following theories?
    a. disorganized neighborhood or social disorganization
    b. strain
    c. labeling
    d. social structure

11. The concept of anomie is associated with
    a. Edwin Sutherland
    b. Cesare Lombroso
    c. Emile Durkheim
    d. Travis Hirschi

12. Which of the following is not one of the lower-class focal concerns identified by Walter Miller?
    a. toughness
    b. disinhibition
    c. excitement
    d. autonomy

13. Which of the following concepts did William Julius Wilson introduce to account for the high crime rates that have long existed in the inner city?
    a. rebellion
    b. anomie
    c. innovation
    d. the truly disadvantaged

14. General strain theory and the concept of negative affect states is associated with:
    a. Robert Merton
    b. Emile Durkheim
    c. Travis Hirschi
    d. Robert Agnew

15. Social process theorists point to research efforts linking family problems to crime as evidence that the key to understanding the onset of criminality is
    a. social bonds
    b. social structure
    c. socialization
    d. all of the above

16. Which of the following is not one of the elements of Travis Hirschi's social bond?
    a. belief
    b. attachment
    c. involvement
    d. conformity

17. Differential association theory is associated with:
    a. Edwin Sutherland
    b. Robert Sampson
    c. Robert Agnew
    d. Travis Hirschi

18. Career, success, and goals are examples of which element of the social bond?
    a. attachment
    b. commitment
    c. involvement
    d. belief

19. Honesty, patriotism, fairness, and responsibility are examples of which element of the social bond?
    a. attachment
    b. commitment
    c. involvement
    d. belief

20. Which of the following concepts is not associated with labeling theory?
    a. primary deviance
    b. degradation ceremonies
    c. stigma
    d. definitions

21. Which of the following is not a branch of critical conflict theory?
    a. peacemaking criminology
    b. left realists
    c. radical feminism
    d. lifestyle theories

22. Conflict theory views the _____ forces operating in society as the fundamental causes of criminality.
    a. economic and political
    b. economic and social
    c. political and social
    d. economic and environmental

23. _____ try to reconcile critical views with the social realities of crime and its impact on the lower-class.
    a. Radical feminists
    b. Left realists
    c. Critical criminologists
    d. Peacemaking criminologists

24. _____ view crime as just another form of violence among others, such as war and genocide.
    a. Radical feminists
    b. Left realists
    c. Critical criminologists
    d. Peacemaking criminologists

25. _____ contend(s) that a certain percentage of the population maintains a personal characteristic that controls their propensity to offend.
    a. Developmental theory
    b. Victim precipitation theory
    c. Latent trait theories
    d. Psychological theories

26. According to life course theory, a criminal career is an _____ process.
    a. unending
    b. evolutionary
    c. stable
    d. intuitive

27. The theory that refers to the fact that victims may have actually initiated the confrontation that led to injury or death is:
    a. victim precipitation theory
    b. routine activities theory
    c. lifestyle theory
    d. developmental theory

28. The term that means the victim exhibits some personal characteristic that unintentionally either threatens or encourages the attacker is:
    a. active precipitation
    b. passive precipitation
    c. precipitation
    d. victim initiation

Essay Questions

1. Compare and contrast specific and general deterrence.

2. Apply the four tactics of situational crime prevention to a contemporary crime problem.

3. Discuss the effects of a disorganized neighborhood on crime.

4. Explain how a deviant subculture forms.

5. Explain Merton's anomie theory and the three models for deviant adaptation.

6. Describe control theory and the role of the four social bonds in preventing crime.

7. List the various conflict theories and explain the differences between them.

8. Explain the concept of low self-control and how it leads to crime.

9. Explain how a victim can be involved in causing crime?

10. Explain why labeling theory sees going to prison a contributing to criminal behavior.

11. Explain routine activities theory as it applies to auto theft at a shopping mall.

CHAPTER 3 ANSWER KEY

FILL-IN-THE-BLANKS

1. political
2. psychopaths
3. alcohol
4. fear, violence, extortion
5. benefits, consequences
6. sure, swift, certain
7. specific deterrence
8. effort, risks, rewards, guilt
9. egos, superegos
10. rewarded, punished
11. anomie
12. social structure
13. excitement, fate, autonomy
14. social control
15. learned, attitudes, behaviors

TRUE/FALSE ANSWERS

1.	F	13.	T
2.	T	14.	F
3.	T	15.	T
4.	T	16.	T
5.	F	17.	T
6.	F	18.	T
7.	F	19.	T
8.	T	20.	F
9.	F	21.	T
10.	F	22.	T
11.	T	23.	F
12.	F	24.	T

MULTIPLE CHOICE ANSWERS

1.	B	15.	C
2.	A	16.	D
3.	D	17.	A
4.	D	18.	B
5.	C	19.	C
6.	A	20.	D
7.	B	21.	D
8.	D	22.	A
9.	A	23.	B
10.	D	24.	D
11.	C	25.	C
12.	B	26.	B
13.	D	27.	A
14.	D	28.	B

Chapter 4

Criminal Law: Substance and Procedure

Learning Objectives

1. Understand the concept of substantive criminal law and its history.

2. Know the similarities and differences between criminal law and civil law.

3. Discuss the differences between felonies and misdemeanors.

4. Know the various elements of a crime.

5. Discuss the concept of criminal intent.

6. Discuss the recent changes in the criminal law.

7. Describe the role and content of the Bill of Rights.

8. Know which constitutional amendments are most important to the justice system.

9. Describe the various insanity defenses.

10. Discuss several major criminal defenses.

11. List the elements of due process of the law.

12. Demonstrate how interpretations of due process affect civil rights.

Keywords and Definitions

Substantive Criminal Law: Defines crime in society. Each state government and the federal government have its own criminal code.

Procedural Law: Outlines criminal process, it consists of the legal steps through which an offender passes beginning with the initial investigation and concluding with release.

Civil Law: The body of rules outside the criminal law that controls the personal relationships between individuals. It includes tort, contract, personal property, maritime, and commercial law.

Criminal Law: The body of rules that defines crimes against the state, defines corresponding punishments, and mandates procedures of the criminal justice process.

Common Law: Early English law, developed by judges. It became the standardized law of the land in England and eventually formed the basis of criminal law in the United States.

Stare Decisis: Latin for "to stand by decided cases." It is a legal principle under which judges follow the law or precedent as it has been judicially determined in prior cases in the justice system.

Mala in se Offense: Latin for "an inherently evil act." Term assigned to crimes such as murder burglary, arson, theft, rape, and robbery that were deemed illegal since common law times or before.

Inchoate Crimes: Offenses based on incomplete criminal acts, including conspiracy and attempts.

Tort Law: The law governing personal wrongs and damages.

Ex Post Facto Laws: Prohibited in the Constitution, these are laws that are created and/or enforced retroactively.

Bill of Attainder: Prohibited by the Constitution, these are legislative acts that inflict punishment without a judicial trial.

Due Process: The fundamental right of a person to be treated fairly and equally.

Felony: A crime that is punishable by death or imprisonment for more than one year.

Misdemeanor: A crime that is punishable by imprisonment for less than one year.

Violations: Least serious or petty criminal offenses, such as traffic violations.

Crime: A legal wrong prohibited by the criminal law and prosecuted by the state in a formal court proceeding in which a criminal sanction or sentence may be imposed.

Corpus Delicti: The "body of the crime." All the elements that together constitute a crime. It includes the *actus reus*, *mens rea*, and the combination of the *actus reus* and *mens rea*.

Actus Reus: Latin for "guilty act." It is the part of a legal statute that defines the forbidden act.

Mens Rea: Latin for "guilty mind." It is the part of a legal statute that specifies the criminal intent required to go along with the forbidden act.

General Intent: The intention of the accused to act purposefully or to accomplish a criminal result.

Specific Intent: The requirement that the actor intended to accomplish a specific purpose as an element of the crime.

Criminal Intent: Instance where an individual willfully and knowingly acts based on conscious wrongdoing.

Public Safety or Strict Liability Crime: Criminal offense where no state of mind is required so the person can be held responsible for the crime independent of the existence of intent to commit the offense, such is the case with traffic laws, drug laws, and statutory rape.

Justification Defense: A criminal defense for a criminal act claiming that the action was reasonable or necessary under the circumstances includes necessity, duress, self-defense, and entrapment.

Excuse Defense: A criminal defense alleging that the accused was in an impaired mental state at the time of the offense and thus unable to form intent, examples include insanity, intoxication, and ignorance.

Ignorance: A form of justification defense in which the accused claims to have been unaware of the law or committed the act by mistake. Generally, ignorance of the law is no excuse.

Insanity: The form of justification defense involving the use of rules and standards to determine if a person's state of mental balance negates criminal responsibility.

Intoxication: A form of justification defense in which the accused claims to have been in a state of involuntary intoxication at the time of the offense, thus nullifying the ability to form intent.

M'Naghten Rule: An insanity test whereby the defendant may be excused from criminal responsibility if at the time the act is committed the accused party suffered under a defect of reason, from a disease of the mind, so as not to know the nature and quality of the act he was doing, or if he did know it, that he did not know that what he was doing was wrong.

Irresistible Impulse: Excuses from criminal responsibility a person whose mental disease makes it impossible to control personal conduct.

Durham Rule: An insanity test whereby the accused is not criminally responsible if the unlawful act was the product of mental disease or defect.

Substantial Capacity Test: The American Law Institute's Model Penal Code insanity test that states a person is not responsible for criminal conduct if at the time of such conduct as a result of mental disease or defect he lacks substantial capacity to appreciate the criminality (wrongfulness) of his conduct or to conform his/her conduct to the requirements of law.

Appreciation Test: Adopted by the federal government, an insanity test whereby the defendant is not required to show lack of control regarding behavior, but the burden of proof is on the defense. The state must show defendant lacks the capacity to appreciate the wrongfulness of his conduct.

Self-Defense: An excuse defense wherein the defendant must have acted under a reasonable belief that he or she was in danger or great harm and had no means of escape from the assailant.

Entrapment: Defense that excuses the defendant from criminal liability when law enforcement agents use traps, decoys, and deception to induce criminal action.

Duress: An excuse defense that may be used when the accused claims to have been forced or coerced into committing the crime as the only means to avoid death or serious harm to his/her self or others.

Necessity: An excuse defense that may be used when the crime was committed under extreme circumstances and could not have been avoided.

Prenumbral Crimes: Offenses that are generally ignored by the public and law enforcement, associated with high levels of non-compliance, minimal stigma, and low levels of enforcement.

Stalking: The willful, malicious, and repeated following, harassing, or contacting of another to the point of invoking fear.

Obitiatry: Helping people take their own lives through assisted suicide.

Criminal Procedure: Consists of the rules and procedures that govern the pretrial processing of criminal suspects and the conduct of criminal trials.

Fourth Amendment: Constitutional amendment affording protection against unreasonable searches and seizures.

Fifth Amendment: Constitutional amendment guaranteeing the right against self-incrimination.

Sixth Amendment: Constitutional amendment guaranteeing the right to a speedy and public trial.

Eighth Amendment: Constitutional amendment guaranteeing protection against excessive bail, fines, and cruel and unusual punishment.

Bail: A money bond put up by the accused to attain freedom between time of arrest and the trial.

Fourteenth Amendment: Constitutional amendment guaranteeing protection against deprivation of life, liberty, or property without due process of law.

Chapter Outline

I.   Introduction
    A.   Laci Peterson case and the concept of a "fair trial"
        1.   Can Scott Peterson get a fair trial?
        2.   Will the celebrity status of the case shape the outcome?
    B.   The rule of law, as applied by the court system, seeks to protect fairness for all

II.   Substantive criminal law
    A.   Criminal law defines crime and punishment in society
        1.   embodied in the criminal code of each legal jurisdiction
        2.   living document that is constantly evolving with society
    B.   Procedural law sets out the rules that guide the steps of the criminal process
    C.   Rule of law governs most all spheres of social existence
        1.   criminal law defines crimes, the associated punishments, and criminal procedure
        2.   civil law are the rules that control personal relationships
           a.   tort law
           b.   contract law
           c.   personal property law
           d.   maritime law

       e.   commercial law

D.   Historical development of criminal law
1.   early criminal codes
    a.   Code of Hammurabi
    b.   Mosaic Code
    c.   twelve Roman Tables
    d.   Justinian's Corpus Juris Civilis
    e.   Napoleonic Code
2.   impact on modern law

E.   Development of common law
1.   originated during King Henry II
2.   circuit judges traveled to specific jurisdictions to hold court
3.   replaced local custom with a national law
4.   judges created crimes by ruling certain actions subject to state control and sanction
5.   decisions eventually produced a body of rules and legal principles about crime and punishment known as precedents
6.   it forms the basis of our early legal system
7.   principle of stare decisis
    a.   decision made by one court generally binding on other courts in subsequent cases
    b.   principle based on judge-made, or case, law created by judicial decisions
8.   mala in se offenses
    a.   inherently bad or evil acts
    b.   common law crimes such as murder, rape, robbery, arson, burglary
9.   Carriers case
    a.   common law case that defined larceny (theft) by unique laws
    b.   birth of crimes such as embezzlement, extortion, and false pretenses

F.   Criminal law and civil law
1.   differences between two
    a.   objective of criminal law is to protect the public by preventing crime
    b.   in civil law it is to compensate injured party for harm done
    c.   injured party in civil law initiates proceedings
    d.   sate initiates legal process and imposes criminal sanctions
2.   common features
    a.   both seek to control people's behaviors
    b.   payment in civil case serves same purpose as paying fine in criminal case
    c.   criminal law confines one to prison
    d.   civil law can confine one in a mental hospital, etc.
    e.   O.J. Simpson case illustrates similarities and differences well

III.   Sources of the criminal law (3)
A.   Common law statutes and case decisions
1.   common law crimes have been adopted into state codes
2.   statutes build on common law meaning
3.   case law and judicial decision making influence and change laws
B.   Administrative rule making - administrative agencies with regulatory power develop measures to control our conduct
C.   Constitutional law and its limits
1.   all criminal laws must conform to the rules and dictates of the constitution
2.   if a law does not comply, it will be stricken from the legal code by judicial order
3.   limitations on ex post facto laws

4. vague and broad laws violate the constitution
5. laws violating due process are unconstitutional
6. Kansas v. Hendericks, Smith et al. v. Doe et al. & Stonegr v. California cases

IV. Classifying crimes
   A. Felonies and misdemeanors
     1. sentence for a felony one year or more and served in prison
     2. sentence for misdemeanor less than one year and served in county jail
     3. felony conviction may bar people from certain employment and professions
     4. felony conviction can affect status as alien, voting, and holding public office
     5. classification according to characteristic of offender, i.e., juvenile delinquent
     6. in presence requirement only for misdemeanors
   B. Legal definition of a crime
     1. a crime can result from commission of an act in violation of the law
     2. a crime can result from omission – failure to act as required by law
     3. the state must prove all the elements of a crime – *corpus delicti*
       a. *actus reus*
         1. physical act
         2. must be a measurable act, not a thought alone
       b. *mens rea*
         1. deals with intent
         2. level of intent often used to categorize crimes – first degree, second degree, etc.
         3. types of intent
           a. general intent
           b. specific intent
       c. relationship *of mens rea* and *actus reus* – offender's conduct must be the proximate cause of any injury resulting from the criminal act
       d. strict liability offenses
         1. usually must prove both criminal intent and wrongful act
         2. for these certain offenses *mens rea* is not essential
         3. can be held responsible independent of the existence of intent to commit the offense

V. Criminal defenses
   A. Defendant must refute one or more of the elements of a crime to succeed in a defense
   B. Legal excuse occurs when accused claims to lack the mental capacity to form intent
   C. Four types of legal excuses
     1. ignorance or mistake
       a. mistake or ignorance of the law is generally no defense to a crime
       b. mistakes of fact may be a valid defense
     2. insanity
       a. a legal concept, not a mental health term
       b. each legal jurisdiction defines insanity as it sees fit
       c. types of insanity defenses
         i. M'Naghten rule
         ii.. irresistible impulse test
         iii.. Durham rule (products test)
         iv. substantial capacity test
         v. present federal law – capacity to appreciate wrong
       d. debate over insanity defense

     i. spurs on crime
     ii. releases offenders
     iii. requires extensive use of expert testimony
     iv. commits more criminals to mental institutions than to prisons
     v. guilty but mentally ill defense
    3. intoxication
     a. being intoxicated by choice is not a defense
     b. defense only viable in the case of involuntarily intoxicated
    4. age and crime
     a. conclusive presumption of incapacity for a child under the of seven to commit a crime
     b. reliable presumption for a child between ages of 7 and 14
     c. no presumption for a child over 14 years old
     d. maximum age of criminal responsibility ranges from 14 to 17
     e. every jurisdiction has established a juvenile court for young offenders
  D. Justifications occurs when accused admits committing the act but claims it was reasonable in this instance
  E. Five types of legal justifications
    1. consent
     a. victim consent alone does not justify offender's action
     b. applicability of consent defense depends on the crime
     c. if consent is a component of the statute, the defense may apply
    2. self-defense
     a. a person engaging in self-defense can use only such force as is reasonably necessary to prevent personal harm
     b. the danger to the defendant must be deemed immediate
     c. obligated to look for alternative means of avoiding the danger
    3. entrapment
     a. police cannot implant criminal ideas, or coerce individuals to bring about a crime
     b. defense was created by court decision and statute in most jurisdictions
    4. duress
     a. coercion may also be a criminal defense under certain conditions
     b. defendant shows that he/she was forced into committing a crime
     c. must demonstrate threat of death or serious injury to self or others
     d. not applicable to murder
    5. Necessity
     a. crime committed under extreme circumstance or unavoidable\
     b. harm avoided must be greater than offense charged

VI. Reforming the criminal law
  A. Ongoing effort to update legal codes to reflect public opinion, social change, technological innovation, and other social issues
    1. example of abortion
    2. weeding out laws that seem archaic in light of what is known about human behavior
  B. Penumbral crimes
    1. crimes ignored by public or police
    2. crimes where non-compliance is high, stigma is low, and enforcement is lax
  C. Creating new penalties
    1. Kevorkian's obitiatry

2. stalking
3. sex offender registry
4. community notification for sex offenders
5. must be careful of the potential fallout for system when writing new laws

VII.   Constitutional criminal procedure
   A. Principles governing criminal procedure
      1. presumption of innocence
      2. right to a defense against criminal charges
      3. requirement that the government act in a lawful manner
   B. The U.S. Constitution of 1776
      1. controls the operations of the criminal justice system
      2. supplemented by Bill of Rights in 1791
   C. The Bill of Rights
      1. first ten amendments to the Constitution
      2. designed to prevent government from usurping personal freedoms
      3. Fourth Amendment
         a. police cannot indiscriminately use their authority to investigate or arrest
         b. both actions must be justified by law and by the facts of the case
      4. Fifth Amendment
         a. limiting illegal confessions designed to control police behavior
         b. *Miranda v. Arizona* and the Miranda warnings against self-incrimination
      5. Sixth Amendment
         a. designed to ensure criminal defendants receive a fair trial
         b. stemmed from abuses to human rights by England
         c. right to an attorney extended to many stages of the justice process
      6. Eighth Amendment
         a. prohibits excessive bail
         b. does not guarantee bail
         c. forbids torture and excessive physical punishment
         d. protects accused and convicted from actions regarded as unacceptable in civilized society
   D. USA Patriot Act of 2001 as a response to terrorism
      1. expands the definition of terrorism (new law)
      2. expands the ability of law enforcement to monitor and apprehend terrorists

VIII.   Due process of law
   A. Due process requires rules and regulations to protect individual rights
   B. Due process is intended to guarantee fundamental fairness in each case
   C. Essence of due process – adequate notice and a fair hearing in both the civil and criminal law

IX.   The Meaning of due process
   A. Due process is shaped by four factors
      1. the facts of each case drive what constitutes due process (facts)
      2. federal and state constitutional and statutory provisions (laws of the land)
      3. previous court cases (precedent)
      4. ideas and principles that society thinks are important at the time (context)
   B. Judicial interpretation is critical to due process determinations

Chapter Summary

The origins of criminal law go back many centuries into ancient times, but American criminal law has its origins in English **common law** which includes a body of rules and legal principles about crime and punishment. One of the major principles that originate in common law is *stare decisis* which makes the decision of one court generally binding on other courts in subsequent cases. In modern society, law can be divided into two broad categories: criminal law and civil law. In **criminal law**, the major objective is to protect the public by preventing crime, while in **civil law**, the purpose is to compensate the injured party for the harm done. Civil law includes tort, contract, personal property, maritime, and commercial law. Both the criminal and civil law seek to control people's behaviors.

In most instances, the common law crimes have been adopted into state penal codes and the various state statutes have built on the common law meanings. Case law and judicial decision making influence and change the laws over time. Regardless of the origins of the law, all criminal laws must conform to the rules and dictates of the U.S. Constitution. If it does not comply, it will likely be challenged and eventually stricken from the code as unconstitutional by judicial order.

A **crime** is a legal wrong prohibited by the criminal law, prosecuted by the state in a formal court proceeding in which a criminal sanction or sentence may be imposed. *Mala in se* offenses are those inherently evil acts that have been outlawed since common law times. All crimes fall into categories and the most common categories are **felony** and **misdemeanor** which are based on the seriousness of the crime. The elements that make up a crime are known as the *corpus delicti* and include the *actus reus*, *the mens rea*, and a concurrence of the *actus reus* and the *mens rea*.

Under the criminal law, adults are presumed to realize the consequences of their actions, but the law does not hold a person criminally responsible if the individual cannot make the requisite **intent** to commit the crime. Such factors as insanity, ignorance, intoxication, or age can excuse a person's criminal responsibility since intent is questioned. Other criminal defenses are based on the concepts of justification including consent, self-defense, entrapment, mistake, compulsion, and necessity. Here, the defendant admits wrongdoing but justifies behavior in this case.

Substantive criminal law has undergone many reforms in an ongoing effort to update the legal codes to reflect current public opinion, social change, technological innovations, and other social issues. One major example has been Dr. Kevorkian's efforts at assisted suicide, also known as obitiatry, stalking laws, sex offender registries, and sex offender community notification laws.

The **Bill of Rights** of the U.S. Constitution provides all citizens their fundamental rights and protections, especially when they are suspects or defendants in a criminal case. Several amendments speak to the legal rights of accused criminals. The **Fourth Amendment** prevents the police from conducting arbitrary searches and seizures of our person or property without a warrant. The **Fifth Amendment** provides protection against self-incrimination and is also designed to control police behavior. The **Sixth Amendment** is designed to ensure that criminal defendants receive a fair trial and it insures that the defendant has access to an attorney at critical stages of the criminal justice process. The **Eighth Amendment** does not guarantee bail, but it does prohibit excessive bail and it also protects against cruel and unusual punishment.

Due process of law requires rules and regulations to protect individual rights. It is designed to guarantee fundamental fairness in each case. The essence of due process is adequate notice and a fair hearing under both the civil law and criminal law. Due process is subject to judicial interpretation based on the facts of the case, existing laws and precedents, and the ideas and principles that society considers important at the time.

Fill-in-the-Blank Questions

1. The _____ law defines crime in U.S. society.

2. Development of formal law in the original colonies was adopted from English _____ _____.

3. One of the principal components of the common law was its recognition of the law of _____.

4. A judicial decision is generally binding on courts in subsequent applicable cases; this legal principle is known as _____ _____.

5. Regardless of its source, all criminal law in the United States must conform to the rules and dictates of the U.S. _____.

6. The Constitution forbids _____ _____ _____ laws, which create crimes and penalties that can be enforced retroactively.

7. _____ are the least serious or petty offenses, often involving criminal traffic offenses.

8. Crime can result from the _____ of an act in violation of the law or from the _____ of a required legal act.

9. The _____ of a crime form what is known as the _____ _____, or "body of the crime."

10. The _____ _____ is Latin for the element of the crime that deals with the defendant's intent to commit a criminal act.

11. The law recognizes that certain conditions of a person's limited mental state might _____ him or her from acts that otherwise would be considered criminal.

12. Criminal _____ is a legal defense involving the use of rules and standards to determine if a person's state of mental balance negates _____ _____.

13. The products test, known as the _____ _____, states that an accused is not criminally responsible if the unlawful act was the product of mental disease or defect.

14. The substantial capacity test states a person is not responsible for criminal conduct if at the time of such conduct as a result of mental _____ or _____ he lacks _____ _____ to appreciate the criminality of his conduct or to conform to the requirements of law.

15. A defendant who becomes _____ intoxicated under _____ or by _____ may be excused for the crimes committed.

16. Mistake or ignorance of the law is generally no _____ to a crime, but mistakes of _____ may be a valid defense.

17. The _____ defense is also known as the compulsion or coercion defense.

18. Dr. Jack Kevorkian uses the term _____ to describe his acts of assisted suicide.

19. _____ _____ laws compel states to make public the private and personal information of registered sex offenders when they move into a community.

20. In 1791, the _____ of _____ was added to the U.S. Constitution to prevent any future government from usurping the personal freedoms of citizens.

True/False Questions

T F 1.   The English common law evolved to fit specific incidents that the judges encountered.

T F 2.   Maritime law fits under the heading of civil law.

T F 3.   The principle of *stare decisis* is not used in interpreting evidence given in trials.

T F 4.   Statutes are a way in which the criminal law is created and modified, but they cannot be used to expunge the criminal law.

T F 5.   A judge may nullify a statute simply because it deals with an act no longer of interest to the public.

T F 6.   An example of an administrative agency is a parole board.

T F 7.   The classification of an offense is important because a person convicted of misdemeanor might be barred from certain fields of employment.

T F 8.   The *mens rea* deals with the "guilty act" or forbidden act itself.

T F 9.   The combination of *actus reus* and *mens rea* is an integral part of the *corpus delicti*.

T F 10.   The right-wrong test is known as the M'Naughten rule.

T F 11.   As a general rule, voluntary intoxication is considered a viable defense.

T F 12. A child under the age of seven generally will not be held criminally responsible for committing a crime.

T F 13. As a general rule, the consent of a victim to a crime justifies or excuses the defendant who commits the action.

T F 14. It is generally forbidden for law enforcement officers to use traps, decoys, and deception to induce criminal action.

T F 15. Compulsion or coercion may be a criminal defense if the defendant shows the actions were the only means of preventing death or serious harm to self or others.

T F 16. Necessity is an acceptable defense only if the harm to be avoided was as great as the offense charged.

T F 17. Age can never be used as a legal defense.

T F 18. The defense of duress could potentially apply in a murder case.

T F 19. The purpose of the separation of powers in the Constitution is to ensure that no single branch of the government could usurp power for itself and institute dictatorship.

T F 20. One way the Constitution affects the operation of the criminal justice system is to guarantee that no one branch of the government can in and of itself determine the fate of those accused of crimes.

T F 21. The Eighth Amendment guarantees a constitutional right to bail.

T F 22. The first ten amendments and the Fourteenth Amendment are commonly referred to as the Bill of Rights.

T F 23. The Fourteenth Amendment's due process clause applies the protection of the Bill of Rights to state governments.

T F 24. The sixth amendment to the United States constitution provides for traditional limits on police behavior.

Multiple Choice Questions

1. The rules designed to implement the substantive criminal law are known as:
   a. criminal process
   b. national statutes
   c. procedural law
   d. civil law

2. Today, personal wrongs and damages are handled under:
    a. tort law
    b. property law
    c. contract law
    d. common law

3. Which of the following is **not** true of criminal law?
    a. crime is a civil wrong
    b. the sanction is incarceration or death
    c. the right of enforcement belongs to the state
    d. the government ordinarily does not appeal

4. Which of the following is **not** a similarity between criminal and civil law?
    a. both seek to control behavior
    b. both impose sanctions
    c. both place emphasis on the intent of the individual committing the crime
    d. they have similar areas of legal action

5. Which of the following is **not** a purpose of the criminal law?
    a. maintain social order
    b. exert social control
    c. regulate punishments
    d. provide compensation to individuals for harm done

6. The Constitution forbids _____, legislative acts that inflict punishment without a judicial trial.
    a. *ex post facto* laws
    b. *corpus delecti*
    c. due process
    d. *stare decisis*

7. The right to be treated fairly and equally is known as:
    a. due process
    b. bills of attainder
    c. *stare decisis*
    d. tort

8. The criminal law of a state:
    a. defines and grades offenses
    b. sets levels of punishment
    c. classifies crimes into different categories
    d. all of the above

9. A crime that is punishable in the statute by death or imprisonment in a state prison for more than one year is a called a:
    a. felony
    b. misdemeanor
    c. violation
    d. strict liability offense

10. The *actus reus*, *mens rea*, and the combination of the *actus reus* and *mens rea* taken together to constitute a crime describe the:
    a. statutory classification
    b. *corpus delicti*
    c. category of crime
    d. a and c

11. Certain statutory offenses exist in which *mens rea* or intent is not essential and these offenses fall within a category known as:
    a. felony offenses
    b. status offenses
    c. strict liability offenses
    d. misdemeanor offenses

12. Under the criminal law, insanity is **not:**
    a. a legal concept
    b. a mental health term
    c. defined by each legal jurisdiction
    d. available as a defense

13. The M'Naghten Rule has been supplemented with the _____ test in many states where it is used.
    a. irresistible impulse
    b. diminished capacity
    c. substantial capacity
    d. both a and c

14. Which of the following is **not** a criticism of the insanity defense?
    a. it spurs crime
    b. it releases criminal offenders
    c. it commits more criminals to mental institutions than to prisons
    d. it is used too often

15. The federal government has adopted a test of criminal responsibility known as the:
    a. appreciation test
    b. products test
    c. irresistible impulse test
    d. substantial capacity test

16. A child under the age of _____ cannot be held criminally responsible.
    a. 5
    b. 7
    c. 14
    d. 16

17. To establish self-defense as a valid defense, the defendant must show all of the following **except** that he or she:
    a. acted under a reasonable belief he or she was in danger of death or great harm
    b. had no means of escape from the assailant
    c. used only such force as was absolutely necessary
    d. was verbally threatened

18. The Fourth Amendment includes the:
    a. right to privacy
    b. right against self-incrimination
    c. right to a speedy and public trial
    d. prohibition of cruel and unusual punishment

19. The Fifth Amendment deals with an individual's:
    a. right to privacy
    b. right against self-incrimination
    c. right to a speedy and public trial
    d. prohibition of cruel and unusual punishment

20. The Sixth Amendment deals with an individual's:
    a. right to privacy
    b. right against self-incrimination.
    c. right to a speedy and public trial
    d. prohibition of cruel and unusual punishment

21. The Eighth Amendment deals with an individual's:
    a. right to privacy
    b. right against self-incrimination
    c. right to a speedy and public trial
    d. prohibition of cruel and unusual punishment

22. The Fourteenth Amendment affords each individual which of the following protections?
    a. due process
    b. equal protection
    c. right to appear in court
    d. a and b

23. Which of the following are not considered a due process procedural safeguard for the offender?
    a. notices of charges
    b. an informal hearing
    c. the right to counsel
    d. the opportunity to present one's own witnesses

24. The philosophical direction of the Supreme Court appears to be veering toward a _____ orientation.
    a. liberal
    b. conservative
    c. middle road
    d. mixed

Essay Questions

1. Differentiate between substantive criminal law and procedural law.

2. Distinguish between criminal law and civil law including their similarities and differences.

3. Describe the various sources of criminal law.

4. Explain the classification of crimes.

5. Explain the elements that constitute the *corpus delicti* of a crime.

6. List the various legal excuses and justifications and briefly explain the requirements of each.

7. Describe the several insanity defenses and how the legal concept has evolved.

8. Explain the relevance of the Miranda v. Arizona case as it applies to the Bill of Rights.

9. List the procedural due process rights that are guaranteed to an individual.

10. Explain the factors that shape judicial interpretation regarding due process issues.

FILL-IN THE BLANK ANSWERS

1. criminal
2. common law
3. precedent
4. stare decisis
5. Constitution
6. ex post facto
7. violations
8. commission, omission
9. elements, corpus delicti
10. mens rea
11. excuse
12. insanity, criminal responsibility
13. Durham rule
14. disease, defect, substantial capacity
15. involuntarily, duress, mistake
16. defense, fact
17. duress
18. obitriatry
19. community notification
20. Bill, Rights

TRUE/FALSE ANSWERS

1.	T	13.	F
2.	T	14.	F
3.	F	15.	T
4.	F	16.	F
5.	T	17.	F
6.	T	18.	F
7.	F	19.	T
8.	F	20.	T
9.	T	21.	F
10.	T	22.	F
11.	F	23.	T
12.	T	24.	F

MULTIPLE CHOICE ANSWERS

1.	C	13.	D
2.	A	13.	D
3.	A	15.	B
4.	C	16.	D
5.	D	17.	A
6.	B	18.	B
7.	A	19.	C
8.	D	20.	D
9.	A	21.	C
10.	B	22.	B
11.	C	23.	A
12.	B	24.	C

Chapter 5

Police in Society: History and Organization

Learning Objectives

1. Describe the concept of the police as gatekeepers for the criminal justice system.

2. Describe the significance of the pledge system and the watch system.

3. Explain the organization and function of the tithing, hundred, and shire.

4. Discuss the eighteenth century developments in English policing and the role of Henry Fielding and Sir Robert Peel.

5. Describe law enforcement in colonial America.

6. Discuss 19th century policing in America and the role of politics in policing.

7. Discuss the 20th century reform of the police departments.

8. Describe policing in each decade for the period 1960 to 1990.

9. List the federal agencies under the jurisdiction of the Justice Department and discuss the role of those agencies.

10. List the federal agencies under the jurisdiction of the Treasury Department and discuss the role of those agencies.

11. Compare and contrast the functions of the metropolitan, county, and state police agencies.

12. Describe several of the recent technological advances with respect to policing.

13. Understand the role of private security in America.

14. Understand the weaknesses in private security and the remedies that might be taken to overcome them.

Keywords and Definitions

Pledge System: Early informal system of policing whereby every person living in the villages scattered throughout the English countryside was responsible for aiding neighbors and protecting the settlement from thieves and marauders.

Tithing: A group of ten families that worked together to protect one another under the pledge system.

Hue and Cry: The alarm given when trouble occurred under the pledge system.

Hundred: A group of ten tithings, supervised by a constable under the pledge system.

Constable: Office originating under the pledge system, it was the person appointed by the local nobleman to supervise a hundred. This office eventually became the primary metropolitan law enforcement agent.

Shire: A geographical area in England of the middle ages, similar to today's county.

Shire Reeve: A forerunner of today's sheriff who pursued and apprehended law violators as part of his duty under early English system of law enforcement.

Watch System: System of security management created in thirteenth century England to help protect property in larger cities and towns.

Justice of the Peace: Office created in 1326 to assist the shire reeve in controlling the county, they eventually took on judicial functions in addition to their primary role as peacekeeper.

Sir Robert Peel: England's Home Secretary who guided the Metropolitan Police Act through Parliament and successfully started the first organized police department in London.

The Metropolitan Police Act: Legislation championed by Sir Robert Peel, it established the first organized police force in London in 1829.

Sheriff: The chief law enforcement officers in a county, a cornerstone of American policing.

Vigilantes: In the old west times, this was the posse of towns peoples formed to chase offenders and eradicate social problems.

International Association of Chiefs of Police (IACP): A professional society started in 1893 to champion the cause of police reform and professionalism.

Community Policing: An approach to law enforcement that seeks to integrate officers into local communities to reduce crime and gain improved police-community relations.

U.S. Department of Justice: The legal arm of the federal government headed by the Attorney General. It is the agency responsible for enforcing all federal laws, representing the United States in court, and conducting independent investigations.

Federal Bureau of Investigations: The arm of the Justice Department that investigates violations of federal law, gathers crime statistics, runs the federal crime laboratory, and helps assist and train local law enforcement officers.

Department of Homeland Security: Formed in 2002, it is a cabinet-level federal agency with the mission of preventing terrorist attacks, reducing vulnerability to terrorism, and minimizing the damage and recovery from terrorist attacks when they occur on U.S. soil.

Drug Enforcement Administration: Federal agency that assists local and state authorities investigate illegal drug behavior, carries out independent drug surveillance and enforcement, and assists foreign governments with source control and interdiction.

Treasury Department: Federal agency under which the Bureau of Alcohol, Tobacco and Firearms, Internal Revenue Service, and Customs Service carries out their various law enforcement functions.

Automated Fingerprint Identification System (AFIS): A computerized automated fingerprint identification system that uses mathematical models to classify and identify fingerprints on up to 250 characteristics.

Crime Mapping: A computer technology used to geographically locate crime events so that law enforcement can effectively identify and monitor crime patterns and related social problems.

DNA Profiling: The technique that allows suspects to be identified on the basis of the genetic material found in hair, blood, and other bodily tissues and fluids.

Chapter Outline

I.   Introduction
    A.   Inter-agency cooperation in law enforcement
        1.   the Green River killer case
            a.   tracking Gary Ridgeway across agency levels
            b.   model of police persistence over a 20 tear investigation
        2.   use of innovative techniques
            a.   DNA testing
            b.   interviewing other serial murderers for insight
    B.   Public perception of police
        1.   expect them to keep crime rates down
        2.   expect them to avoid abuses of the office
            a.   shy away from corruption
            b.   proper use of police force
            c.   respect civil liberties
                i.   no racial profiling
                ii.   driving while black phenomenon
        3.   public is generally supportive and appreciative of police
        4.   policing as a job opportunity of increasing demand

II.   The history of police
    A.   Origin of American policing can be traced to early English society
        1.   informal pledge system of the pre-Norman Conquest era
            a.   protection of property and life was a function of self-sufficiency
            b.   the pledge system was in use
            c.   families banded together in for self-protection
            d.   individuals were expected to raise the "hue and cry" to warn of trouble and to pursue suspected criminals

   e. a group of ten families was called a "tithing"

   f. ten tithings formed a "hundred" which was supervised by the constable

   g. shires, similar to modern counties, were supervised by the shire reeve

  2. the watch system of the 13th century

   a. watch system was a more formal organization than the earlier pledge system

   b. used watchmen to protect property against fire and robbery

   c. the justice of the peace was also created during this century

    i. took on judicial duties

    ii. constables served as their assistants

   d. the watch system continued to operate for about 500 years

  3. eighteenth-century developments

   a. effects of the industrial revolution

   b. dramatic increase in crime exposed the inadequacies of the watch system

   c. London began to experiment with more centralized and professional types of police forces

    i. Henry Fielding creates the Bow Street Runners

    ii. improved record keeping and investigation function

B. Sir Robert Peel and his Bobbies

  1. 1829 passage of the Metropolitan Police Act formalize police under the authority of Home Secretary and Parliament

   a. creates the first organized police force of over 1,000 men

   b. force was structured along formal, military model

    i. clean cut with distinctive uniforms

    ii. grew to provide assistance to outlying areas

    iii. growing pains of corruption and incompetence

  2. by 1856 every borough and county in England formed its own force

C. Law enforcement in colonial America

  1. county sheriff was the most important law enforcement agent

   a. paid by the fee system

   b. investigated citizen complaints, ran the jail & collected taxes

  2. town marshal policed the urban areas

   a. relied on the aid of constables, watchmen, police justices & council members

   b. little power and administration in generals at the local level

   c. Post-American Revolution, elected official model emerges

  3. regional individual initiatives

   a. slave patrols of the rural south capture runaway slaves

   b. bounty hunters and vigilantes of the "wild west"

D. Early police agencies

  1. first US police department in Boston in 1838

   a. New York in 1844

   b. Philadelphia in 1854

  2. local politics & politicians often controlled early urban departments

   a. politics often determined hiring and promotion decisions

   b. connections trumped qualifications in hiring decisions

  3. early American police work was often primitive in nature

   a. most officers patrolled on foot

         b.   corruption and brutality were everyday occurrences

         c.   there was little formal training and minimal supervision

         d.   advances of the 19th century and early 20th century

- i. detective bureau
- ii. first telegraph police boxes were installed in 1867
- iii. bicycles and motorcycles were introduced
- iv. first police car was used in Akron, Ohio, in 1910

E.   Twentieth-century reform

    1.   public concern about police corruption lead to a reform efforts

        a.   administrative review boards or tribunals were created

        b.   state legislators took control of some police departments

        c.   police officer strikes heightened interest in reform

    2.   local, state and Federal crime commissions investigated police corruption and suggested reform measures

    3.   Boston police strike of 1919 leads to reforms\

F.   The emergence of professionalism

    1.   the International Association of Chiefs of Police was formed in 1893

    2.   August Vollmer, chief from Berkeley, CA was a famous reformer

    3.   O.W. Wilson, chief from Wichita, KS enhances management and administration of policing

III.   The modern era of policing: 1960 to present day

A.   Policing in the 1960's

    1.   turmoil and crisis in society pressures police

        a.   Supreme Court decisions invoke the rights of the accused

        b.   civil unrest over race relations, civil rights & Vietnam war

        c.   growing crime rate

    2.   police resent demands of the public & public dissatisfied with police

B.   Policing in the 1970's

    1.   many structural changes to police agencies

        a.   responding to minority group threat

        b.   increased federal support for police agencies

- i. Law Enforcement Assistance Administration
- ii. federally funded program to finance college educations for many criminal justice practitioners

        c.   technological innovations such as computers

        d.   recruitment and promotion of women and minorities

    2.   police-community relations remain rocky

C.   Policing in the 1980s

    1.   emergence of community policing

    2.   growth of police unions

    3.   budget cutbacks

    4.   police-community relations still a problem in urban areas

D.   Policing in the 1990s

    1.   Rodney King incident as a defining event

        a.   videotaped six officers deliver 56 baton blows to King

        b.   officers tried and acquitted in suburban court

        c.   resulting South Central riots kill 54 and injure 2,383

        d.   officers later tried and convicted in federal court

2. community policing model stresses cooperation and collective problem solving

IV. Police and law enforcement today (4 levels of policing)
   A. Federal law enforcement agencies
      1. designed to protect the rights and privileges of U.S. citizens
      2. multiple agencies with no particular rank or order
         a. Department of Justice (DOJ)
            i. headed by the U.S. Attorney General
            ii. enforces all federal laws
            iii. represents the U.S. in court actions
            iv. Civil Rights Division
            v. Tax Division
            vi. Criminal Division
         b. Federal Bureau of Investigation (FBI)
            i. principle federal investigative agency
            ii. the Mann Act and the Bureau of Investigation in 1908
            iii. Director J. Edgar Hoover (1924-1972)
            iv. 28,000 employees in 56 domestic and & 40 foreign offices
            v. identification division
            vi. crime laboratory
            vii. post 9/11 reformulation of priorities
         c. Department of Homeland Security (DHS)
            i. product of the 9/11 incident
            ii. cabinet level agency to prevent terrorism combining law enforcement and national security functions
            iii. Border and Transportation Safety branch
            iv. Emergency Preparedness branch
            v. Science and Technology branch
            vi. Information Analysis and Infrastructure Protection branch
            vii. Management branch
         d. other independent agencies reporting to DHA
            i. US Coast Guard
            ii. US Secret Service
            iii. Bureau of Citizenship and Immigration Services
            iv. Office of State and Local Government Coordination
            v. Office of Inspector General
         e. Drug Enforcement Administration (DEA)
            i. Harrison Act of 1914 establishes federal jurisdiction over drugs
            ii. Bureau of Narcotics and Dangerous Drugs was predecessor
            iii. DEA created in 1973
            iv. assists local and state authorities with drug investigations
            v. carries out independent investigations of drug rings
            vi. works with foreign governments on source eradication
            vii. Operation X-Out targets party and predatory drugs
         f. Treasury Department (3 law enforcement branches)
            i. Bureau of Alcohol, Tobacco, and Firearms (ATF)
            ii. Internal Revenue Service (IRS)
            iii. Customs Service

B. State police
   1. legislatively created agencies
   2. Texas Rangers were one of the first agencies
   3. the first modern state police were formed in Pennsylvania in 1905
   4. generally responsible for highway safety, law enforcement and provide technical support to local and county agencies
   5. 80,000 state police employees (55,000 officers, 25,000 staffers)
C. County law enforcement
   1. generally known as the county sheriff, but some counties have created a county police department
   2. usually responsible for law enforcement, corrections, civil law authority, and court-related duties
   3. rural departments are more likely to have law enforcement duties
   4. 3,1000 sheriff's offices nationwide (290,000 staffers, 165,000 officers)
D. Metropolitan police
   1. comprise the majority of personnel
   2. New York City is largest police agency (40,000 officers, 10,000 staffers)
   3. 441,000 sworn police personnel (120,000 staff) at local level nationwide
   4. most local departments have less than 50 sworn officers
   5. most departments perform standard functions and services
   6. multiplicity of roles and duties over time

V. Technology and Law Enforcement
A. Application of sophisticated electronic gadgetry
B. Computer software
   1. data mining to identify crime patterns and links to suspects
   2. crime mapping programs identify problem locales
      a. 36% of agencies use the technology
      b. Chicago's ICAM program
   3. information technology
      a. computer support systems link agencies to data repositories
      b. computerized imaging systems replace mug books of offenders
   4. criminal identification
      a. enhanced booking processes
      b. two-dimensional mug shots
   5. automated fingerprint identification systems (AFIS)
      a. mathematical models classify prints on up to 250 characteristics
      b. AFIS files are regionalized to allow inter-agency usage
      c. national database taps prints from all 50 states
      d. agencies scan repository of prints for matches
   6. DNA testing
      a. genetic evidence
      b. RFLP technique
      c. PCR technique
      d. recent court decisions upheld the legality of DNA testing
      e. ethical and practical questions
         i. can't be used to solve the majority of serious crimes
         ii. potential threat to civil liberties
   7. communication
      a. computers
      b. HUD in patrol cars

      c.   cellular phones
      d.   monitoring stolen cars
      e.   electronic bulletin boards
      f.   CALEA system aids in monitoring terrorists
   8.   biometric technology
      a.   digital technology used to identify the faces of known offenders
      b.   popular in post 9/11 terrorist identification in airports
      c.   identification mode identifies person from population
      d.   verification mode taps previous registered patterns

Chapter Summary

The police are considered the gatekeepers of the criminal justice process in America. Their origins, as was the case with the criminal law, can be traced back to early English society. Before the Norman Conquest, there were no English police so every town used the **pledge** system which called for every person to be responsible for aiding neighbors in crime-related problems. Under this system, families were divided into groups of ten called **tithings**. Ten tithings were grouped into a **hundred** and were supervised by a constable, who could be considered the police officer. The crown or local landowner appointed the **shire reeve** to control the **shire**, similar to the counties of today. The shires were to supervise the territory and ensure that order would be kept. The shire reeve, forerunner of today's sheriff, soon began to pursue and apprehend law violators as part of his duties. Various forms of policing evolved until 1829 when **Sir Robert Peel** organized the first police department in London via the **Metropolitan Police Act** in 1829. This proved so successful that by 1856 every borough and county in England was required to form its own police force.

Law enforcement in colonial America paralleled that of the British model. The county **sheriff** became the most important law enforcement agent in the land. The sheriff did not patrol or seek out crime. Law enforcement belonged to the town marshal who supervised night watchmen on patrol. In the south, slave patrols performed policing duties, while in the west, it was left to vigilantes.

The modern police department was born out of urban mob violence in the nation's cities in the nineteenth century. These early police departments were concerned with dangerous classes, those immigrants, free Blacks, and urban poor whom the middle class feared. Boston created the first formal U.S. police department in 1838. During this time, politics dominated the departments and determined the recruitment of new officers and promotion of supervisors. Politicians gave away jobs to their friends, and these jobs were coveted because of their high salary. However, the job was not secure because one stayed on only as long as the politician who gave the person the job held office. Police during the nineteenth century were generally incompetent, corrupt, and disliked by the people they served.

The 20th century brought reform. Efforts to reduce corruption were evident everywhere. The **International Association of Chiefs of Police** spearheaded the work with its first president, District of Columbia police Chief Richard Sylvester. The most famous reformer was **August Vollmer**, the police chief of Berkeley, California, who was instrumental in the advent of university-level training and education for law enforcement officers. Their efforts led to a goal of developing police departments that were incorruptible, tough, highly trained, rule-oriented, and organized along militaristic lines. Police departments now wanted incorruptible crime fighters who would not question the authority of central command.

The 1960s were characterized by turmoil and crisis, especially civil unrest that brought tensions between the police and the public. In addition, the U.S. Supreme Court handed down many court decisions designed to control police operations. The 1970s brought a reduction in tensions, but the relationship between the police and minority communities was still rocky. However, the 1970s also brought higher education to the police, especially through the **Law Enforcement Education Program** of the **Law Enforcement Assistance Administration**. The 1980s saw the police moving to community policing, but it also brought a rise in police unions and dramatic state and local budget cutbacks. The 1990s brought a new outlook to policing, namely the development of community cooperation and problem solving. Two major problems continued namely police corruption and over-enforcement in minority communities. The videotaped beating of Rodney King crystallized law enforcement reforms in the 1990 and fueled **community policing** efforts aimed at improving police-community relations by integrating officers in local communities.

The **U.S. Department of Justice** is the legal arm of the United States Government. Headed by the Attorney General, it is empowered to enforce federal laws, represent the United States when it is party to court action, and conduct independent investigations through its law enforcement services. One branch of the Department of Justice is the **Federal Bureau of Investigation** (FBI), an investigative agency with jurisdiction over all matters in which the United States is, or may be, an interested party. It limits its jurisdiction to federal laws including all federal statutes not specifically assigned to other agencies. The **Drug Enforcement Administration** (DEA) is an agency which assists local and state authorities in their investigation of illegal drug use and carries out independent surveillance and enforcement activities to control the importation of narcotics. The **Department of Homeland Security** (DHS) was formed shortly after the terrorist attacks of September 11, 2001. This cabinet-level agency seeks to prevent and respond to terrorist acts on U.S. soil. Other federal law enforcement agencies under the jurisdiction of DHS include the **Coast Guard**, the **Secret Service**, the **Bureau of Citizenship and Immigration Services**, the **Office of State and Local Government Coordination**, the **Office of Private Sector Liaison**, and the **Office of the Inspector General**. The U.S. Treasury Department also has a law enforcement function, as it maintains the following enforcement branches: the **Bureau of Alcohol, Tobacco, and Firearms** (ATF), the **Internal Revenue Service** (IRS), and the **Customs Service.**

State police agencies were legislatively created to deal with crime in non-urban areas. One of the first state police agencies was the Texas Rangers. There are currently 55,000 sworn state police officers and 25,0000 civilian staffers across the 50 United States An elected sheriff heads county law enforcement in all states except Rhode Island and Hawaii. There are 3,100 sheriff's offices with 165,000 sworn law enforcement officers and 295,000 staffers. Most sheriffs are full-service departments whose duties include law enforcement, corrections, and judicial matters. Some may perform only law enforcement, some only judicial duties, and others may perform judicial duties and corrections. However, city police comprise the majority of the nation's authorized law enforcement personnel. Patrol officers spend a great deal of time in areas other than crime fighting, including traffic enforcement, emergency medical care, jail operation, crowd control, and other community services. Metropolitan police departments have jurisdiction over law enforcement functions in urban areas. New York City has the largest police force with 40,000 sworn officers. There are an estimated 441,000 sworn law enforcement officers at the local level and an additional 120,000 civilian staffers.

There is an increasing reliance on technology in law enforcement. Technological advances include **crime mapping**, **criminal identification systems**, **automated fingerprint identification systems** (AFIS), **DNA profiling**, **biometric technology** and communication-based technologies that aid in counter-terrorism efforts.

Private security consists of two major categories. **Propriety security** is undertaken by an organization's own employees and includes both plainclothes and uniformed agents directed by the organization's head of security. The second category of private security is **contractual services** such as guards, investigators, and armored cars that are provided by private companies. The **Hallcrest Report** has suggested several steps that might improve private security, including mandatory training and statewide regulatory agencies.

Fill-in-the-Blank Questions

1. The police are the _____ of the criminal justice process.

2. The police initiate contact with law violators and decide whether or not to formally _____ them, to settle the issue in an _____ way, or to simply take _____ _____ at all.

3. Under the _____ _____, every person living in the villages scattered throughout the countryside was responsible for aiding neighbors and protecting the settlement from thieves and marauders.

4. People were grouped into collectives of ten families, called _____, and when trouble occurred, the citizen was expected to make a _____ and _____.

5. The _____ _____ was implemented in 13th century England in which watchmen patrolled at night and helped protect against robberies, fires, and disturbances.

6. _____ _____ was the forerunner to today's sheriff who was appointed by the local landowner in England to pursue and apprehend law violators.

7. _____ _____ _____ was the British Home Secretary responsible for championing the _____ _____ _____ that lead to the creation of the first organized police department in London in 1829.

8. The salary of the sheriff was related to his _____ and was paid on a _____ system.

9. Unfortunately, the sheriff's _____ _____ chores were more lucrative than fighting crime, so law enforcement was not one of his primary concerns.

10. In the south, _____ _____ were an early form of law enforcement charged with capturing escaped _____.

11. The _____ is the chief law enforcement officer at the county level.

12. _____ _____ was the Chief of Police in Washington, D.C. who served as the first president for the International Association of Chiefs of Police.

13. During the reform period, professionalism was equated with an _____, tough, highly-trained, _____, department organized along _____ lines.

14. During the 1970s, the _____ _____ _____ Program helped thousands of officers further their education as hundreds of college education programs were developed on college campuses around the country.

15. The Department of Justice is headed by the _____ _____.

16. J. Edgar Hoover served as the first Director of the _____ _____ _____ _____.

17. The Commandant of the U.S. Coast Guard reports directly to the head of the _____ _____ _____ _____.

18. The ATF, IRS, and _____ _____ are the three law enforcement branches of the _____ _____.

True/False Questions

T F 1.   Citizens are especially likely to look favorably on the police if they credit local law enforcement agencies with keeping their neighborhoods safe.

T F 2.   The origins of U.S. police agencies can be traced to early French society.

T F 3.   The pledge system was created to help protect property in England's larger cities and towns.

T F 4.   The constable might be considered the first real police officer.

T F 5.   The office of justice of the peace was created to assist in controlling the hundred.

T F 6.   Thief takers only captured thieves.

T F 7.   The Bow Street Runners of London was one of the first local police agencies to investigate crimes and attempt to bring offenders to justice.

T F 8.   The London bobbies were named after their creator, Sir Robert Peel.

T F 9.   Law enforcement in colonial America was distinct from the British model.

T F 10. In colonial America, the watchmen replaced the constable as the main law enforcement officer.

T F 11.   In 19th century America, police work paid more than most other blue-collar jobs.

T F 12.   The major role of the 19th century police officer was maintaining order.

T F 13.   As a result of 20th century reforms to fight corruption, some jurisdictions created police administrative boards to reduce local officials' control over the police.

T F 14.   The Boston police strike of 1919 reduced the interest in police reform.

T F 15.   The International Association of Chiefs of Police was a leading voice for police reform in the 20th century.

T F 16.   During the reform era, the most respected police department was the New York City Police Department.

T F 17.   The 1960s were a relatively stable period for police in America.

T F 18.   During the 1960s the police were unable to control the crime rate and police officers resented the demands placed on them by dissatisfied citizens.

T F 19.   The Federal Bureau of Investigation is the one single federal agency that has unlimited jurisdiction.

T F 20.   Police departments are evolving because leaders recognize that traditional models of policing have not been effective.

T F 21.   Criminal investigation will be enhanced in the future by the application of technology.

T F 22.   Computerized crime mapping allows police officers to detect patterns of crimes and pathologies of related problems.

T F 23.   Technology seems to be an important method of increasing police productivity at a relatively low cost.

T F 24.   Some police departments are using computerized imaging to replace mug books.

Multiple Choice Questions

1.   The public is concerned by media reports of police officers who:
     a.   abuse their power
     b.   use unnecessary force or brutality
     c.   use "racial profiling"
     d.   all of the above

2.   A "hundred" in England's pledge system consisted of 100:
     a.   men
     b.   adults
     c.   families
     d.   children

3. The justice of the peace was created to assist the:
   a. constable
   b. shire reeve
   c. nobleman
   d. all of the above

4. A local nobleman could appoint which of the following individuals?
   a. shire reeve
   b. constable
   c. justice of the peace
   d. both a and b

5. The Bow Street Runners of London were an example of a group of:
   a. police officers
   b. thief takers
   c. corrupt politicians
   d. shire reeves

6. _____ is most well known for organizing the London Metropolitan Police.
   a. Sir Robert Peel
   b. O.W. Wilson
   c. August Vollmer
   d. Sir John Fielding

7. Which of the following was not a function performed by the colonial sheriff?
   a. investigation of crimes that occurred.
   b. patrolling
   c. tax collecting
   d. arrest

8. In the cities of colonial America, who did **not** aid the town marshal?
   a. constable
   b. watchman
   c. city council member
   d. sheriff

9. In the 19th century, one might find police departments performing which of the following functions?
   a. maintaining the public health
   b. street sweeping
   c. engaging in politics
   d. all of the above

10. Which of the following is **not** a characteristic of 19th century American policing?
    a. The job depended on the local political machine
    b. The work was primitive
    c. Job security was certain
    d. Officers were not respected

11. All of the following **except** _____ were as characteristic of the police in the second half of the 19th century.
    a. use of police cars
    b. use of uniforms
    c. use of key (call) boxes
    d. use of bicycles

12. Which of the following was a hallmark of law enforcement in the wild west?
    a. slave patrols
    b. vigilance committees
    c. shire reeves
    d. pledge system

13. Which of the following occurred as a result of the Boston police strike of 1919?
    a. Police unionism ended for decades
    b. Power was solidified in the hands of police administrators
    c. Federal crime commissions began to investigate the extent of crime
    d. All of the above occurred

14. Which of the following individuals in associated with the International Association of Chiefs of Police as its first president?
    a. O. W. Wilson
    b. Richard Sylvester
    c. August Vollmer
    d. J. Edgar Hoover

15. The most famous police reformer of the 20th century was:
    a. O. W. Wilson
    b. Richard Sylvester
    c. August Vollmer
    d. J. Edgar Hoover

16. During the _____, the police role seemed to be changing, the police were called upon to have a more awareness of community issues, and police unions began to grow.
    a. 1960s
    b. 1970s
    c. 1980s
    d. 1990s

17. During the _____, strict guidelines for police to interrogate and search were handed down from the U. S. Supreme Court, growing tension between the police and the public began, civil unrest was widespread, anti-Vietnam War demonstrations were occurring, and a rising crime rate.
    a. 1960s
    b. 1970s
    c. 1980s
    d. 1990s

18. During the _____, police departments scrambled to institute reforms in the face of the Rodney King beatings and the subsequent trials and riots.
    a. 1960s
    b. 1970s
    c. 1980s
    d. 1990s

19. The Attorney General serves as the chief law enforcement officer in this country and heads up which federal law enforcement agency?
    a. Department of Homeland Security
    b. Department of Justice
    c. Federal Bureau of Investigations
    d. Treasury Department

20. The _____ performs the functions of representing the United States when it is party to court action.
    a. Federal Bureau of Investigation
    b. Justice Department
    c. Treasury Department
    d. Secret Service

21. Which of the following is **not** true concerning the Federal Bureau of Investigation?
    a. It is a police agency
    b. It limits its jurisdiction to federal laws
    c. It operates a crime laboratory
    d. It publishes the Uniform Crime Reports

22. The Drug enforcement Agency conducts which of the following activities?
    a. It assists state and local authorities in investigating illegal drug use
    b. It works with foreign governments to destroy opium and marijuana crops
    c. It targets drug transportation organizations
    d. All of the above are included in their activities

23. Which of the following is **not** a law enforcement branch of the Treasury Department?
    a. U.S. Marshals
    b. Internal Revenue Service
    c. Customs Service
    d. Bureau of Alcohol, Tobacco, and Firearms

24. Which of the following is **not** an agency at least partly under the jurisdiction of the Department of Homeland Security?
    a. Customs Service
    b. Office of the Inspector General
    c. Office of Private Sector Liaison
    d. Secret Service

25. The majority of the nation's authorized law enforcement personnel work for:
    a. federal police
    b. metropolitan police
    c. county sheriff
    d. state police

26. The overwhelming number of police departments actually employ fewer than
    _____ full-time law enforcement officers.
    - a. 10
    - b. 30
    - c. 50
    - d. 100

27. Which of the following computer networks is used in fingerprint identification?
    - a. CODIC
    - b. NCIC
    - c. ICAM
    - d. AFIS

28. Which of the following law enforcement technologies is used in airports to aid in the facial
    identification of terrorists?
    - a. crime mapping
    - b. biometric technology
    - c. data mining
    - d. DNA profiling

29. Which of the following law enforcement technologies gained national attention because of its
    central role on the O.J. Simpson case?
    - a. crime mapping
    - b. biometric technology
    - c. data mining
    - d. DNA profiling

30. Which 1994 federal act aimed to make it easier for law enforcement officers to conduct
    surveillance on suspected terrorists living in the United States?
    - a. Patriot Act
    - b. LEAA
    - c. LEEP
    - d. CALEA

Essay Questions

1. Describe the concept of the police as gatekeepers for the criminal justice system.

2. Discuss the significance of the pledge and watch systems of policing.

3. Explain the role of Sir Robert Peel in the development of 18th century English policing.

4. Describe the impact of politics on 19th century American policing.

5. Discuss the movement to reform 20th century American policing.

6. Compare and contrast American policing during the 1960s and 1990s.

7. Discuss the law enforcement functions of Justice Department and the U.S. Attorney General.

8. Discuss the branches and functions of newly formed Department of Homeland Security.

9. Discuss the way that the terrorist attacks of 9/11/01 changed American policing.

10. Discuss the impact of the Rodney King case on police practice in the 1990s and beyond.

CHAPTER 5 ANSWER KEY

FILL-IN-THE-BLANK QUESTIONS

1. gatekeepers
2. arrest, informal, no action
3. pledge system
4. tithings, hue, cry
5. watch system
6. shire reeve
7. Sir Robert Peel, Metropolitan Police Act
8. effectiveness, fee
9. tax collecting
10. slave patrols, slaves
11. sheriff
12. Richard Sylvester
13. incorruptible, rule-oriented, militaristic
14. Law Enforcement Education, college education, criminal justice
15. Attorney General
16. Federal Bureau of Investigations
17. Department of Homeland Security
18. Customs Service, Treasury Department

TRUE/FALSE QUESTIONS

1.	T	13.	T
2.	F	14.	F
3.	F	15.	T
4.	T	16.	F
5.	F	17.	F
6.	F	18.	T
7.	T	19.	F
8.	T	20.	T
9.	F	21.	T
10.	F	22.	T
11.	T	23.	T
12.	T	24.	T

MULTIPLE CHOICE QUESTIONS

1.	D	16.	C
2.	C	17.	A
3.	B	18.	D
4.	D	19.	B
5.	B	20.	B
6.	A	21.	A
7.	B	22.	D
8.	D	23.	A
9.	D	24.	A
10.	C	25.	B
11.	A	26.	C
12.	B	27.	D
13.	D	28.	B
14.	B	29.	D
15.	C	30.	D

CHAPTER 6

THE POLICE: ORGANIZATION, ROLE, AND FUNCTION

Learning Objectives

At the conclusion of this chapter, the student should possess sufficient knowledge to achieve the following learning objectives:

1.   Describe the organization of a typical police department in terms of chain of command and structure.

2.   Know the similarities and differences between patrol and detective operations.

3.   Describe patrol activities and discuss the effectiveness of police patrol to deter crime.

4.   Have an understanding of the inherent role conflict of proactive and reactive policing.

5.   Understand the concept of community policing and the various strategies that go along with the approach.

6.   Describe basic investigative practices and activities, including the specialized technique of undercover work.

7.   Understand the concept of problem-oriented-policing.

8.   Understand the various police subsystems.

9.   Identify the factors that may be used to improve police productivity.

10. List and describe the duties of support and administrative positions in a typical police department.

Keywords and Definitions

Time-In-Rank System: The system used by most police departments for determining promotion eligibility. It is a seniority-based system in which an officer must spend a certain amount of time in the next lowest rank before being promoted. Productivity is a secondary factor in promotion decisions.

Beat: The specific area of the jurisdiction a police officer is charged with patrolling.

Order Maintenance (Peacekeeping): The process of maintaining order and civility within an officer's assigned jurisdiction, usually accomplished by informal means instead of arrest.

Discretion: The authority that a police officer has to decide whether or not to pursue formal or informal social control efforts against offenders.

Selective Enforcement: The policy of police officers to concentrate on some crimes, but handling the majority in an informal manner.

Kansas City Patrol Study: The study that evaluated the effects of variations in patrol techniques and the effectiveness of patrol.

Displacement: An effect that occurs when criminals relocate their offending to a different area in response to increased police presence.

Proactive Policing: An aggressive law enforcement style that encourages officers to stop motor vehicles to issue citations and to aggressively arrest and detain suspicious persons in order to reduce crime rates.

Detective Division: The unit in a police department that is responsible for conducting detailed investigations on crimes reported to the police.

Vice Squad: The unit within the police department that is responsible for the enforcement of morality-based laws such as prostitution, gambling, and pornography.

Sting Operations: Organized groups of detectives who deceive criminals into openly committing illegal acts or conspiring to engage in criminal activity.

Forensics: The use of comprehensive chemical, biological, and physical analyses on evidence submitted by law enforcement agencies.

Broken Windows Model: Founded by James Q. Wilson and George Kelling, it is a new approach to improving police relations that emphasizes the role of police as maintainers of community order and safety.

Police-Community Relations: The interaction and ongoing relationship between law enforcement and private citizens that is aimed at identifying, combating, and preventing criminal activity.

Community-Oriented Policing (COP): The police model that emphasizes community preservation, public safety, and order maintenance rather than crime fighting. Under this model, police administrators deploy their forces where they can encourage public confidence, strengthen feelings of safety, and elicit cooperation from citizens.

Foot Patrol: A deployment approach that takes officers out of cars and puts them on walking beats in an effort to strengthen their ties with the community.

Neighborhood-Oriented Policing (NOP): An approach that is based on decentralized, flexible, and adaptive decision making to deal with the particular needs of each neighborhood.

Problem-Oriented Policing (POP): A proactive type of policing that police agencies employ to identify particular long-term community problems and develop strategies to eliminate them.

Hot Spots of Crime: Those few locations where a great deal of urban crime is concentrated; those relatively few locations in metropolitan areas from where a significant portion of all police calls typically radiate.

Gang Tactical Detail: A police unit created to combat youth gang problems by targeting known offenders and tracking their gang-related behavior.

Internal Affairs: The branch charged with policing the police.

Civilian Review Board: An oversight entity comprised of private citizens that hears allegations of police wrongdoing and seeks to improve police-community relations.

Consolidation: The combining of small departments in adjoining areas into a "superagency" that services the previously fragmented jurisdictions.

Informal Arrangements: Unwritten cooperative agreements made between localities to perform a task collectively that would be mutually beneficial.

Pooling: The combining of resources by two or more agencies to perform a specified function under a predetermined, often formalized arrangement with direct involvement by all parties.

Service Districts: Areas within a given police jurisdiction where a special level of service is provided and financed through a special tax or assessment.

Differential Police Response: Strategies to maximize resources by differentiating among police requests for services in terms of the form the police response takes. Some calls will result in the dispatch of a sworn officer, others in the dispatching of a less highly trained civilian, or by asking citizens to walk in or mail in their requests for low priority services.

Chapter Outline

I.   Introduction
        A.   Chief Charles Moose
                1.   point man of the Washington-area sniper case
                2.   model of successful law enforcement career
        B.   Law enforcement as a challenging job
                1.   patrol the mean streets
                2.   risk their lives to protect citizens
        C.   Police are subject to unrealistic expectations

II.   The police organization
        A.   Police departments are independent agencies under the executive branch of government
                1.   some cooperative efforts take place across departments
                2.   each department has its own set of rules, policies, procedures, norm & budget

B.   Militaristic, hierarchical structure
1.   chain of command
2.   police chief is at the top setting policy and maintaining administrative control
3.   numerous operating divisions and decision-making practices can exist

C.   Promotions based on the time-in-rank system
1.   provides stability and cost savings to the department
2.   frustrates the educated officer and administrators who want to promote young officers
3.   once granted, rank is rarely taken away

III.   The police role
    A.   Media portrayals
        1.   fearless crime fighters
        2.   the reality is the great bulk of police patrol efforts is devoted to order maintenance or peacekeeping, not crime fighting
        3.   police as community problem solvers
    B.   Service vs. Enforcement
        1.   reality is a large number of calls for service handled each year
        2.   social-service and administrative tasks take up more than half the officer's time
        3.   crime-related calls make up 5 to 20 percent of total activity
    C.   Law enforcement activity
        1.   many officers (1/3) serve support roles and don't patrol or make arrests
        2.   the average officer makes two arrests a month and less than one felony arrest every two months

IV.   Patrol function
    A.   Patrol personnel
        1.   patrol officers comprise 2/3 of the force and are a highly visible component
        2.   they work in "beats"
        3.   they work shifts, 24 hours a day
        4.   major purposes of patrol
            a.   deter crime with a visible police presence
            b.   maintain public order
            c.   respond quickly to crime and emergencies
            d.   arrest criminals
            e.   provide aid to citizens in distress
            f.   facilitate the movement of people and traffic
            g.   create a sense of safety and security

        5.   patrol activities
            a.   order maintenance and peacekeeping makes up the bulk of the work
            b.   the use of discretion and selective enforcement
    B.   Does patrol work?
        1.   research efforts questioned the basic assumptions that patrol deters crime
        2.   Kansas City Patrol Study
            a.   little differences in crime rates were found in reactive, proactive and normal patrol districts

           b.   variations in patrol had little effect on citizen's attitudes toward the police and fear of crime

C.   Improving patrol
    1.   proactive patrol
        a.   incorporate social service in with crime deterrence
        b.   aggressive patrol
        c.   targeting specific crimes
            i.   zero tolerance in New York City
            ii.   "life-style" crimes
        d.   making arrests to deter crime
        e.   adding patrol officers to reduce crime
    2.   critical success of proactive policing model

V.   The investigation function
    A.   First detective bureau established in London in 1841
    B.   Detectives and crime scene investigators are romantic figures
    C.   Detective divisions may be subdivided into sections or bureaus
      1.   crimes against persons (homicide, robbery, sex crimes)
      2.   property crimes (burglary, auto theft, forgery, felony theft)
      3.   investigative support (evidence, crime scene, polygraph)
      4.   special operations (narcotics, school drugs taskforce, liaison detectives)
    D.   Vice squads
      1.   plainclothes or detectives who focus on victimless crimes
      2.   conduct covert operations that are criticized by civil libertarians
    E.   Sting operations
      1.   organized groups of detectives deceive criminals into engaging in criminal activity
      2.   operations have netted millions of dollars in recovered property
      3.   involve deceit & other questionable practices by the officer
    F.   Undercover work
      1.   lone agent infiltration into a criminal organization
      2.   officer may pose as a victim
      3.   personal danger to the officer
      4.   psychological problems
    G.   Evaluating Investigation
      1.   study estimates that half of all detectives could be replaced without affecting clearance rates
      2.   subsequent research finds that most cases are solved because the suspect was positively identified at the scene of the crime
      3.   as time elapses so does the chance of arrest
    H.   Improving investigation effectiveness
      1.   give patrol officers responsibility to conduct preliminary investigations
      2.   use of specialized units
      3.   technological advances
      4.   limitations in investigative practices
        a.   unsolved cases
        b.   length of investigation
        c.   sources of information
        d.   effectiveness

5. Crime Scene Investigation (CSI)
    a. popularized by TV shows on the topic
    b. use of science, mathematics and complex instruments in investigation
        i. controlled substance and toxicology of blood
        ii. biology of the crime lab
        iii. chemistry of forensics and trace evidence
        iv. document examination
        v. firearm and toolmark identification
6. using technology
    a. streamline and enhance investigations
    b. catalog and compare evidence through Coplink system

VI. Community policing
    A. Police-community relations (PCR)
        1. cooperative efforts between police and citizens
        2. make citizens more aware of policing activities
        3. enhance methods of self-protection in the community
        4. improve public attitudes toward police
    B. Broken windows model
        1. Kelling and Wilson's 3 observations
            a. neighborhood disorder creates fear
            b. neighborhoods give out crime-promoting signals
            c. police need citizen's cooperation
        2. core police role must be altered to achieve community involvement
        3. call for a return to earlier patrol function that stressed intimate contact with citizens
    C. Implementing community-oriented policing (COP) programs
        1. foot or bicycle patrols
        2. organizational elements
        3. tactical elements
        4. external elements
    D. Neighborhood-oriented policing (NOP)
        1. reconsider recruitment, organization, and operating procedures
        2. emphasize results, not bureaucratic process
        3. decentralize decision making to the neighborhood level
        4. be flexible and adaptive
    E. Changing the police role
        1. sharing power with local groups and individuals
        2. citizens must actively participate with police in crime fighting
        3. top-down management style replaced by bottom-up model
        4. recruit community savvy officers

VII. Problem-oriented policing (POP)
    A. Proactive orientation to policing
        1. identify long-term community problems
        2. develop strategies for problem elimination
    B. "Hot spots" of crime
    C. Criminal acts and criminal places
        1. focus on specific areas and specific criminal acts

        2.   combating auto theft
                 a.   GPS technology
                 b.   bait cars
        3.   reducing violence
                 a.   gang tactical details
                 b.   Operation Ceasefire
                 c.   displacement issues

VIII.   The challenges of community policing
       A.   Challenges that must be addressed to implement effective community policing
            1.   defining community
            2.   defining roles
            3.   emphasizing supervision style
            4.   reorient police values
            5.   revise training
            6.   reorient recruitment
       B.   Overcoming obstacles
            1.   still unclear if community policing is the crime control solution its backers claim it to be
            2.   many definitions of community policing
            3.   COP has become a staple of municipal police departments

IX.   Support functions
       A.   Support and administration functions that aid patrol, investigation, and traffic
            1.   personnel service
                 a.   recruitment
                 b.   Behavioral-Personnel Assessment Device (B-PAD)
            2.   internal affairs
                 a.   process citizen complaints
                 b.   investigate corruption and criminal activity in the police department
            3.   budget office
                 a.   administer to payroll
                 b.   purchase equipment
                 c.   planning
                 d.   auditing
            4.   data management systems
                 a.   wanted offenders
                 b.   stolen merchandise
                 c.   traffic violations
            5.   dispatch
            6.   emergency services
            7.   crime lab
            8.   planning and research
       B.   Citizen oversight of police: civilian review boards
            1.   citizens investigate allegations of police misconduct
            2.   citizens review investigations of the department
            3.   complainants may appeal findings of the agency to the civilian review board

X.   Issues in police productivity
        A.   Police seek to increase productivity of line officers through various efforts
                1.   consolidation of smaller agencies into larger ones
                2.   informal arraignments between agencies that are mutually beneficial
                3.   sharing via mutual aid pacts
                4.   pooling resources
                        a.   community mapping, planning, and analysis for safety
                                strategies (COMPASS)
                        b.   data sharing and common site for data analysis
                        c.   Boston Gun Project or New York's Comstat program map
                                crimes
                5.   contracting to other jurisdictions
                6.   service districts using special taxes or assessments
                7.   civilian employees for administrative support or supplemental
                        police services
                8.   multiple tasking of the public safety officer
                9.   special assignments
                10.   differential police response for prioritized call type
        B.   Departments now implement a variety of creative designs to stretch resources
                and improve effectiveness

Chapter Summary

Most police departments are independent agencies, operating without specific administrative control from any higher governmental authority. The majority are organized in militaristic, hierarchical manner. Most departments employ a **time-in-rank** system for determining promotion eligibility. Under this approach, an officer must spend a certain amount of time in the next lowest rank before he or she can be considered for advancement and productivity is of secondary importance.

Most research efforts show that a police officer's **crime-fighting** efforts are only a small part of his or her overall activities. The **police role** involves a preponderance of noncrime-related activities and is similar in both larger and small departments. Uniformed patrol officers are the backbone of the police department, accounting for about two-thirds of a department's personnel. Patrol officers are charged with supervising specific areas of their jurisdiction, called **beats**, whether it be on **foot patrol**, in a patrol car, or by motorcycle, horse, helicopter, plane or boat. The greatest bulk of police patrol efforts are devoted to what has been described as **order maintenance**, or **peacekeeping**. Police officers exercise their decision-making **discretion** and practice a policy of **selective enforcement**, concentrating on some crimes but handling the majority in an informal manner.

An evaluation of the effectiveness of patrol was measured by the **Kansas City Patrol Study** that indicated that variations in patrol techniques had little effect on crime. It was discovered that increasing the number of patrol cars in a beat did not reduce crime, fear of crime, or enhance citizen satisfaction with the police. The study set the stage for the implementation of a **proactive policing**, aggressive law enforcement style in order to achieve crime rate reductions. A proactive approach to crime fighting requires officers to initiate actions against law violators, but the downside of aggressive tactics is resentment of minority communities. Such proactive approaches have been shown to have deterrent effects in cases of domestic violence, but another major study concluded that adding police officers had little impact on the crime rate.

The modern criminal investigator, or **detective**, is most likely an experienced civil servant, trained in investigatory techniques, knowledgeable about legal rules of evidence and procedure, and somewhat cautious about the legal and administrative consequences of his or her own actions. Detective divisions are typically organized into sections or bureaus such as homicide, robbery, or rape. Criticism has been leveled at the nation's detective forces for being bogged down in paperwork and being relatively inefficient at clearing cases. However, police detectives do make a valuable contribution to police work because of their skilled interrogation and case-processing techniques are essential to eventual criminal conviction.

Police agencies have been trying to use **police-community relations** programs to gain the cooperation and respect of the communities they serve for more than thirty years. Wilson and Kelling articulated the **"broken windows" model** in an attempt to improve police-community relations. They contend that the core police role must be altered to gain community involvement is to be gained and maintained. The **community-oriented policing approach** holds that police administrators would be well served by deploying their forces where they can encourage public confidence, strengthen feelings of safety, and elicit cooperation from citizens. To achieve the goals of community policing, some agencies have tried to decentralize, an approach known as **innovative neighborhood-oriented policing**. A key element of the community policing philosophy is that citizens must actively participate with the police to fight crime. **Problem-oriented policing** is closely associated, yet independent from the community policing concept and requires police agencies to identify particular long-term community problems and help develop strategies for their elimination.

A large part of police resources is devoted to support and administrative functions, including: personnel services; internal affairs; budget and finance; records and communications; training; community relations; crime prevention; laboratory; planning and research; property; and detention.

Police productivity refers to the amount of actual order, maintenance, crime control, and other activities provided by individual police officers, and concomitantly, by police departments as a whole. **Consolidation** of police services combines small departments, usually with less than ten employees, in adjoining areas into a super-agency that services the previously fragmented jurisdictions. Some of the techniques used to accomplish this include: informal arrangements, sharing, **pooling**, contracting, **service districts**, civilian employees, multiple-tasking, special assignments, budget supplements, and **differential police response**.

Fill-in-the-Blank Questions

1. Most police departments are _____ agencies, operating without specific administrative control from any _____ governmental authority.

2. The majority of police departments are organized in a _____, _____ manner.

3. The majority of formal police-citizen interactions take shape as _____ _____ _____.

4. _____ _____ _____ are the backbone of the police department, usually accounting for about two-thirds of a department's personnel.

5. Patrol officers are charged with patrolling specific areas of their jurisdiction, which is known as a _____.

6. Most experts today agree that the bulk of police patrol efforts are devoted to _____ maintenance or _____ functions.

7. Data from the _____ _____ Patrol Study indicated that variations in _____ techniques had little effect on crime patterns.

8. _____ occurs when heightened police presence in one neighborhood inclined offenders to move their operations to a nearby location with lighter patrol levels.

9. _____ _____ is an aggressive form of law enforcement in which patrol officers take the initiative against crime instead of waiting for acts to occur.

10. Efforts have been directed at improving the relationships between police departments and the public through programs known as _____ - _____ relations.

11. A _____ _____ involves an organized group of detectives who deceive criminals into openly committing their illegal acts and then swoop in to make the arrests.

12. According to the _____-_____ _____ approach, community relations and crime control effectiveness cannot be the province of a few specialized units housed within the traditional police department.

13. Problem-oriented policing (POP) models are supported by the fact that a great deal of urban crime is concentrated in a few _____ _____ of crime.

14. The branch charged with policing the police is _____ _____.

15. _____ means combining small departments in adjoining areas into a _____ that services the previously fragmented jurisdictions.

True/False Questions

T F 1. It is quite easy for citizens to determine who is actually responsible for the police department's policies and operations.

T F 2. Most police departments use a time-in-rank system for determining promotion eligibility.

T F 3. Many educated and ambitious officers seek private employment because of an inability to advance through the ranks through simple hard work and personal initiative.

T F 4. Crime fighting efforts comprise the majority of a police officer's overall activities.

T F 5. Order maintenance refers to an officer being adept at "handling the situation" informally.

T F 6. Aggressive policing decreases the community perception that police arrest a lot of criminals and that most violators get caught.

T F 7. Proactive policing may also help control crime because it results in conviction of more criminals.

T F 8. The actual number of law enforcement officers on patrol in a jurisdiction has a great impact on area crimes.

T F 9. The Kansas City Patrol Study revealed that increased police presence can deter criminals.

T F 10. The investigative function of the detective requires very little input from the regular patrol officer.

T F 11. Once a crime has been completed and the investigation is placed in the hands of the detective, the chances of identifying and arresting the perpetrator diminish rapidly.

T F 12. George Kelling was one of the scholars who set forth the "broken windows" approach to policing.

T F 13. An evaluation of foot patrol indicated that it was effective in bringing down crime rates.

T F 14. Community policing programs have been implemented in large cities, suburban areas, but not often in rural areas.

T F 15. Community policing emphasizes results, not bureaucratic process.

T F 16. Internal affairs investigators are generally feared and distrusted by fellow officers.

T F 17. Police departments use forensic laboratories to identify substances and classify fingerprints.

T F 18. Police productivity simply refers primarily to the number of arrests made by the police over a certain time period.

T F 19. Pooling refers to unwritten cooperative arrangements made between localities to perform a task collectively that would be mutually beneficial.

T F 20. Service districts are set aside areas, usually within an individual county, where a special level of service is provided and financed through a special tax or assessment.

Multiple Choice Questions

1. The time-in-rank method for determining promotion requires an officer to do which of the following before he/she is eligible for a promotion?
   a. Serve at least 3 years on patrol
   b. Spend time as a community service officer
   c. Achieve a certain number of felony arrests
   d. Spend a certain amount of time in the next lowest rank

2. All of the following concerning the time-in-rank system are true **except:**
   a. it determines promotion eligibility
   b. it promotes administrative flexibility
   c. it promotes fairness
   d. it prohibits rapid advancement

3. Which of the following is true concerning the police officer's overall activities?
   a. Crime-fighting takes up the majority of his or her overall activities
   b. Social service and administrative tasks take less than one-fourth of the officer's time
   c. Social service and administrative tasks consume more than half of the officer's calls
   d. All of the above are true

4. All of the following concerning the police role are correct **except:**
   a. Less attention will be paid to special populations
   b. The police role is similar in both large and small departments
   c. Officers in large urban departments handle more felony cases than those in small towns
   d. In the future, police will handle more social problems

5. The majority of a police officer's efforts are devoted to which of the following type of activities?
   a. selective enforcement
   b. order maintenance
   c. crime fighting
   d. providing services

6. Which of the following is not a proposed method for improving patrol functions?
   a. increased civilian patrols
   b. targeting certain types of crime
   c. proactive policing efforts
   d. adding patrol officers

7. The policy of a police officer concentrating on some crimes but handling the majority in an informal manner is known as:
   a. order maintenance
   b. selective enforcement
   c. aggressive patrol
   d. crime fighting

8. _____ is the practice of responding only when summoned by citizens to the scene of a particular crime.
   a. proactive patrol
   b. selective enforcement
   c. reactive patrol
   d. positive patrol

9. The Kansas City Patrol study indicated that variations in patrol techniques?
   a. they had a significant effect on crime patterns
   b. they greatly improved citizen's attitude toward police
   c. they had little effect on citizens fear of crime
   d. they improved patrol officer morale

10. Organized groups of detectives who deceive criminals into openly committing illegal acts or conspiring to engage in criminal activity is a(n):
    a. sting operation
    b. undercover operation
    c. entrapment operation
    d. all of the above

11. Which branch of the police force is generally responsible for enforcing prostitution laws?
    a. vice squad
    b. detective bureau
    c. foot patrols
    d. liaison detectives

12. Research shows that if a crime is reported while in progress, the police have about a _____ chance of making an arrest.
    a. 10%
    b. 25%
    c. 33%
    d. 50%

13. The community-oriented policing (COP) approach holds that police administrators would be well served by deploying their forces where they can:
    a. encourage public confidence
    b. strengthen feelings of safety
    c. elicit cooperation from citizens
    d. do all of the above

14. In community policing all of the following must take place **except:**
    a. citizens must actively participate with the police to fight crime
    b. maintain the same design of the police department
    c. patrol officer is the manager of the beat
    d. police department must alter recruitment and training requirements

15. The relationship between problem-oriented policing and community policing is which of the following?
    a. Problem-oriented policing is related with community policing
    b. Problem-oriented policing is independent from community policing
    c. both a and b are correct
    d. There is no relationship between the two

16. Problem-oriented policing (POP) strategies require which of the following?
    a. police agencies to identify particular, long-term community problems
    b. police agencies to identify efficient and effective solutions to the problems
    c. police managers to become advocates as well as agents of reform
    d. all of the above

17. Defining the community is a challenge in community policing because:
    a. the police do not know what a community is
    b. it must be an ecological area with common norms and shared values
    c. community policing projects should cross boundaries of communities
    d. all of the above

18. Which of the following is said to be a significant challenge of community-oriented policing (COP) as we move forward with this approach?
    a. defining what is meant by community
    b. defining the roles of community police officers
    c. reorienting police norms and values to embrace the COPs approach
    d. all of the above

19. The internal affairs division handles which of the following offenses?
    a. citizen complaints of police corruption
    b. unnecessary use of force by police officers
    c. allegations of police officer participation in criminal activity
    d. all of the above

20. Which of the following is the innovative new approach being used to track and respond to allegations of police misconduct?
    a. civilian review boards
    b. selective enforcement protocols
    c. multiple tasking approaches
    d. neighborhood-oriented policing

21. Which of the following is **not** a support function in a police department?
    a. budget
    b. information dissemination
    c. traffic
    d. training

22. Which of the following is not part of the police department's training?
    a. training academy
    b. field training officer
    c. on-the-job training
    d. college training

23. Which of the following practice(s) is/are used to increase police productivity?
    a. multiple-tasking
    b. civilian employees
    c. pooling
    d. all of the above

24. _____ is the provision or reception of services that aid in the execution of a law enforcement function.
    a. pooling
    b. sharing
    c. contracting
    d. consolidation

25. All of the following are characteristics of differential police response **except:**
    a. some calls will result in the dispatch of a highly trained civilian
    b. it is designed to maximize resources
    c. some calls will result in the dispatch of a sworn officer
    d. citizens may be asked to mail in their requests

Essay Questions

1. Explain the major purposes of proactive and reactive policing practices.

2. Describe the relationship between patrol officers and detectives when it comes to solving crimes.

3. Discuss the Kansas City Patrol study and what is has to say about police patrol efforts.

4. Discuss the pros and cons of undercover police operations.

5.   Explain the three key points to Wilson and Kelling's broken windows model.

6.   Compare and contrast problem-oriented policing, neighborhood-oriented policing and community-oriented policing.

7.   Discuss the major administrative challenges that face the community-oriented policing approach moving forward.

8. Describe the major support functions performed in the typical police department.

9. Discuss the prospects and limitations of civilian review boards as a means of addressing police wrongdoing.

10. Identify five innovative approaches to improve police productivity and explain each one.

CHAPTER 6 ANSWER KEY

FILL-IN-THE-BLANK QUESTIONS

1. independent, higher
2. militaristic, hierarchal
3. motor vehicle stops
4. uniformed patrol officers
5. beats
6. order, peacekeeping
7. Kansas City, patrol
8. displacement
9. proactive policing
10. police, community
11. sting operation
12. community oriented policing
13. hot spots
14. internal affairs
15. consolidation, superagency

TRUE/FALSE QUESTIONS

1.	F	11.	T
2.	T	12.	T
3.	T	13.	F
4.	F	14.	F
5.	T	15.	T
6.	F	16.	T
7.	T	17.	T
8.	F	18.	F
9.	F	19.	F
10.	F	20.	T

MULTIPLE CHOICE QUESTIONS

1.	D	14.	B
2.	B	15.	C
3.	C	16.	D
4.	A	17.	B
5.	B	18.	D
6.	A	19.	D
7.	B	20.	A
8.	C	21.	C
9.	C	22.	D
10.	A	23.	D
11.	A	24.	B
12.	C	25.	A
13.	D		

Chapter 7

Issues in Policing

Learning Objectives

1. Describe the unique characteristics of the police culture and its core beliefs.

2. Describe the traits of the police personality and provide some explanation of how those traits are developed.

3. Recognize and describe the different styles of policing and how they can affect job performance.

4. Describe factors which influence police discretion and discuss the controversy surrounding the control of discretion.

5. Understand the concept of police profiling and its relationship to police discretion.

6. Describe the role of women in police agencies and how it has evolved over time.

7. Understand the problems faced by minority police officers and how they have evolved over time.

8. Understand the causes and manifestations of job stress among police and what can be done to combat it.

9. Understand the problem of police brutality and police shootings and the different formal and informal mechanisms that are used to control these actions.

10. Know the varieties of police corruption that exist, there causes, and the measures that are being used to control police corruption.

Keywords and Definitions

Police Culture: The banding together of police officers caused by the experience of becoming a police officer and by the nature of the job itself.

Blue Curtain: The police culture characterized by cynicism, clannishness, secrecy, and insulation from others in society.

Cynicism: The adoption and maintenance of negative values and attitudes by a police officer.

Police Style: The working attitude through which a police officer approaches his/her work.

Crime Fighter: The style of policing that sees investigating serious crime and apprehending criminals as the most important aspect of police work.

Social Agent: The style of policing that believes that the police should be involved in a wide range of activities without regard for their connection to law enforcement.

Law Enforcer: The style of policing that believes that the officer's duty is clearly set out in the law and believes that officers should "play it by the book."

Watchman: The style of policing that is characterized by an emphasis on the maintenance of public order as the police goal, rather than on law enforcement or general service.

Discretion: Police officer's ability to make her or his own decisions in carrying out daily tasks.

Low-visibility decision making: The high degree of personal discretion used by the majority of police officers in carrying out daily tasks that generally go without administrative review.

Demeanor: The manner in which an offender conducts himself or herself when dealing with a police officer.

Racial Profiling: The aggressive campaign of street searches that singles out Blacks and Hispanic citizens.

Double Marginality: Coined by Nicholas Alex, it refers to black police officers suffering from expectations by black offenders that the black officer would give them a break and from overt racism from white police officers.

Defeminization: The process by which women who prove themselves tough enough to gain respect as police officers are then labeled as "lesbians" or "bitches."

Police Stress: The strain placed on a police officer because of the ambiguity of the police role, social isolation, and the ever present threat of danger.

Police Brutality: Unethical actions by police officers that include abusive language, unnecessarily using force or coercion, making threats, prodding with nightsticks, stopping people to harass them, etc.

Deadly Force: The actions of a police officer who shoots and kills a suspect who is fleeing from arrest, assaulting a victim, or attacking the officer.

Fleeing Felon Rule: The standard put forth in English Common Law that allowed for the use of deadly force by a police officer trying to arrest a felon who was resisting or running away.

Suicide by Cop: A phenomenon whereby distraught citizens attack the police in hopes of producing a victim-precipitated killing by the officers.

Tennessee v. Garner: The Supreme Court case ruling that the use of deadly force against apparently unarmed and non-dangerous fleeing felons may not be used unless it is necessary to prevent the escape and the officer has probable cause to believe the suspect poses a significant threat of death or serious injury to the officer or others.

Graham v. Connor: The Supreme Court case that created a reasonableness standard for the use of force.

Pepper Spray: A non-lethal weapon system made from peppers that is sprayed in the eyes of perpetrators by police officers to gain compliance.

Bean Bag Gun: A non-lethal weapon system that uses a tea bad sized projectile filled with lead birdshot to assist police in immobilizing perpetrators.

Taser: A non-lethal weapon system that fires electrified darts into perpetrators to deliver a 50,000 volt charge that allows police to immobilize the individual.

Knapp Commission: The special commission that investigated corruption among New York City police officers and concluded that most corrupt police officers are "grass eaters."

"Meat Eaters:" Chronically corrupt officers who aggressively misuse police power for personal gain by demanding bribes, threatening legal action, or cooperating with criminals.

"Grass Eaters:" Police officers who are willing to accept payoffs when their everyday duties place them in a position to be solicited by the public.

Mollen Commission: The commission investigating corruption among New York City police officers in the 1990s and found some police officers actively involved in violence and drug dealing.

Rotten Pockets: This type of police department has a corrupt officers who band together to perpetrate and cover up their corrupt activities.

Chapter Outline

I. Introduction
   A. Public concern
      1. video taped police violence against citizens
      2. high profile cases such as the Rodney King & Donovan Jackson cases raise awareness and unrest
   B. Public confidence in the Police
      1. 60% of Americans surveyed say they have a great deal of confidence in police
      2. minority citizens report less confidence and are less likely to report crimes
      3. police agencies have begun to reach out to the African American community
   C. Experts and law enforcement administrators
      1. raise effectiveness and efficiency concerns
      2. question the optimal social composition of police force

3. concerned over the problems that officers face in their interactions with citizens

II. The police profession
   A. Police Culture
      1. police subculture (the "blue curtain")
         a. unique characteristics that exists among police officers
         b. marked by cynicism, clannishness, secrecy, insulation from others in society
         c. police tend to socialize together and cut themselves off from outsiders
         d. become preoccupied with the dangers and violence inherent in the job
      2. six core beliefs of the police subculture
         a. they are the only real crime fighters
         b. no one else understands us
         c. loyalty to each other
         d. it is difficult to win the war against crime
         e. public is unsupportive
         f. patrol work is the pits
      3. believed to develop from work experiences in response to dangerous public
      4. naïve will to help people & fight crime is replaced by seasoned cynicism
      5. fellow officers provide guidance and support within the police subculture
   B. Police personality
      1. officers develop a unique set of personality traits
         a. dogmatic
         b. authoritarian
         c. suspicious
         d. cynical
      2. negative values and attitudes cause officers to buy into the blue curtain
   C. Origins of the police personality
      1. police work attracts people with these personality traits
      2. the nature of the work causes traits to develop
   D. Police style
      1. the working personality of the police officer
         a. departmental rules and procedures exist for potential guidance
         b. police subculture serves as another source of guidance
         c. individuals styles emerge out of experience and interpretation
      2. the "Dirty Harry" problem
         a. stress their central role as protector of society
         b. "thin blue line" mentality stresses "any means necessary"
      3. four common styles of policing have been proposed
         a. the crime fighter
            i. investigates crimes and prosecutes criminals
            ii. focuses on major personal crime
            iii. disregards property crime and misdemeanors
            iv. also known as enforcers, supercops or old-style crime fighters
         b. the social agent
            i. feels responsible for a wide range of services
            ii. problem-solvers
         c. the law enforcer
            i. emphasizes detection and apprehension
            ii. does not distinguish between major and minor crimes
            iii. plays it by the book

   d. the watchman
     i. emphasizes maintenance of public order
     ii. ignores infractions and service requests
  4. some question that police styles exist?
   a. argue that police force is too diverse for common styles to emerge
   b. question whether officers are actually able to choose between styles

II. Police discretion
 A. Each police officer possesses personal discretion as part of their professional responsibility
 B. Low-visibility decision making
  1. most officers decision-making is not generally subject to administrative review
  2. several factors shape police discretion
   a. legal factors
     i. greatest discretion exists for minor offenses
     ii. officer must diagnose the severity of the offense on the spot
   b. victim factors
     i. relationship between the offender & victim influences response
     ii. acquaintances treated more casually than strangers
     iii. severity of offense also plays a role here as well
   c. environmental factors
     i. living and working environment shapes officer response
     ii. officers that live in the community uses more leniency
     iii. perceptions of community alternatives to arrest also factor in
     iv. look for alternative agencies or persons to handle the problem
   d. departmental factors
     i. policies, practices & customs of the department shape responses
     ii. departmental directives focus officers on specific problems
     iii. written rules often limit or direct discretionary options
   e. supervisory factors
     i. number of eyes overseeing officer operations shape behaviors
     ii. supervisory styles trickle down to patrol officers
   f. peer factors
     i. peer pressure from fellow officers shape decisions
     ii. direct pressure through comments and approval
     iii. indirect pressure through desire for respect and admiration
   g. situational factors
     i. officer's in-the-moment interactions shape decisions
     ii. offender attitude and demeanor can shape officer decisions
     iii. physical resistance by the offender shapes decisions
     iv. the way that the officer comes into contact with the offense can shape their response
     v. officer's personal matters can spill over into work decisions
   h. extralegal factors
     i. race, class, and gender of actors can influence decisions
     ii. social debate surrounds the appropriateness of this situation

III. Who are the police?
 A. Traditional police officer
  1. white male

       2.   high school education

       3.   family members also police officers

       4.   increasing levels of college education

B.   Police education

       1.   majority of departments do not require a college education

           a.   most departments prefer and appreciate college educated officers

           b.   number of departments requiring college education is on the rise

       2.   education makes for a better police officer

           a.   improved verbal communication skills

           b.   improved writing skills

           c.   improves professionalism

           d.   increases chances for promotion

           e.   increases self-confidence

       3.   does higher education matter?

           a.   dissuades minority applicants

           b.   costly to recruit and pay

           c.   lack of evidence that education is a benefit to police work

C.   Minorities in policing

       1.   departments seek to field a police force that approximates citizenry

       2.   diverse police force more readily gains public trust

       3.   minority officers possess special knowledge & skills

           a.   know the culture

           b.   know the language

D.   Minority police officers

       1.   first minority officer hired in Washington, D.C. in 1861

       2.   early officers served restricted roles and had limited promotion potential

           a.   assigned to minority communities

           b.   white officer was often required for an arrest to occur

           c.   not permitted to partner or ride with white officers

       3.   Nicholas Alex's 1969 book "Black in Blue"

           a.   described the plight of the black police officer

           b.   black officers face double marginality in eyes of citizens & fellow officers

       4.   numbers of minority officers is on the rise

       5.   minority officers are becoming more aggressive and self-assured

       6.   minority officers are more likely to seek aid from fellow minority officers

       7.   affirmative action caused dissention amongst the ranks

       8.   public is more concerned with effectiveness than racial composition of force

E.   Women in policing

       1.   first women officer with arrest powers hired in Los Angeles in 1910

       2.   early women faced separate selection criteria, menial tasks & declined promotion

       3.   courts forced a revision of entrance requirements

       4.   women currently make up about 11% of all sworn officers

       5.   promotion and acceptance problems

       6.   experience more stress and are targeted for disciplinary actions

       7.   female officer job performance

           a.   exhibit satisfactory work performance

           b.   receive support from community

           c.   less likely to be charged with improper conduct

           d.   female and male arrest rates identical

           e.   work best when paired with another female

            f.   less likely to use firearm
        8.   gender conflicts
            a.   males complain that females lack emotional and physical strength
            b.   "macho" atmosphere of police work
            c.   catch-22 in the eyes of male officers
        9.   minority female officers
            a.   black women comprise less than 5% of police officers
            b.   perceive more racial discrimination but less sexual discrimination

IV. Problems of policing
    A.   Job stress
        1.   cause of stress
            a.   job related sources
                i.   being on duty 24 hours a day
                ii.   dangers of the job
            b.   internal conflicts with administrative policies
            c.   poor training
            d.   poor pay
            e.   lack of promotion opportunities
            f.   job dissatisfaction
            g.   role conflict
            h.   fears
        2.   categories of police stressors
            a.   external stressors from public or judiciary
            b.   organizational stressors from administration
            c.   duty stressors from job roles and responsibilities
            d.   individual stressors from personal problems
        3.   combating stress
            a.   enhanced coping strategies
            b.   wellness programs
            c.   involving family members and support systems
            d.   stress reduction programs focus on positives of the job
    B.   Police violence
        1.   police brutality against citizens
            a.   high profile cases (Abner Louima & Rodney King) showcase the problem
            b.   use of force is at the core of the police role
            c.   departments have trouble regulating violent contacts with citizens
            d.   a particularly sensitive topic among the minority community
                i.   75% of all citizen complaints involve nonwhite male citizen
                ii.   departments such as the LAPD have a long history
        2.   how common is the use of force?
            a.   an estimated 43 million police-citizen contacts each year
                i.   1% (422,000) are said to involve force or threat of force
                ii.   most cases of force are minor
                iii.   less than 20% produce injury
            b.   intrusive force measures
                i.   4 in 1,000 officers shoot at civilians
                ii.   6,600 civilians killed by officers since 1976
        3.   race and forces
            a.   inconclusive evidence on the relationship between race & the use of force

b. minority community perceives disparity in stops and hassling by police
4. who are the problem cops?
   a. a minority of chronic offenders account for a large number of complaints
   b. young, inexperienced officers responsible for bulk of the complaints
   c. little evidence of racial motivation
   d. 3-part early warning system to deal with bad cops
      i. selecting officers
      ii. intervention
      iii. monitoring subsequent performance
5. curbing brutality
   a. train officers to be prepared for all types of calls
   b. implementing neighborhood and community policing models
   c. creating detailed rules of engagement for the use of force
   d. force-related integrity testing programs
   e. threat of public video taping and civil suits
6. deadly force
   a. police officer who shoots and kills a suspect who is either fleeing from arrest, assaulting a victim, or attacking the officer
   b. best guess is that police kill 250 to 300 suspects each year
7. factors related to police shootings
   a. violence levels in the community
   b. officer's exposure to violence
   c. workload factors
   d. firearms availability in the community
   e. social conflict in the community
   f. poorly written or ambivalent use of force policies
   g. levels of officer racial prejudice and discrimination
8. controlling deadly force
   a. fleeing felon standard
      i. English common law rule
      ii. in the process of arresting a felon on the run
   b. Tennessee v. Garner standard
      i. deadly use of force against an unarmed, nondangerous suspect deemed an illegal seizure
      ii. deadly force to prevent escape of a dangerous suspect
   c. Graham v Connor standard
      i. court created a reasonable officer standard to guide rulings
      ii. focuses on circumstances of the case and officer awareness
   d. FLETC use-of-force model
      i. outlines proper model to escalate force in response to threat
      ii. uses training scenarios to model responses
   e. administrative review boards
      i. investigate and adjudicate all firearm discharges by officers
      ii. departmental recommendation can lead to criminal prosecution
9. non-lethal weapons
   a. wood, rubber, or polyurethane bullets
   b. pepper spray
   c. bean bag guns
   d. tasers

10. police as victims
　　　　a. about 50 officers are killed each year
　　　　b. officer killings usually stem from routine police-citizen interactions
　C. Corruption
　　　1. illegal and unprofessional behavior by officers for personal gain for self or others
　　　2. urban forces have faced charges since the early 19th century
　　　　a. Knapp Commission on corruption in the NYPD of the 1970s
　　　　　i. limited numbers of chronic meat eaters
　　　　　ii. far more limited and minor grass eaters
　　　　b. Mollen Commission on corruption in the NYPD of the 1990s
　　　　　i. corruption was still a problem
　　　　　ii. some officers were actively involved in violence and drug dealing
　　　3. varieties of corruption
　　　　a. internal corruption
　　　　b. selective enforcement or non-enforcement
　　　　c. active criminality
　　　　d.. bribery and extortion
　　　4. causes of control of corruption
　　　　a. police personality
　　　　b. institutions and practices
　　　　c. moral ambivalence
　　　　d. corrupt departments with rotten pockets
　　　5. controlling corruption
　　　　a. strengthen internal review process within departments
　　　　b. implementing accountability systems
　　　　c. anti-corruption guidelines
　　　　d. outside review boards or special prosecutors
　　　　e. change the social context of policing to provide more visibility &
　　　　　decriminalization of vice crimes

Chapter Summary

Researchers have found that the process of becoming a police officer and the nature of the police work cause police officers to band together into a distinct **police culture** that is characterized by cynicism, clannishness, secrecy, and insulation from others. Research on policing has also found that there is a unique **police personality**, one that includes traits such as authoritarianism, suspicion, hostility, racism, conservatism, **cynicism,** and insecurity. There are two opposing viewpoints on the cause of this phenomenon. One holds that the police profession attracts people who have these traits before their policing careers. The other argues that socialization and on the job experience causes these traits to develop.

Part of the socialization of police officers includes the development of a particular working attitude or **police style**. Researchers have identified four such styles. The **crime fighter** stresses the investigation of serious crimes and the apprehension of criminals as a way to guarantee a secure society. The **social agent** believes that the police should be involved in a wide range of activities and that law enforcement is only one activity among the many the police should perform. The **law enforcer** believes that an officer's duty is clearly set out in the law and tends to emphasize playing it "by the book." The **watchman** emphasizes the maintenance of public order as the police goal rather than law enforcement or general service activities. The style a police officer adopts influences the manner in which the officer carries out duties and may affect the exercise of discretion.

Police officers use a tremendous amount of **discretion** in carrying out their daily duties. There are several factors which influence police discretion. **Legal** factors influencing discretion include the seriousness of the crime, the type of crime, use of a weapon, and the extent of injury to the victim. **Victim** factors have to do with the nature of the relationship between the offender and the victim; acquaintances are afforded more leeway than strangers. **Environmental** factors, such as the social climate, community attitudes, and treatment alternatives influence discretion. **Departmental** factors that influence discretion include peer pressure, supervisors, and the policies, practices, and customs of the local police department. **Supervisory** factors have to do with the way that the styles and practices of supervisors influence patrol officers' decisions. **Peer** factors have to do with the way that fellow patrol officers exert peer pressure on each other's discretionary practices. **Situational** factors attached to a particular crime provide another important influence on police actions and behavior. Studies have found that officers rely heavily on the offender's **demeanor** (the attitude and appearance of the offender), the nature of the crime, type of encounter, presence of witnesses, and the presence of back-up in making decisions. **Extralegal** factors also have an influence on officer discretion; factors such as class, race, gender, and age can influence arrest decisions.

Since 1931, many national commissions on policing have recommended that police officers enter the police force with a **college education**. Despite the growth of educational opportunities for police, the issue of requiring advanced education for the field is not a simple one. For example, the evidence is not clear that a college degree provides any benefits or that a college education is the preferred educational requirement. Today, most departments welcome and value advanced education but require no more than a high school degree.

Another key issue in policing includes the growing population of women and minority officers. For the past two decades, police departments have made a concerted effort to attract minority police officers and there have been many gains. In many cities with high minority populations, the percentage of minorities on police forces generally reflects their representation in the population. However, the number of female officers in American police departments is still far below what it should be. Recent research indicates that women are becoming highly successful police officers. There is, however, a slowly increasing number of women and minorities in supervisory positions. Discrimination is an issue police departments will continue to address for many years to come. African American officers often describe experiencing a sense of **double marginality** whereby they face prejudice at the hands of fellow officers as well as community members.

Job stress is another problem in police departments because the effects of stress can lead to alcoholism, divorce, depression, and even suicide. Police psychologists have divided stressors into four distinct categories. **External** stressors include verbal abuse from the public, justice system inefficiency and liberal court decisions favoring the criminal. Among **organizational** stressors are low pay, excessive paperwork, arbitrary rules and limited opportunity for advancement. **Duty** stressors consist of rotating shifts, work overload, boredom, fear and danger. **Individual** stressors are discrimination, marital difficulties, and personality problems. Police departments are attempting to deal with stress by training officers to cope with its effects. The training often includes diet information, biofeedback, relaxation and meditation, and exercise for stress reduction. Most often the training is part of an overall "wellness" program.

Today, **police brutality**--from abusive language to the unnecessary use of force--and the use of **deadly force** in apprehending fleeing or violent offenders, are critical issues with respect to public safety. Both of these areas continue to be of concern to police administrators as they attempt to develop policies and procedures to eliminate and control abusive or illegal actions. In 1985, the U.S. Supreme Court outlawed the use of deadly force against non-violent felons with its decision in the case of *Tennessee v. Garner*. This was followed by the *Graham v. Conner* case that established the reasonable officer standard to guide deadly use of force cases. Recently, the Federal Law Enforcement Training Center (FLETC) established the use-of-force model to map out the various perceptions and responses that should guide the use of force by police officers. There are several approaches that can be taken to control brutality and the use of deadly force such as the use of restrictive policies, but the greatest control may come from the threat of civil litigation. These range from review boards to the use of non-lethal weapons. Since their inception, U.S. police departments have wrestled with the problem of controlling **corruption**, the illegal and unprofessional behavior of police officers. There are several methods that can be used to control police corruption. One is to strengthen internal administrative review procedures within the department. Another is the use of outside review boards and special prosecutors that respond to allegations of abuses.

Fill-in-the-Blank Questions

1. Police experts have found that the experience of becoming a police officer and the nature of the job causes officers to band together into a police _____, characterized by cynicism, clannishness, secrecy, and insulation from others in society. This is referred to as the _____ _____.

2. The _____ _____ problem refers to those officers who routinely and successfully violate all known standards of police work to protect the public and apprehend known criminals.

3. The policeman's "_____ _____" is his/her working personality that is shaped by constant exposure to danger and the need to use force and authority to reduce and control threatening situations.

4. _____ is the belief that most people's actions are motivated solely by personal needs and selfishness. This core sentiment permeates all levels of policing.

5. The _____ _____ style of policing can be distinguished from the _____ _____ style in that the latter does not separate between major and minor crimes.

6. The _____ _____ style of policing states that the police should get involved in a wide range of activities and assist special needs populations.

7. The _____ style emphasizes the maintenance of public order as the primary police goal.

8. Police use _____ when they decide to arrest one suspect for disorderly conduct but escort another home.

9. Better communication with the public, especially minority and ethnic groups, is believed to be one of the benefits of _____ _____ for police officers.

10. Nicholas Alex uses the term "_____ _____" in reference to the black officer's dilemma of expectations to give members of his own race a break, and overt racism from his police colleagues.

11. Efforts to control _____ _____ and discrimination are now ongoing in most major police departments.

12. _____ _____ is a negative label that male officers assign to female officers who work in the station and are limited to administrative duties.

13. _____ _____ is a label that male police officers often assign to a female officer who displays courage and aggressiveness, thus suggesting that she can handle dangerous calls.

14. A _____ police force can be instrumental in gaining the minority community's confidence.

15. In the Washington D.C. study of police women, it was found that women were more likely than their male colleagues to receive _____ from the community and were less likely to be charged with _____ conduct.

16. _____ is the process of labeling women who prove themselves tough enough so as to neutralize their threat to male dominance.

17. Rotating shifts, work overload, boredom, fear, and danger are forms of _____ stressors.

18. _____ _____, _____ _____ _____, and _____ are three forms of non-lethal weapons that emerged in the wake of *Tennessee v. Garner* to curb the need for deadly force to capture fleeing felons.

19. In the case of _____ v. _____ the U.S. Supreme Court ruled that deadly force may not be used unless it is necessary to prevent an offender's escape and only if the officer has probable cause to believe that the suspect poses a significant threat of death or serious injury to the officer or others.

20. According to the Knapp Commission _____ aggressively misuse police power for personal gain by demanding bribes, threatening legal action, or cooperating with criminals.

True/False Questions

T F 1. One of the core beliefs in the police culture is that it is possible to win the war on crime without bending the rules.

T F 2. At the heart of the police culture is the belief that loyalty to colleagues counts above everything else.

T F 3. According to Arthur Neiderhoffer, police cynicism decreases with length of service.

T F 4. Those who internalize the Crime Fighter style view themselves as the "thin blue line" that protects citizens from criminals.

T F 5. According to the Watchman style of policing, vice and gambling are problems only when the currently accepted standards of order are violated.

T F 6. An officer who operates under the Law Enforcer style is most likely to aspire to command rank.

T F 7. Unlike members of almost every other criminal justice agency, police are heavily regulated in their daily performance of duties.

T F 8. Police discretion is inversely related to the severity of the offense.

T F 9. The relationship between the victim and offender often influences the decisions made by police officers.

T F 10. Peer pressure has very little influence on the discretion of police officers.

T F 11. There is no clear-cut evidence that college educated police perform better on their daily activities than do non-educated officers.

T F 12. There is no difference in the number of citizen complaints against college-educated officers as compared to those officers without a college education.

T F 13. Minority police officers often possess special qualities that can serve to improve police performance.

T F 14. African-American citizens report having less confidence in the police than Hispanics and Caucasians.

T F 15. Research by Nicholas Alex has shown that black officers did not have to deal with the expectation by African-American offenders that they would give a break to members of their own race.

T F 16. There are many successful role models on which female recruits can shape their career aspirations.

T F 17. Studies show that female officers report significantly lower levels of job related stress than male officers.

T F 18. The Mollen Commission investigated allegations of corruption within the Los Angeles Police Department in the wake of the Rodney King beating.

T F 19. According to research, physical abuse of citizens by police officers is more frequent than commonly imagined.

T F 20. Force is considered excessive when, considering all the circumstances known to the officer at the time he acted, the force was unreasonable.

Multiple Choice Questions

1. The style of policing that sees handling minor social service and non-enforcement duties as harmful to police efforts to create a secure society is that of a:
   a. Crime Fighter
   b. Social Agent
   c. Watchman
   d. Law Enforcer

2. The style of policing in which the officer ignores many infractions and requests for service unless they believe that the social or political order is jeopardized is
   a. Crime Fighter
   b. Social Agent
   c. Watchman
   d. Law Enforcer

3. The style of police work in which police officers see themselves as general law enforcement agents is that of a:
   a. Crime Fighter
   b. Social Agent
   c. Watchman
   d. Law Enforcer

4. The style of police work in which police officers are troubleshooters who patch the holes that appear where the social fabric wears thin is that of a:
   a. Crime Fighter
   b. Social Agent
   c. Watchman
   d. Law Enforcer

5. Directives, supervisors, and peers are examples of _____ factors that have an influence on discretion exercised by the police.
    a. environmental
    b. departmental
    c. legal
    d. situational

6. Crime seriousness, serious injury, and use of a weapon are examples of _____ factors that have an influence on discretion exercised by the police.
    a. environmental
    b. departmental
    c. legal
    d. situational

7. Of all the following, _____ is **not** an example of a situational factor that influences discretion exercised by police.
    a. demeanor
    b. manner in which a crime is encountered
    c. personal matters
    d. social climate

8. Race, gender, and economic status are _____ factors that can relate to police discretion.
    a. environmental
    b. situational
    c. extralegal
    d. departmental

9. Today, about _____ percent of all police departments recognize that college education should be an important factor in promotion decisions.
    a. 82
    b. 66
    c. 25
    d. 33

10. Today, about _____ percent of all sworn officers are minorities.
    a. 8
    b. 16
    c. 22
    d. 33

11. Today, about _____ percent of all sworn officers are females.
    a. 6
    b. 10
    c. 15
    d. 35

12. Recent surveys of male officers show that more that _____ do not think that women can handle the physical requirements of the job as well as men.
    a. one-fourth
    b. one-third
    c. half
    d. three-fourths

13. Which of the following is **not** one of the four distinct categories of stress that impacts the psyche of the average police officer?
    a. external stressors
    b. organizational stressors
    c. duty stressors
    d. judicial stressors

14. Which of the following is **not** an organizational stressor?
    a. arbitrary rules
    b. low pay
    c. excessive paper work
    d. rotating shifts

15. All of the following are individual stressors **except**:
    a. boredom
    b. discrimination
    c. personality problems
    d. marital problems

16. Which of the following is **not** a duty stressor?
    a. rotating shifts
    b. boredom
    c. fear
    d. arbitrary rules

17. Deadly force refers to the actions of a police officer who shoots and kills a suspect who is:
    a. fleeing from arrest
    b. assaulting a victim
    c. attacking the police officer
    d. all of the above

18. Evidence suggests that actual instances of physical abuse of citizens by police officers are _____ than commonly imagined by the public.
    a. more frequent
    b. less frequent
    c. more vicious
    d. less vicious

19. Which of the following is not one of the factors that predict the shooting of police officers?
    a. violence levels in the community
    b. firearms availability in the community
    c. the number of police officers patrolling the community
    d. levels of social conflict in the community

20. Deadly force refers to the actions of a police officer who shoots and kills a suspect who is:
    a. fleeing from arrest
    b. assaulting a victim
    c. attacking the police officer
    d. all of the above

21. Which of the following factors does **not** relate to police shootings?
    a. firearm availability
    b. social variables
    c. police workload
    d. all of the above relate to police shootings

22. The U.S. Supreme Court case that created a reasonableness standard for the use of force is:
    a. *Tennessee v. Garner*
    b. *Graham v. Connor*
    c. *U.S. v. Paradise*
    d. *Gregg v. Georgia*

23. The category of corruption that takes place among police officers themselves, involving the bending of departmental rules and outright performance of illegal acts is:
    a. internal corruption
    b. selective enforcement – abuse of power
    c. rotten apples
    d. pervasive organized corruption

24. The category of corrupt police department in which a majority of personnel are corrupt, but have little relationship to one another is:
    a. rotten apples and rotten pocket
    b. pervasive organized corruption
    c. pervasive unorganized corruption
    d. rotten apples

Essay Questions

1. Describe the police culture and explain the six core values associated with it.

2. Compare and contrast the four major styles of police work; explain how these styles influence police discretion.

3. Explain the eight different factors that commonly influence an officer's use of discretion.

4. Explain how a college degree contributes to the effectiveness of being a police officer.

5. Identify and describe the four distinct categories of stressors that impact police officers.

6. Identify and describe the seven factors that have been related to police shootings.

7. Compare and contrast the "fleeing felon," and "Garner" rules as they relate to police use of deadly force.

8. Discuss the five levels of perception and response that make up the Federal Law Enforcement Training Center's (FLETC) use-of-force model.

9. Review the six different dispositions that are available to the New York Firearm Discharge Review Board.

10. Discuss the differences between grass eaters and meat eaters as they relate to police corruption.

CHAPTER 7 ANSWER KEY

FILL-IN-THE BLANK QUESTIONS

1. subculture, blue curtain
2. Dirty Harry
3. police style
4. cynicism
5. Crime Fighter, Law Enforcer
6. Social Agent
7. Watchman
8. discretion
9. higher education
10. double marginality
11. racial profiling
12. station queen
13. hard charger
14. heterogeneous
15. support, improper
16. Defeminization
17. duty
18. pepper spray, bean bag guns, and tasers
19. *Tennessee v. Garner*
20. "meat eaters"

TRUE/FALSE QUESTIONS

1.	F	11.	T
2.	T	12.	F
3.	F	13.	T
4.	T	14.	T
5.	T	15.	F
6.	T	16.	F
7.	F	17.	F
8.	T	18.	f
9.	T	19.	F
10.	F	20.	T

MULTIPLE CHOICE QUESTIONS

1.	A	13.	D
2.	C	14.	D
3.	D	15.	A
4.	B	16.	D
5.	B	17.	D
6.	C	18.	B
7.	D	19.	C
8.	C	20.	D
9.	A	21.	D
10.	C	22.	B
11.	A	23.	A
12.	C	24.	C

Chapter 8

Police and the Rule of Law

Learning Objectives

At the conclusion of this chapter, the student should possess sufficient knowledge to achieve the following learning objectives:

1. Discuss the process through which legal control over the police is achieved.

2. Discuss the constitutional rights afforded by the Fourth Amendment and how they relate valid searches and seizures by the police.

3. Describe the constitutional and court imposed restrictions placed on law enforcement's use of informants.

4. Explain the concept of the totality of the circumstances.

5. Explain the limits placed on conducting searches without a warrant.

6. Explain the stop and frisk rule.

7. Describe the rules associated with conducting postarrest warrantless searches.

8. Describe the rules that govern police searches of an automobile.

9. Explain the Miranda v. Arizona decision and its impact on questioning suspects.

10. Identify the ways that incriminating statements can be used in the absence of a Miranda warning.

11. Explain the processes and procedures associated with a police lineup.

Keywords and Definitions

Search and Seizure: The legal term, contained in the Fourth Amendment to the U.S. Constitution, that refers to the searching for and carrying away of evidence by the police during a criminal investigation.

Search Warrant: An order issued by judge, directing police officers to conduct a search of a specified premises for specified objects or persons and bring them before the court.

Reasonableness: Legal standard that requires the existence of probable cause to believe the item searched for was involved in criminal activity and will be located at the site to be searched.

Probable Cause: The evidentiary criterion necessary to sustain an arrest or the issuance of an arrest or search warrant; less than absolute certainty or "beyond a reasonable doubt," but greater than mere suspicion or "hunch."

Particularity: The specificity of the search; the Fourth Amendment requires that a search warrant specify the place to be searched and the reasons for searching it.

Hearsay Evidence: Testimony that is not firsthand but relates information told by a second party; it also refers to information provided by an informant that becomes the basis for the request for a search warrant.

Aguilar v. Texas: The Supreme Court articulated a two-part test for issuing a warrant on the word of an informant: (1) the police had to show why they believed the informant, and (2) how the informant acquired personal knowledge of the crime had to be explained.

Illinois v. Gates: The U.S. Supreme Court case that replaced the two-pronged test of *Spinelli* and *Aguilar* with the "totality of circumstances" test.

Alabama v. White: The U.S. Supreme Court case that deemed a search based on an anonymous tip with independent police corroboration legal.

Totality of the Circumstances Test: To obtain a search warrant, the police must prove to a judge that, considering the "totality of the circumstances," an informant has relevant and factual knowledge that a fair probability exists that the evidence of a crime will be found in a certain place.

Exigent Circumstances: An immediate or emergency situation that precluded the ability of police to obtain a warrant.

Kirk v. Louisiana: The U.S. Supreme Court case that acknowledged but did not specifically define exigent circumstances as a legitimate reason for a warrantless search.

Stop and Frisk: The procedure where police officers who are suspicious of an individual run their hands lightly over the suspect's outer garments to determine if the person is carrying a concealed weapon.

Threshold Inquiry: Another term for a stop and frisk episode.

Terry v. Ohio: The U.S. Supreme Court upheld the right of the police to conduct brief threshold inquiries of suspicious persons when they have reason to believe that such persons may be armed and dangerous to the police or others.

Search Incident to a Lawful Arrest: An exception to the search warrant rule; limited to the immediate surrounding area.

Chimel v. California: The U.S. Supreme Court ruled that the police can search a suspect without a warrant after a lawful arrest to protect themselves from danger and to secure evidence.

Plain-View Doctrine: Police officers may make a warrantless seizure of contraband found in plain view during a lawful search for other items.

United States v. Ross: U.S. Supreme Court case that deemed warrantless searches of an automobile, including the search of closed compartments, constitutional.

Carroll v. United States: The United States Supreme Court ruled that distinctions should be made between searches of automobiles, persons, and homes so warrantless searches of automobiles are valid if the police have probable cause to believe that the car contains evidence they are seeking.

United States v. Ross: The U.S. Supreme Court ruling that if probable cause exists to believe that an automobile contains criminal evidence, a warrantless search by the police is permissible, including the search of closed containers in the vehicle.

Delaware v. Prouse: The U.S. Supreme Court forbade the practice of random stops of vehicles in the absence of any reasonable suspicion that some traffic or motor vehicle law has been violated.

City of Indianapolis v Edmund: U.S. Supreme Court case that deemed routine stops of all motorists in hope of finding drug criminals unconstitutional.

Michigan Department of State Police v. Sitz: U.S. Supreme Court case that deemed brief, suspiciousless seizures at highway drunk driving check points legal as they serve a public health role.

Maryland v. Wilson: Supreme Court ruling extending *Pennsylvania v. Mimms* by stating that police officers could order passengers out of cars during routine traffic stops.

Pennsylvania v. Mimms: U.S. Supreme Court case that deemed the search of drivers and passengers during routine traffic stops constitutional.

U.S. v. Green: Court case that deemed the warrantless search of a vehicle unconstitutional where the driver is confronted outside of said vehicle.

Ohio v. Robinette: The U.S. Supreme Court ruling that a search is reasonable even if police officers do not tell the detained driver that he or she is "free to go" before asking for consent to search the vehicle.

Pretext Stops: Traffic stops where police use traffic violations as the excuse to stop a vehicle.

Whren v. United States: The U.S. Supreme Court ruling that if probable cause exists to stop a person for a traffic violation, the motivation of the police officers is irrelevant.

Bumper v. North Carolina: The U.S. Supreme Court upheld a lower court ruling that a search is illegally obtained if the police falsely claim they had a search warrant.

Schneckloth v. Bustamonte: The U.S. Supreme Court decision that the issue of voluntariness of the consent to a search is a question of fact to be determined from all the circumstances of the case.

Bus Sweep: The drug interdiction technique of boarding buses, and without suspicion of illegal activity, questioning passengers, asking for identification, and requesting to search luggage.

Florida v. Bostick: The U.S. Supreme Court upheld the police drug interdiction technique of bus sweeps.

Plain View Doctrine: Legal principle stating that a police officer may lawfully seize without a warrant any evidence that is in his/her plain view.

Arizona v. Hicks: The U.S. Supreme Court ruling that moving a stereo component in plain view a few inches to record the serial number constituted a search under the Fourth Amendment and had to be justified by probable cause, and not by reasonable suspicion.

Curtilage: The fields or grounds adjacent to or attached to a home.

Oliver v. United States: The U.S. Supreme Court distinguished between the privacy granted persons in their own home or its adjacent grounds and a field by ruling that police can use airplane surveillance to spot marijuana fields and then send in squads to seize the crops, or they can peer into fields from cars for the same purpose.

California v. Ciraola: The U. S. Supreme Court ruling that flying over the yard of a home in a private plane at an altitude of one thousand feet to ascertain whether it contained marijuana plants is not a violation of a defendant's privacy.

Florida v. Riley: The U.S. Supreme Court ruled that police do not need a search warrant to conduct low-altitude helicopter searches of private property.

Minnisota v. Dickerson: U.S. Supreme Court that established the "plain touch" doctrine as a corollary to the plain view doctrine, thus allowing for warrantless seizures of evidence that is felt through clothing during a lawful pat down.

Bonds v. United States: U.S. Supreme Court case stating that the plain touch doctrine does not extend to personal luggage.

Katz v. United States: The U.S. Supreme Court ruling that the government must obtain a court order if it wishes to listen in on conversations in which the parties have a reasonable expectation of privacy, such as in their own homes or on the telephone because electronic eavesdropping is a search, even though there is no actual trespass.

Arrest Warrant: An order issued by the court determining that an arrest should be made and directing the police to bring the named person before the court.

Riverside County v. McLaughlin: The U.S. Supreme Court ruled that the police may detain an individual arrested without a warrant for up to forty-eight hours without a court hearing on whether the arrest was justified.

Atwater et al. v. City of Lago Vista et al.: The U.S. Supreme Court case that deemed a warrantless arrest of an individual pursuant to noncriminal acts such as a traffic violation constitutional.

Miranda v. Arizona: The U.S. Supreme Court ruling that before questioning, the police must warn a person in custody that they have the following rights: (1) the right to remain silent; (2) that if they decide to make a statement, the statement can and will be used against them in a court of law; (3) they have the right to have an attorney present at the time of interrogation, or they will have the opportunity to consult with an attorney; (4) if they cannot afford an attorney, one will be appointed for them by the state.

Inevitable Discovery Rule: States that evidence obtained in violation of the Miranda rule can be used in court if it can be established that the police would have discovered it anyway via other means or sources.

Public Safety Doctrine: States that a suspect can be questioned in the field without a Miranda warning so long as the information being obtained is needed to protect public safety.

Chavez v. Martinez: U.S. Supreme Court case establishing that the failure to give a suspect a Miranda warming is not illegal unless the case becomes a criminal matter.

Dickerson v. United States: The recent U.S. Supreme Court ruling reaffirming the *Miranda* decision and ruling that the an Act of Congress cannot overrule the constitutional decision contained in *Miranda*.

United States v. Bin Laden: The U.S. Supreme Court case stating that the Miranda rule applies to interrogations of foreign nationals conducted abroad by U.S. authorities.

Booking: The administrative record of an arrest that lists descriptive information about the offender and may be accompanied by fingerprints and photographs.

Lineup: A suspect is placed in a group for the purpose of being viewed and identified by a witness.

United States v. Wade: The U.S. Supreme Court ruled that a defendant has a right to counsel if the lineup takes place after a suspect has been formally charged with a crime.

Simmons v. United States: The U.S. Supreme Court ruled that the primary evil to be avoided in any lineup is a very substantial likelihood of irreparable misidentification.

Neil v. Biggers: The U.S. Supreme Court established the following general criteria to judge the suggestiveness of a pretrial identification procedure: (1) the opportunity of the witness to view the criminal at the time of the crime; (2) the degree of attention by the witness and the accuracy of the prior description by the witness; (3) the level of certainty demonstrated by the witness; (4) the length of time between the crime and the confrontation; and (5) the weighing all these factors, the court determines the substantial likelihood of misidentification.

Exclusionary Rule: All evidence obtained by illegal searches and seizures is inadmissible in criminal trials; it also excludes the use of illegal confessions under Fifth Amendment prohibitions.

Weeks v. United States: The U.S. Supreme Court held that evidence obtained by unreasonable search and seizure must be excluded in a <u>federal</u> criminal trial.

Mapp v. Ohio: The U.S. Supreme Court made the decision in *Weeks* applicable to <u>state</u> courts.

Illinois v. Gates: The U.S. Supreme Court ruling allowing an anonymous letter to be used as evidence in support of a warrant.

Good Faith Exception: Evidence obtained with less than an adequate search warrant may be admissible in court if the police officers acted in good faith on obtaining court approval for their search.

United States v. Leon: U.S. Supreme Court case responsible for establishing the good faith exception.

Chapter Outline

I.   Introduction
  A.   The police charge
    1.   preventing crime
    2.   identifying and arresting criminals
  B.   Means to achieve goals
    1.   gather evidence
    2.   seize contraband
    3.   interrogate witnesses and suspects

II.   Police and the courts
  A.   Search and seizure
    1.   Fourth Amendment protections
      a.   protects individuals from unreasonable searches and seizures
      b.   specifies warrant requirement under normal circumstances
    2.   officer may search with a warrant or under one of many exceptions to the warrant requirement
    3.   a search warrant is an order, issued by a judge, directing officers to conduct a search of a specified place for specified objects or persons
    4.   Fifth Amendment protects against forcing people to incriminate themselves
  B.   Search warrant requirements
    1.   unreasonableness exists when an officer exceeds the scope of police authority, generally from a lack of probable cause
      a.   can't search through stealth, deception, or disguise
      b.   can't search on the basis of the offender's past behavior or status
      c.   can't search because person simply looks like a criminal
    2.   the officer must establish probable cause to convince a magistrate that a crime was or is being committed
      a.   probable cause established through written affidavits to a judge
      b.   officer must provide factual evidence to define & identify activities
      c.   officer must show how he/she obtained the information
    3.   sources for a warrant
      a.   informant testimonials
      b.   firsthand accounts
      c.   co-conspirator implication
      d.   victim testimonial

<ol type="e" start="5">
<li>witness testimonial</li>
<li>law enforcement officer testimonial</li>
</ol>

    4.   particularity refers to the requirement that a warrant specify the precise place to be searched, the reasons for searching, and the property to be seized

C. Procedural requirements for obtaining a search warrant
1. request warrant from the court
2. submit affidavit
3. state place to be searched and items to be seized

D. Use of informers
1. many search warrant requests are based on information provided by a police informer, generally known as hearsay evidence
2. *Aguilar v. Texas* - establishes a two-pronged test for warrant
    a. must establish informant's direct contact with police
    b. must establish that the informant's information is
3. *Illinois v. Gates* - creates a totality of circumstances test to determine probable cause
4. *Alabama v. White* – establishes that anonymous tips are valid if they can be independently corroborated
5. *Florida v. J.L.* – establishes that, in absence of independent corroboration, an anonymous tip must include specific information to establish its reliable

III. Warrantless searches

A. Exceptions to the search warrant requirement of the Fourth Amendment
1. exigent or emergency circumstances
    a. *Kirk v. Louisiana* – exigent circumstances must be accompanied by warrant or probable cause
    b. no clear cut definition of what constitutes exigent circumstances
2. court has identified a number of exigent circumstances that preclude the need for a warrant

B. Field interrogation
1. exigent circumstance rule also known as the stop and frisk or threshold inquiry
    a. stop = briefly detaining suspect in crime prevention or detection effort
    b. frisk = patting down the stopped person for officer's safety
2. may investigate suspicious persons and circumstances without making an arrest
    a. lesser reasonable suspicion requirement replaces probable cause
3. *Terry v. Ohio* - police may conduct brief threshold inquiries of suspicious persons when they have reason to believe that such persons may be armed and dangerous to the police or others
4. *Illinois v. Wardlow* – suspicious behavior in a high crime area are grounds for stop & frisk

C. Search incident to a lawful arrest
1. after a lawful arrest, no warrant required for search of the suspect and immediate surrounding area for weapons or to preserve evidence
2. search pursuant to a lawful arrest is governed by two rules:
    a. must be conducted immediately after arrest is made

    b. search must be limited to the suspect & area in his/her immediate control

 D. Automobile searches
   1. certain circumstances allow for warrantless automobile searches on the street
    a. *Carroll v. United States* - deemed car searches distinct from those of persons and homes and allowed search based on probable cause alone
    b. *United States v. Ross* – deemed search of vehicle and closed containers in it when probable cause exists
   2. roadblock searches
    a. *Delaware v. Prouse* - forbids random stops; tacit approval granted for checkpoints conducted in a systematic fashion
    b. *City of Indianapolis v. Edmund* – routine random drug stops are illegal; stop must be accompanied by individualized suspicion
    c. *Michigan Dept. of State Police v Sitz* – systematic drunk driving stops & suspiciousless seizures are reasonable to protect public safety
     i. checkpoints must target a predetermined number of cars
     ii. may request license, registration, and proof of insurance
     iii. may check for outward signs of intoxication
   3. searching drivers and passengers during traffic stops
    a. *Pennsylvania v Mimms* - officers can order drivers from car
    b. *Maryland v Wilson* - passengers can be searched
    c. *U.S. v. Green* – search of auto must come pursuant to auto stop
    d. *Ohio v. Robinette* – must not inform suspect that he/she is free to go before invoking search of an auto
   4. pretext stops
    a. stopping suspected criminal on the pretext of a minor offense
    b. *Whren v United States*- deemed pretextual stops and searches legal so long as probable cause exists for minor offense
    c. *Arkansas v. Sullivan* - actual motivation for the officer's search is irrelevant as long as a legal custodial arrest is present
 E. Consent searches
   1. warrantless search where person in control of area or object offers legal consent
    a. consent must be voluntarily given
    b. consent must be given intelligently
    c. some jurisdictions require that suspect be given the option to refuse
   2. *Bumper v. North Carolina* – false claim of a warrant invalidates consent
   3. *Schneckloth v. Bustamonte* – voluntariness is determined by the circumstances of the case
    a. helping officers search demonstrates consent
    b. officers are under no obligation to inform of right to refuse
 F. The bus sweep
   1. searches of bus or train without suspicion to question and search passengers
   2. *Florida v. Bostick* - nature of bus sweep search does not invalidate consent

G. The doctrines of plain view and curtilage
   1. police may seize evidence or contraband if it is plain view
      a. *New York v. Class* - lawful checking of VIN# on car justifies plain view of items located on dash of car
      b. *Arizona v. Hicks* - plain view search and seizure requires probable cause, not just reasonable suspicion
   2. police may search the curlitage or open fields and grounds adjacent to home
      a. *Oliver v. United States* – distinguishes between privacy of a home and curlitage via airplane or ground level surveillance
      b. *California v. Ciraola* – altitude of flight and height of fence not important
      c. *Florida v. Riley* - low altitude helicopter searches are permissible
   3. like plain view, police may seize contraband that is subject to plain touch
      a. *Minnesota v. Dickerson* – search for weapons can legally uncover contraband that is in plain touch or feel of officer
      b. *Bond v. United States* – personal items and luggage are not subject to the plain touch rule

IV. Electronic surveillance
   A. Use of electronic devises to intercept & record conversations or actions of a suspect
      1. wiretaps on phones or physical locations
      2. pen registers to record phone numbers dialed
      3. trap and trace devices link source and destination of phone calls
      4. email taps
      5. video surveillance
      6. computer data transmission taps
      7. thermal imaging and infrared searches of structures
   B. Surveillance is deemed an invasion privacy unless prior approval obtained from the courts
      1. *Katz v. United States* - monitoring of home or phone must be preceded by warrant
      2. *Kyllo v. United States* – use of thermal imaging or other devises beyond general public use require a warrant

V. Arrest
   A. Arrests may be made by police officers within their jurisdiction, or by Private citizens in whose presence a crime is committed
   B. Actual arrest conditions
      1. police officer has probable cause and intends to restrain a suspect
      2. officer deprives individual of freedom
      3. suspect believes he or she is in custody
      4. person deprived of liberty is under arrest
   C. Conditions under which a lawful arrest can be made
      1. with or without a warrant
      2. must be based on probable cause
      3. arrest without a warrant requirements
         a. probable cause exists
         b. law allows such an arrest

D. Time-frames
  1. arrestee must be brought promptly before a magistrate
  2. *Riverside County v. McLaughlin* - police may detain an individual for up to 48 hours without a warrant or court hearing
E. Arrests in non-criminal acts
  1. police can arrest someone for a non-criminal or minor acts
  2. *Atwater v. City of Lago Vista et al.* – court upheld arrest pursuant to a traffic stop

VI. Custodial interrogation
  A. A suspect must be warned of Fifth Amendment rights when taken into police custody
  B. *Miranda v. Arizona* – suspects in custody must be informed of rights before Questioning
    1. right to remain silent
    2. any statements can be used against you
    3. right to an attorney during questioning
    4. if you can't afford an attorney, one will be appointed for them by the state
  C. Further limits and extensions of the *Miranda* rule
    1. suspect can choose to stop at any time or refuse to answer questions
    2. waiver of rights must be voluntary
    3. an attorney must be present if the suspect cannot understand rights or questions
    4. all questioning must stop once suspect requests an attorney
    5. police may question for a second crime without an attorney if valid waiver exists
    6. may ask questions of anyone not in custody
    7. voluntary confession after warning is admissible
    8. evidence obtained in violation of *Miranda* can still be used to establish perjury
    9. inevitable discovery rule permits evidence obtained in violation of *Miranda*
    10. initial errors can be overcome by a proper implementation of *Miranda* warning
    11. evidence from a mentally impaired suspect is admissible if the preponderance of evidence suggests that he understood the warnings
    12. right to counsel only applies to attorneys, not priests, probation officers, or others
    13. field questioning without waiver is permissible where public safety concern exists
    14. suspects need not be aware of all possible outcomes associated with waiver
    15. suspect, not an attorney, friend, or family must affect the waiver
    16. *Chavez v. Martinez* – *Miranda* rule applies only to investigation of criminal matters
  D. Impact of *Miranda*
    1. police have come to rely on other forms of evidence beyond confessions
    2. *Dickerson v. United States* – recently solidified the standing of the *Miranda* rule

3. police have slowly grown to accept the *Miranda* rule
4. *United States v. Bin Laden* – Miranda applies to non-citizens interrogated abroad

E. Pretrial identification process
   1. "booking process" immediately follows arrest
      a. time and date of arrest is recorded
      b. arrangements are made for bail, detention or removal to court
      c. information for identification of suspect is obtained
      d. defendant may be fingerprinted, photographed, and put into a lineup
   2. *United States v. Wade* and *Kirby v. Illinois*
      a. establied the right to counsel at post-indictment lineup
      b. no right to counsel in pre-indictment or precomplaint lineup
   3. *Simmons v. United States* - must avoid suggestive lineups and irreparable misidentification
   4. *Neil v. Biggers* - sets reliability standards to judge the suggestiveness of lineups
      a. may provide opportunity of witness to view criminal at crime scene
      b. degree of attention and accuracy of prior descriptions by witness matter
      c. witness certainty matters
      d. time between crime and confrontation matters

VII. The exclusionary rule
  A. Provides that all evidence obtained by illegal searches, seizures, or confessions is inadmissible in court
  B. *Weeks v. United States* - established the exclusionary rule for the federal court
  C. *Mapp v. Ohio* – deemed that the exclusionary rule applies to state courts
  D. Current status and controversy
   1. *Illinois v. Gates* - anonymous letter establishes probable cause for search warrant
   2. *United States v. Leon* – set good faith exception based on magistrates warrant
   3. *Arizona v. Evans* - good faith reliance on apparently valid warrant is admissible
   4. as a general rule, recent courts place public safety above exclusionary rights
  E. The future of the exclusionary rule
   1. criticisms of the exclusionary rule
      a. it has no direct impact on police practices
      b. it does not control police harassment
      c. it allows guilty to go free
   2. dealing with violations
      a. criminal prosecution of officers
      b. internal police controls
      c. civil lawsuits
      d. federal lawsuits

Chapter Summary

The primary investigative tools of the police are criminal detection, apprehension and arrest to collect the facts and evidence needed to identify, arrest and convict the criminal. Statutes and constitutional law place limitations on police investigation methods such as **search and seizure**, **warrantless searches**, **arrest**, **custodial interrogation**, and **lineups**.

The search and seizure requirements of the Fourth Amendment to the U.S. Constitution govern evidence collected by the police. The police can undertake a proper search and seizure if a valid **search warrant** has been obtained from the court. To be valid, the warrant must meet the criteria of **reasonableness (probable cause)** and **particularity**. The searches and seizures that exceed the authority of the police are considered unreasonable.

There are some significant **exigent circumstance** exceptions to the search warrant requirement of including **searches incident to a lawful arrest**, **heresay evidence**, field interrogation (**threshold inquiry** or **stop-and-frisk**), automobile searches, consent searches, **pretext stops**, **bus sweeps**, **roadblock searches**, **curtilage**, and evidence in **plain view** or **plain touch**. Supreme Court cases such as *Aguilar v. Texas, CIllinois v. Gates, Chimel v. California, Terry v. Ohio, Delawar v. Prouse, Florida v. Bostick, Carroll v. United States, Minnisota v. Dickinson*, and *United States v. Ross* have clarified the scope of these exceptions.

Electronic eavesdropping by wiretapping, pen registers, electronic communication devises, video surveillance, or by trap and tracer represent an invasion of an individual's right to privacy unless a court gives permission to intercept conversations in this manner. In *Katz v. United States*, and other cases, the U.S. Supreme Court concluded that electronic eavesdropping is a search, even though there is no actual trespass, so a warrant is needed to do so.

The police can initiate arrests with or without an **arrest warrant** and both must be based on **probable cause**. The police may arrest without a warrant only if the law of the given jurisdiction allows for warrantless arrests, and probable cause has been established. Once an arrest without a warrant is made, the person arrested must be brought before a magistrate promptly for a probable cause hearing. The Supreme Court defined promptness in *Riverside County v. McLaughlin* as within forty-eight hours.

As a result of the landmark case of *Miranda v. Arizona*, suspects taken into custody must be warned of their Fifth Amendment rights against self-incrimination before they are questioned. Numerous issues surrounding the *Miranda* ruling continue to be litigated, and the Supreme Court recently upheld it in *Dickerson v. United States*. Exceptions to the Miranda rule include the **inevitable discovery rule** and the **public safety doctrine**. The Supreme Court has also reviewed the legal issues related to **lineups** that occur at the **booking** stage and other identification procedures, and ruled in *United States v. Wade* that a defendant has the right to counsel if the lineup takes place after suspect has been formally charged with a crime.

Under the **exclusionary rule**, any evidence obtained in violation of the Fourth Amendment can be excluded from use in a criminal prosecution. The future of the exclusionary rule is one of the most controversial issues in the criminal justice system. While the Supreme Court has limited its application in recent years by establishing exceptions such as the **good faith exception**, the exclusionary rule still generally prohibits the admission of evidence that violates a defendant's constitutional rights.

Fill-in-the-Blank Questions

1. The U.S. Supreme Court has taken an active role in considering the _____ of police operations, and of primary concern has been police _____ in obtaining and serving search and arrest warrants.

2. Evidence collected by the police is governed by the _____ and _____ requirements of the _____ Amendment to the U.S, Constitution.

3. A _____ _____ is an order from the court authorizing and directing the police to _____ a designated place for property stated in the order and to bring that property to court.

4. The _____ of searches and seizures generally refers to whether an officer has exceeded the _____ of his police authority.

5. _____ _____ is the evidentiary criteria necessary to sustain a lawful arrest or the issuance of an _____ or _____ warrant.

6. Police request warrants during investigations of many offenses when they are reasonably sure that the evidence sought cannot be _____ from the premises, _____, or _____ by the suspect.

7. If an arrest is found to have been invalid, then any warrantless search made incident to arrest would be considered _____, and the evidence obtained from the search would be _____ from the trial.

8. The _____ _____ or stop-and-frisk procedure applies to the _____ _____ in which stopping a suspects allows for brief _____ of the person and frisking affords the officer an opportunity to avoid the possibility of attack.

9. The landmark 1968 Supreme Court case _____ v. _____ was the first to shape the contours of the stop and frisk procedure.

10. In *Ohio v. Robinette*, the Supreme Court said that the touchstone of the Fourth Amendment is _____, and it is assessed by examining the _____ of the _____, and not by applying rigid rules.

11. Electronic eavesdropping constitutes a _____, even though there is no actual _____, so it is unreasonable and a warrant is needed.

12. The basic principle of the law of electronic surveillance is the wiretapping and other devices that violate _____ are contrary to the _____ Amendment.

13. The _____ power of the police involves taking a person into _____ in accordance with lawful authority and _____ that person to answer for violation of the criminal law.

14. The interrogation process is protected by the _____ Amendment.

15. The landmark 1984 Supreme Court case United States v. Leon was central to the development of the _____ _____ exception to the exclusionary rule.

True/False Questions

T F 1. The order for a search warrant must be based on sworn testimony of the police officer that the facts on which the request for the search warrant are trustworthy.

T F 2. Reasonableness requires the existence of personal knowledge to believe the item searched for was involved in criminal activity.

T F 3. The legality of a search incident to an arrest depends entirely on the lawfulness of the arrest.

T F 4. The stop-and-frisk procedure is also known as a threshold inquiry.

T F 5. Under *Minnesota v. Dickerson*, a police officer may squeeze a suspect's pocket to what is within it.

T F 6. One important purpose of the decision in *Delaware v. Prouse* was to eliminate the practice of random traffic stops in absence of reasonable suspicion of a law violation.

T F 7. Pretext stops are those where the police use traffic violations as an excuse to stop a vehicle.

T F 8. *Pennsylvania v. Mimms* allows police officers to order drivers and passengers out of their cars during routine traffic stops.

T F 9. In *Ohio v. Robinette*, the Supreme Court ruled that police officers must tell drivers they are "free to go" before asking consent to search the vehicle.

T F 10. Those who consent to search essentially waive their constitutional rights under the Fourth Amendment.

T F 11. A pen register is a device that ascertains the number from which calls are placed to a particular telephone.

T F 12. Electronic eavesdropping by police represents an invasion of an individual's right to privacy unless a court gives permission to intercept conversations.

T F 13. Statutory provisions provide for the suppression of evidence when voice recordings are obtained in violation of the law.

T F 14. Private citizens do not have the right to make an arrest.

T F 15. Legally, arrests can be made only with a warrant.

T F 16. A misdemeanor arrest requires probable cause and the officer's presence at the time of the offense.

T F 17. The plain touch doctrine is an extension or corollary of the plain view doctrine.

T F 18. If an accused decides to answer any questions, the accused may not stop at any time and refuse to answer further questions.

T F 19. *Brown v. Mississippi* held that statements obtained by physical coercion were inadmissible evidence.

T F 20. The inevitable discovery doctrine is directly related to the *Miranda* rule.

T F 21. *Dickerson v. United States* reaffirmed the *Miranda* decision.

T F 22. Some evidence obtained by illegal searches is admissible in a criminal trial.

T F 23. The exclusionary rule was designed as a means of deterring police misconduct.

T F 24. The exclusionary rule does not apply to interrogations conducted by U.S. authorities outside of the borders of the United States.

Multiple Choice Questions

1. Particularity generally refers to the _____ of the search.
    a. specificity
    b. reasonableness
    c. probable cause
    d. all of the above

2. Information that comes from a police informer is called:
    a. reasonable
    b. curtilage
    c. invalid evidence
    d. hearsay evidence

3. Which of the following Supreme Court cases pertains to the issue of a warrant issued on the basis of informant information?
    a. *Kirk v. Louisiana*
    b. *Aguilar v. Texas*
    c. *U.S. v. Ross*
    d. *Florida v. Bostick*

4. The "totality of the circumstances" test to determine probable cause for issuing a search warrant is found in which U.S. Supreme Court case?
   a. *Spinelli v. United States*
   b. *Aguilar v. Texas*
   c. *Richards v. Wisconsin*
   d. *Illinois v. Gates*

5. Which U.S. Supreme Court applies to roadblock searches?
   a. *Delaware v. Prouse*
   b. *City of Indianapolis v. Edmund*
   c. *Michigan Department of State Police v. Sitz*
   d. all of the above

6. Which Supreme Court case authorized the search without a warrant after a lawful arrest to protect the officer and to secure evidence?
   a. *Chimel v. California*
   b. *Terry v. Ohio*
   c. *Carroll v. United States*
   d. *Illinois v. Gates*

7. In _____, the Supreme Court case that permitted police officers to stop-and-frisk.
   a. *Minnesota v. Dickerson*
   b. *Terry v. Ohio*
   c. *Carroll v. United States*
   d. *United States v. Ross*

8. In _____, the Supreme Court ruled that "patdowns" must be limited to a search for weapons and that the officer may not extend the "feel" beyond that necessary to determine if it is a weapon.
   a. *Minnesota v. Dickerson*
   b. *Terry v. Ohio*
   c. *Carroll v. United States*
   d. *United States v. Ross*

9. Which Supreme Court case decided that distinctions should be made between searches of automobiles, persons, and homes?
   a. *United States v. Ross*
   b. *Delaware v. Prouse*
   c. *Pennsylvania v. Mimms*
   d. *Carroll v. United States*

10. Which Supreme Court case decided that a warrantless search of an automobile is valid if the police have probable cause to believe that the car contains the evidence they are seeking?
    a. *United States v. Ross*
    b. *Delaware v. Prouse*
    c. *Pennsylvania v. Mimms*
    d. *Carroll v. United States*

11. Which Supreme Court case decided that if probable cause exists that an automobile contains criminal evidence, a warrantless search by the police is permissible, including the search of closed containers in the vehicle?
    a. *United States v. Ross*
    b. *Delaware v. Prouse*
    c. *Pennsylvania v. Mimms*
    d. *Carroll v. United States*

12. In _____, the United States Supreme Court forbade the practice of random stops in the absence of any reasonable suspicion that some traffic or motor vehicle law has been violated.
    a. *United States v. Ross*
    b. *Delaware v. Prouse*
    c. *Pennsylvania v. Mimms*
    d. *Carroll v. United States*

13. In _____, the United States Supreme Court authorized the police to order passengers out of the cars during routine traffic stops.
    a. *Pennsylvania v. Mimms*
    b. *Whren v. United States*
    c. *Maryland v. Wilson*
    d. *Carroll v. United States*

14. _____ is the Supreme Court case that said voluntariness of a search is a fact to be determined from all the circumstances of the case.
    a. *Bumper v. North Carolina*
    b. *Schneckloth v. Bustamonte*
    c. *Florida v. Bostick*
    d. *Arizona v. Hicks*

15. In *Florida v. Bostick*, the Supreme Court upheld the use of _____.
    a. stop-and-frisk
    b. breathalyzers
    c. curitlage searches
    d. bus sweeps

16. Which Supreme Court case decided that moving a stereo to view the serial number was contrary to plain view?
    a. *Oliver v. United States*
    b. *Arizona v. Hicks*
    c. *California v. Ciraola*
    d. *Florida v. Riley*

17. Which Supreme Court case upheld using airplane surveillance to spot marijuana fields and can peer into fields from cars for the same purpose?
    a. *Oliver v. United States*
    b. *Arizona v. Hicks*
    c. *Katz v. United States*
    d. *Florida v. Riley*

18. Which Supreme Court case ruled that police officers do not need a search warrant to conduct low-altitude helicopter searches of private property?
    a. *Oliver v. United States*
    b. *Arizona v. Hicks*
    c. *Katz v. United States*
    d. *Florida v. Riley*

19. Which Supreme Court case held that the government must obtain a warrant to listen in on conversations in which the parties have a reasonable expectation of privacy, such as their home or on the telephone?
    a. *Oliver v. United States*
    b. *Arizona v. Hicks*
    c. *Katz v. United States*
    d. *Florida v. Riley*

20. In the Supreme Court case _____, the court said that the police may detain an individual arrested without a warrant for up to 48 hours without a court hearing on whether the arrest was justified.
    a. *Oliver v. United States*
    b. *Riverside County v. McLaughlin*
    c. *Miranda v. Arizona*
    d. *Terry v. Ohio*

21. The police must give the Miranda warning upon:
    a. arrest
    b. arrival
    c. questioning
    d. all of the above

22. Which of the following cases addressed an issue related to the *Miranda* rule?
    a. *Chavez v. Martinez*
    b. *Delaware v. Prouse*
    c. *Mapp v. Ohio*
    d. *Terry v. Ohio*

23. Which Supreme Court case held that a defendant has the right to counsel if the lineup takes place after the suspect has been formally charged with a crime?
    a. *Kirby v. Illinois*
    b. *Simmons v. United States*
    c. *Neil v. Biggers*
    d. *United States v. Wade*

24. Which court case established the general criteria to judge the suggestiveness of a pretrial identification procedure?
    a. *Kirby v. Illinois*
    b. *Simmons v. United States*
    c. *Neil v. Biggers*
    d. *United States v. Wade*

25. _____ is the court case that held that evidence obtained by unreasonable search and seizure must be excluded in a federal criminal trial.
    a. *Mapp v. Ohio*
    b. *Weeks v. United States*
    c. *United States v. Leon*
    d. *Illinois v. Gates*

26. _____ is the case that articulated the good faith exception.
    a. *Mapp v. Ohio*
    b. *Weeks v. United States*
    c. *United States v. Leon*
    d. *Illinois v. Gates*

27. _____ is the case that articulate the exclusionary rule to the state courts.
    a. *Mapp v. Ohio*
    b. *Weeks v. United States*
    c. *United States v. Leon*
    d. *Illinois v. Gates*

Essay Questions

1. Explain the two rules a police officer must observe when searching a suspect incident to a lawful arrest.

2. Explain the constitutional requirements for stop and frisk.

3. Explain consent searches and the constitutional requirements for them to be considered voluntary.

4. Discuss the constitutional issues in electronic surveillance.

5. Explain the conditions that must exist to have an actual arrest.

6. Discuss the circumstances where an arrest may be made without a warrant.

7. Explain the constitutional rights that must be covered in the *Miranda* warning.

8. Discuss the general criteria used to judge the suggestiveness of a pretrial identification procedure.

9. Discuss the suggested approaches by opponents of the exclusionary rule to violations of search and seizure requirements.

10. Discuss the relevance of the exclusionary rule to the war on terrorism.

CHAPTER 8 ANSWER KEY

FILL-IN-THE BLANK QUESTIONS

1. legality, conduct
2. search, seizure, Fourth
3. search warrant, search
4. reasonableness, scope
5. probable cause, arrest, search
6. removed, destroyed, damaged
7. illegal, excluded
8. threshold inquiry, street encounter, questioning
9. Terry, Ohio
10. reasonableness, totality, circumstances
11. search, trespass
12. privacy, Fourth
13. arrest, custody, holding
14. Fifth
15. good faith

TRUE/FALSE QUESTIONS

1.	T	13.	T
2.	F	14.	F
3.	T	15.	F
4.	T	16.	T
5.	F	17.	T
6.	T	18.	F
7.	T	19.	T
8.	T	20.	T
9.	F	21.	T
10.	T	22.	F
11.	T	23.	T
12.	T	24.	F

MULTIPLE CHOICE QUESTIONS

1.	A	15.	D
2.	D	16.	B
3.	B	17.	A
4.	D	18.	D
5.	D	19.	C
6.	A	20.	B
7.	B	21.	C
8.	A	22.	A
9.	D	23.	D
10.	D	24.	C
11.	A	25.	B
12.	B	26.	C
13.	C	27.	A
14.	B		

Chapter 9

The Courts and the Judiciary

Learning Objectives

At the conclusion of this chapter, the student should possess sufficient knowledge to achieve the following learning objectives:

1. Understand the structure of the state and federal court systems.

2. Know the difference between limited and general jurisdiction courts.

3. Understand the function of the appellate court system.

4. Describe the federal judicial system in terms of structure and jurisdiction.

5. Describe the process by which an appeal is accepted by & decided on in the U.S. Supreme Court.

6. Provide details on court caseloads and case overload.

7. Describe the judiciary in terms of duties, qualifications, and selection methods.

8. Describe the Missouri Plan for judicial selection.

9. Discuss the different types of judicial selection.

10. Describe the impact that modern technology has on court administration.

Keywords and Definitions

Adjudication: The determination of guilt or innocence; a judgment concerning criminal charges.

Appeal: A review of a lower-court's proceedings by a higher court.

Appellate Court: Courts that consider a case that has already been tried to determine whether the measures used complied with accepted rules of criminal procedure and were in line with constitutional doctrines.

Plea Negotiations: The discussion between the defense counsel and the prosecution by which the accused agrees to plead guilty for certain considerations.

Adversarial Procedure: The procedure used to determine truth in the adjudication of guilt or innocence in which the defense is pitted against the prosecution, with the judge acting as arbiter of the legal rules.

Assembly-Line Justice: The view that the justice process resembles and endless production line that handles most cases in a routine and perfunctory fashion.

Courts of Limited Jurisdiction: Courts that handle misdemeanors and minor civil complaints.

Lower Courts: A generic term referring to those courts that have jurisdiction over misdemeanors.

Courts of General Jurisdiction: Courts that try felony offenses and more serious civil matters.

de Novo Trial: The granting of a new trial by a court of general jurisdiction after hearing an appeal from a court of limited jurisdiction.

Specialty Courts: Courts that focus on one type of criminal act (drug courts or gun courts) and all cases within the jurisdiction that involve this particular type of crime are funneled to the specialty court where presumably, they will get prompt attention.

Drug Court: A specialty court given jurisdiction over cases involving illegal substances; drug court judges are skilled in finding alternative treatment programs for defendants.

Federal District Court: The trial courts of the federal system having jurisdiction over cases involving violations of federal laws, including civil rights abuses, interstate transportation of stolen vehicles, drug trafficking, and so on.

U.S. Circuit Courts: The courts that handle the first level of appeal in the federal system.

Court of Last Resort: A court that handles the final appeal on a matter. The U.S. Supreme Court is the official court of last resort for criminal matters.

Writ of Certiorari: Literally, "to be informed of, to be made certain in regard to." It isan order of a superior court requesting that the record of an inferior court (or administrative body) be brought forward for review or inspection.

Legal Briefs: Written materials submitted to the Supreme Court after a case has been accepted for review by writ of certiorari.

Case Conference: After the material is reviewed and the oral arguments heard, the justices of the Supreme Court meet to discuss the case and vote to reach a decision.

Missouri Plan: A way of picking judges through nonpartisan elections as a means of ensuring judicial performance standards.

Chapter Outline

I.   The criminal court process
      A.   Role of the courts
            1.   provide an open and honest forum for regulating human behavior and settling disputes
            2.   provide fair & just hearings that maintain a sense of impartiality and objectivity
            3.   interpret the Constitution
      B.   Complex social agency with independent but interrelated subsystems
            1.   governed by precise rules to ensure fairness and uniformity
            2.   functioning of the system is compromised by restraints
                  a.   chronically under budgeted
                  b.   chronically overburdened with cases
            3.   court becomes a scene of accommodation
                  a.   plea bargains
                  b.   discretionary powers produce dissimilar treatment
      C.   Chief Justice Roy Moore and the Ten Commandments case
            1.   separation of church and state issue
            2.   illustrates that even judges must obey the court

II.   State courts
      A.   High volume
            1.   processed 92 million cases in 2001
                  a.   56 million traffic and ordinance violations
                  b.   20 million civil and domestic cases
                  c.   14 million criminal cases
                  d.   2 million juvenile cases
            2.   overall caseloads are steadily increasing
                  a.   up 28% from 1987 to 2001
                  b.   some types of cases experienced increases, others decreased
      B.   Lower trial courts: courts of limited jurisdiction
            1.   approximately 14,000 in the U.S.
            2.   most organized at the town, municipal or county level, some controlled by the state
            3.   outnumber general jurisdiction courts 5 to1
            4.   referred to as misdemeanor, municipal or lower courts
            5.   handle misdemeanors, violations, and small civil suits
                  a.   restricted in the penalties that they can impose
                  b.   refer serious cases to a higher level
            6.   conduct preliminary hearings in felony cases for higher level
            7.   specialty courts
                  a.   juvenile and family
                  b.   probate courts (divorce, estate issues, custody)
                  c.   drug courts
            8.   process and punishment in the lower trial courts
                  a.   most often accused of assembly-line justice
                  b.   "handling the situation" and resolving minor disputes
                  c.   dangerous offenders can slip through the cracks

C.   Felony courts: courts of general jurisdiction
        1.   approximately 3,000 in the U.S.
        2.   process roughly 5 million felony cases each year
                a.   for example murder, rape, robbery
                b.   highest state trial court for felony cases to be adjudicated
        3.   also handle the more serious civil matters
        4.   most (90%) are controlled by the state
        5.   review appeals from courts of limited jurisdiction
        6.   use the trial de novo process

D.   Appellate courts
        1.   appellate courts do not retry cases
        2.   review case procedure of lower courts to determine if errors exist
                a.   defendant thinks the law violates constitutional standards
                b.   defendant believes due process rights were violated
                c.   most focus on trial convictions, sentences, and pleas
        3.   appellate court options
                a.   order a new trial
                b.   allow defendant to go free
                c.   uphold original verdict
        4.   each state has at least one court of last resort (usually called the supreme court)
        5.   39 states also have intermediate appellate courts
        6.   appellate overflow?
                a.   criminal appeals are small percentage of appellate caseload but are increasing rapidly
                b.   number of new judges can't kept up with added caseload
                c.   many jurisdictions limiting the number of appeals

E.   Model state court structure
        1.   each state has its own slightly unique court structure
        2.   all have some sort of tiered (lower, upper, appellate) structure
        3.   generic structure displayed in Figure 9.3
                a.   Texas system depicted in Figure 9.4
                b.   New York system depicted in Figure 9.5

III.   The structure of the federal courts
    A.   Legal basis and jurisdiction
        1.   legal basis is found in Article 3, section 1 of the U.S. Constitution
        2.   jurisdiction over laws of the United States
        3.   jurisdiction over treaties
        4.   jurisdiction over admiralty and maritime law
        5.   jurisdiction over controversies between two states
        6.   jurisdiction over civil suits between citizens of different states
        7.   jurisdiction over civil suits citizens and a federal agency
    B.   Federal district courts
        1.   trial courts of the federal system
        2.   jurisdiction over:
                a.   violations of federal laws
                b.   civil rights abuses
                c.   interstate transportation of stolen vehicles
                d.   kidnaping
                e.   citizenship and alien rights

        f.   interstate or federal civil suits

        g.   occasionally overlaps with state courts

    3.   originally organized under the Judicial Act of 1789

    4.   there are 94 district courts

    5.   each state plus DC has at least one Federal district court

C.   Federal appellate (circuit) courts

    1.   12 appeals courts

    2.   hear roughly 40,000 appeals from District Courts annually

    3.   usually located in major cities

    4.   review federal and state appellate court cases

    5.   appeal must invoke a constitutional guarantee

    6.   also enforce regulatory orders

D.   The U.S. Supreme Court

    1.   the court of last resort for all cases tried in state and federal courts

    2.   9 members with lifetime appointments subject to Senate approval

    3.   discretion to hear appeal

    4.   generally hears 300 of the 5,000 appeals presented annually

    5.   writ of certiorari indicates a willingness to hear a case

    6.   rulings are determined by majority opinion & become precedent

    7.   sometimes the ruling is referred to as a landmark decision

    8.   court has power to influence procedures criminal justice matters

E.   How a case gets to the Supreme Court

    1.   uniqueness

        a.   the only court established by constitutional mandate

        b.   decides important cases with grave consequences

        c.   shapes the meaning of the Constitution

    2.   history of judicial review

        a.   did not review state court decisions initially

        b.   *Martin v. Hunter's Lessee*

    3.   selecting a case to hear

        a.   use of writ of certiorari

        b.   less than 100 cases receive a full opinion annually

        c.   four justices must vote to hear a case

        d.   written and oral arguments are presented

        e.   reach a decision in a case conference

F.   Supreme Court decision making

    1.   factors considered when reading a decision

        a.   state statutes

        b.   U.S. Constitution

        c.   referencing previous case decisions

    2.   writing the opinion

        a.   assigned by chief justice

        b.   majority opinion

        c.   minority or dissenting opinion

IV.   Court congestion

    A.   Communities aggressively prosecuting minor offenses

    B.   Numbers are dramatically increasing causing congestion and wait time

    C.   Reducing court congestion

        1.   causes of congestion

            a.   excessive number of continuances

      b. pretrial motions

      c. mandatory sentencing

      d. civil litigation

      e. complexity of criminal cases

   2. solutions to congestion

      a. better court management

      b. mandating speedy trials

      c. unified state court into single administrative structure

V. The judiciary

  A. Duties

    1. rule on appropriateness of conduct

    2. settle questions of evidence and procedure

    3. guide questioning of witnesses

    4. jury instruction

    5. formally charge the jury

    6. decide the case

    7. sentencing

    8. control of probation officers and court clerks

    9. influence the police and prosecutor's office

  B. Judicial qualifications

    1. vary from state to state and court to court

    2. typically they must be:

      a. resident of the jurisdiction

      b. licensed to practice law

      c. member of the jurisdiction's bar

      d. age requirements

    3. general or appellate court judges usually must to have a law degree

    4. municipal or town judges may not be trained attorneys

  C. Judicial alternatives

    1. retired judges

    2. dispute resolution systems

      a. 700 programs in effect nationally

      b. handle minor domestic conflicts, landlord-tenant issues, misdemeanors

    3. quasi-judicial officers

      a. referees or magistrates positions are created

      b. handle civil cases where both parties agree

      c. Magistrate Act of 1968

    4. part-time judges

      a. attorneys who carry out their duties pro bono

      b. maintain an active law practice but help out the court

  D. Systems of judicial selection

    1. appointment

      a. appointed directly by the chief executive

      b. chief executive recommendation followed by confirmation process

        i. Senate confirmation model

        ii.. Governor's council model

        iii. special confirmation committee model

        iv. executive council model

                            v.   elected review board model

        2.   popular election

                a.   partisan and non-partisan models exist

                b.   terms of appointment vary by court jurisdiction

                c.   concerns exist over conflict of politics and independence

        3.   the Missouri Plan

                a.   nominating committee produces a list of candidates

                b. ·   appointment by elected official from the commission's list

                c.   appointees subject to subsequent noncompetitive confirmation elections

    E.   Problems of judicial selection and quality

        1.   political appointments

        2.   limited requirements

        3.   concern over judicial qualifications

VI.   Court administration

    A.   Court management goals improve efficiency and reduce congestion

        1.   improve organization and scheduling of cases

        2.   efficient allocation of resources

        3.   administration of fees and monies

        4.   preparing budgets

        5.   overseeing personnel

    B.   The Administrative Office of the U.S. Courts

        1.   created by Administrative Office Act of 1939

        2.   collects statistics on court operations

        3.   prepares budget

        4.   judicial council provides general supervision

    C.   Court management problem areas

        1.   individualism

        2.   judicial independence

        3.   many actors are not employed by the judiciary

        4.   conflicting goals

        5.   low profile of the courts

    D.   Technology and court management

        1.   computers perform many tasks

                a.   maintain case histories

                b.   monitor and schedule cases

                c.   prepare documents

                d.   index cases

                e.   issue summonses

                f.   notify witnesses

                g.   select jurors

                h.   prepare budgets

        2. ·   SEARCH is an example of a court computer network

        3.   other computerized technology

                a.   videotaped testimony

                b.   information and data-processing

                c.   fax services

                d.   closed-circuit arraignments

                e.   video conferencing

                f.   internet

Chapter Summary

The **criminal court process** is the system through which many of the most important decisions in the criminal justice system are made, including the determination of bail, trial, **plea negotiations**, **adjudication**, and **sentencing**. There are currently two views of the criminal justice process. The first view is that it is an **adversarial procedure** in which the defendant and the state are opponents in a type of contest and so it uses procedures that are fair and formalized by following the laws of criminal procedure and rules of evidence. The second view sees a simple, quick, and efficient system where the case is handled with little fuss. According to this latter view, the defense attorney, the prosecutor, the judge, and other court personnel are a work group that encourages plea negotiations or some other "quick fix."

Usually three (or more) separate systems exist in each state jurisdiction. The **courts of limited jurisdiction**, commonly called **lower courts**, are restricted in the types of cases they hear. These courts handle misdemeanors and include special courts such as juvenile, family, and probate. In contrast, the **courts of general jurisdiction** are the trial courts that handle serious civil and criminal matters. A growing phenomenon in the United States is the creation of **specialty courts** that focus on only one type of criminal act, for example, **drug courts** and gun courts. The **appellate courts** review questions of law appealed from the trial courts and each state has a **court of last resort**, usually called the state supreme court.

The federal government has established a three-tiered hierarchy of court jurisdiction. The **Federal District Courts** are the trial courts of the federal system. Appeals from the district courts are heard in one of twelve federal appeals courts, sometimes referred to as **U.S. Circuit Courts**. These federal appellate courts also enforce orders of federal administrative agencies. The **U.S. Supreme Court** is the nation's highest appellate body. Rulings of the Supreme Court become a precedent that must be honored by all lower courts and are called landmark cases that set legal precedents for all lower courts to follow. The Supreme Court hears only those cases that it selects to review by a **writ of certiorari**. It requires four justices to vote to hear the case.

Both the state and federal courts have experienced an explosion in the number of cases being heard. The case overload is the result of an excessive number of continuances requested by attorneys, the increasing number of pretrial motions, and the recent explosion in civil litigation. Relief will come by better administrative and management techniques or by the unification of existing state courts into a single administrative structure.

The **judge** is the senior officer in a court of criminal law. Judges have a variety of duties including rulings on conduct, evidence, procedure, jury instructions, and sentencing. The states use several methods to select their state court judges including appointments by governors or legislatures, popular election, and the three-part approach known as the **Missouri Plan**.

There has been a nationwide recognition of the need for improved court administration to reduce the current congestion facing the courts. The goals that must be accomplished are the improvement in the organization and scheduling of cases, improved methods to allocate court resources, the administration of fines and monies due the court, preparation of budgets, and overseeing court personnel.

Fill-in-the-Blank Questions

1. The _____ _____ _____ is the setting in which the most important decisions in the criminal justice system are made.

2. Those accused of crime (defendants) call on the tools of the legal system to provide them with a fair and just hearing with the _____ _____ _____ resting on the state.

3. A _____ _____ is a nonjudicial alternative that is far more common than the formal trial and serves to alleviate caseload pressure.

4. State courts of limited limted jurisdiction are restricted in the criminal penalties that they can impose. In most jurisdictions, they can impose a _____ fine or a _____ term of less than _____.

5. State courts of limited jurisdiction are also called _____ courts or _____ courts.

6. Admitting into evidence illegally seized materials, improperly charging a jury, and allowing a prosecutor to ask witnesses improper questions are all examples of _____ _____ that can serve as grounds for an appeal.

7. The federal government has established a three-tiered hierarchy of court jurisdiction that, in order of ascendancy, consists of the U.S. _____ _____, the U.S. _____ _____ _____, and the U.S. _____ _____.

8. Circuit courts do not actually _____ cases, nor do they determine whether the facts brought out during the trial support _____ or _____.

9. The U.S. Supreme Court is the nation's _____ appellate body and the court of _____ _____.

10. The U.S. Supreme Court has discretion over most of the cases it will consider and may choose to hear only those it deems _____, _____, and _____ of its attention.

11. When the U.S. Supreme Court decides to hear a case, it grants a _____ _____ _____.

12. Decisions by the U.S. Supreme Court represent the legal precedents that _____ to the existing body of law on a given subject, _____ it, and/or _____ its future development.

13. _____ programs, _____ of certain offenses, and _____ _____ are possible avenues of relief for court overcrowding.

14. Typically, the potential judge must be a _____ of the state, be _____ to practice law, be a member of the state _____ _____, and be between the ages of _____ and _____ years of age.

15. Some jurisdictions have created new quasi-judicial officers, such as _____ or _____ to relieve the traditional judge of time-consuming responsibilities.

True/False Question

T F 1.   The criminal court process is designed to provide an open and impartial forum for deciding the truth of the matter and reaching a solution which, though punitive, is fairly arrived at and satisfies the rule of law.

T F 2.   Since 1987, criminal court case filings have risen but traffic cases have declined in state courts.

T F 3.   If, upon appeal, a determination is made that criminal procedure has been violated, the appellate court cannot dismiss the charge outright.

T F 4.   The formal trial process is slightly more common than the plea negotiation as a means of resolving criminal cases.

T F 5.   Probate court is an example of a specialty court

T F 6.   Defendants are encouraged to plea bargain because cases drag on for a long time.

T F 7.   Specialty courts fall under the heading of courts of general jurisdictionl.

T F 8.   Some states separate courts of limited jurisdiction into those that handle civil cases only and those that settle criminal cases.

T F 9.   The nation's courts of general jurisdiction are the ones most often accused of providing assembly-line justice.

T F 10.   Courts of limited jurisdiction shoulder the largest caseloads of all the types of courts.

T F 11.   All courts of general jurisdiction in the states are state-administered.

T F 12.   All courts of general jurisdiction hear both serious civil and criminal matters.

T F 13.   Family courts and municipal courts are considered specialty courts.

T F 14.   Appellate courts do not try cases.

T F 15.   The U.S. Supreme Court sometimes uses a jury trial format.

T F 16.   The U.S. Supreme Court must hear all cases appealed to it.

T F 17.   The U.S. Supreme Court justices can shape the future meaning of the U.S. Constitution.

T F 18.   To receive a hearing before the U.S. Supreme Court, at least four justices must vote to hear the case.

T F 19.   There are three primary systems of judicial selection in operation in the United States.

T F 20.   Judges have extensive control and influence over the other agencies of the court: probation, the court clerk, the police, and the district attorney's office.

T F 21.   Research efforts have failed to find consistent bias in judicial decision making.

T F 22.   Some jurisdictions use practicing attorneys as part-time judges.

Multiple Choice Questions

1.   Within the confines of the court, the primary concern of the agents of the criminal justice system is to find solutions that benefit:
    a.   the victim
    b.   the defendant
    c.   society
    d.   they seek to balance all of the above

2.   The adversarial procedure pits the:
    a.   defendant against the state
    b.   defendant against the victim
    c.   defense counsel against victim
    d.   all of the above

3.   The _____ have original jurisdiction over misdemeanor cases.
    a.   courts of general jurisdiction
    b.   courts of limited jurisdiction
    c.   appellate courts
    d.   all of the above

4.   The _____ conduct preliminary hearings for felony cases.
    a.   courts of general jurisdiction
    b.   courts of limited jurisdiction
    c.   appellate courts
    d.   all of the above

5.   Felony court is another name used to describe:
    a.   courts of limited jurisdiction
    b.   courts of general jurisdiction
    c.   circuit courts
    d.   specialty courts

6. According to the text, what is the primary reason for defendants plea bargaining?
   a. to avoid the pains of imprisonment
   b. to avoid a prolonged trial
   c. to avoid the pains of the court process
   d. to avoid dealing with the prosecutor

7. Felony appeals from state courts of general jurisdiction are generally handled by:
   a. state courts of limited jurisdiction
   b. state courts of last resort
   c. state appellate courts
   d. federal circuit courts

8. How many U.S. District Courts are there?
   a. 51
   b. 94
   c. 121
   d. 152

9. Defendants can appeal under all of the following circumstances **except** which?
   a. They believe the procedures violated their constitutional rights
   b. They were tried under a law that violates constitutional standards
   c. The judge improperly charged the jury
   d. All of the above are grounds for appeal

10. The U.S. Courts of Appeal are organized into _____ judicial circuits.
    a. 7
    b. 12
    c. 25
    d. 50

11. A total of _____ justices preside over the U.S. Supreme Court.
    a. 3
    b. 6
    c. 9
    d. 12

12. The legal basis for the federal court system is the:
    a. case of *Martin v. Hunter's Lessee*
    b. Bill of Rights
    c. U.S. Constitution
    d. Declaration of Independence

13. The _____ are the trial courts of the federal system.
    a. Federal District Courts
    b. U.S. Circuit Courts
    c. U.S. Claims Courts
    d. all of the above

14. _____ is the current Chief Justice of the U.S. Supreme Court.
    a. Warren Burger
    b. Earl Warren
    c. Clarence Thomas
    d. William H. Renquist

15. The U.S. circuit courts are empowered to review federal and state appellate court cases on _____ issues involving rights guaranteed by the Constitution.
    a. substantive
    b. procedural
    c. factual
    d. a and b

16. Which of the following is **not** one of the primary systems used for selecting state judges?
    a. Missouri Plan
    b. appointment by a committee of the House of Representative
    c. popular election
    d   appointment by the governor

17. Which of the following is **not** true concerning a ruling by the Supreme Court?
    a. It is referred to as a de novo decision.
    b. Its rule becomes a precedent.
    c. It must be honored by all lower courts.
    d. It can influence the everyday operating decisions of the police, courts, and corrections.

18. In *Martin v. Hunter's Lessee*, the U.S. Supreme Court reaffirmed the legitimacy of the Court's jurisdiction over _____ court decisions when such courts handled issues of federal or constitutional law.
    a. all
    b. military
    c. state
    d. federal

19. When a case is heard by the U.S. Supreme Court, the justices review:
    a. oral arguments by attorneys
    b. submitted legal briefs
    c. new testimony by witnesses
    d. both A and B

20. The overflow of court cases in the United States is due to:
    a. excessive number of continuances demanded by attorneys
    b. increasing number of motions on evidence and procedural issues
    c. recent explosion in civil litigation
    d. all of the above

21. The _____ is the senior officer in a court of criminal law.
    a. victim
    b. prosecutor
    c. defense counsel
    d. judge

22. The qualifications for appointment to one of the existing state judgeships:
    a. vary from state to state
    b. are uniform at the state level
    c. are uniform from court to court
    d. are set by the federal government

23. Which of the following is **not** part of the Missouri Plan of judicial selection?
    a. nominations by a judicial nominations commission
    b. appointments by an elected official
    c. nonpartisan and noncompetitive elections for incumbent judges
    d. senate confirmnation

24. _____ states select judges of the courts of general jurisdiction by non-partisan elections.
    a. 7
    b. 10
    c. 17
    d. 32

25. How do federal judges reach the bench?
    a. they are elected in a non-partisan elections
    b. they are appointed by the President and confirmed by the senate
    c. they are appointed by the President without confirmation
    d. they are appointed by a senate committee and confirmed by the President

Essay Questions

1. Explain the two competing views of the criminal justice process.

2. Explain the significance of the concept of "assembly-line" justice.

3. Explain the role of specialty courts in the state court system.

4. Describe the functions of the three-tiered federal court system.

5. Explain how the writ of certiorari is issued by the Supreme Court.

6. Explain the significance of the decision of the U.S. Supreme Court in *Martin v. Hunter's Lessee.*

7. Describe the problem of court overload and congestion; discuss some possible steps to overcome the problem.

8. Explain the role of the judge.

9. Describe the various methods of judicial selection at the state level.

10. Describe the use of alternatives to the traditional judge.

CHAPTER 9 ANSWER KEY

FILL-IN-THE-BLANK QUESTIONS

1. criminal court process
2. burden of proof
3. plea negotiation
4. $1,000, jail, 12 months
5. municipal, lower
6. judicial error
7. district courts, courts of appeals, Supreme Court
8. retry, conviction, dismissal
8. federal administrative agencies
9. highest, last resort
10. important, appropriate, worthy
11. writ of certiorari
12. add, change, guide
13. diversion, decriminalization, bail reform
14. resident, licensed, bar association, twenty-five, seventy
15. referees, magistrates

TRUE/FALSE QUESTIONS

1.	T	12.	T
2.	T	13.	F
3.	F	14.	T
4.	F	15.	F
5.	T	16.	F
6.	T	17.	T
7.	F	18.	T
8.	T	19.	T
9.	F	20.	T
10.	T	21.	T
11.	F	22.	T

MULTIPLE CHOICE QUESTIONS

1.	D	14.	D
2.	A	15.	B
3.	B	16.	B
4.	B	17.	A
5.	B	18.	C
6.	C	19.	D
7.	C	20.	B
8.	A	21.	D
9.	D	22.	A
10.	B	23.	D
11.	C	24.	C
12.	C	25.	B
13.	A		

Chapter 10

The Prosecution and the Defense

Learning Objectives

At the conclusion of this chapter, the student should possess sufficient knowledge to achieve the following learning objectives:

1.   Provide a description of the formal and informal role of the prosecutor in the criminal process.

2.   Compare and contrast the various types of prosecutors.

3.   Describe the role of prosecutorial discretion in the justice system.

4.   Describe the role that politics plays in prosecutorial discretion.

5.   Discuss the concept of right to counsel.

6.   Provide a description of the different types of defender services.

7.   Know the case law associated with the right to counsel issue.

8.   Describe the role that the defense attorney plays in the criminal process and his or her duties as a part of that role.

9.   Discuss the issues involved in legal ethics.

10.   Explain what it means to be a legally competent attorney.

Keywords and Definitions

Prosecutor: The public official, usually a licensed attorney, who represents the government's case against a person accused of a crime. Depending on the jurisdiction, this individual may go by the title District Attorney, County Attorney, Solicitor, State's Attorney, or U.S. Attorney.

Harmless Error Doctrine: The doctrine established by the Supreme Court that holds a conviction valid despite some errors committed by the judge or prosecutor.

Career Criminal Prosecution Program: A form of priority prosecutions that involve identifying dangerous offenders who commit a higher rate of crime so that prosecutors can target them for swift prosecution.

Attorney General: The chief prosecutor of each state and of the United States.

District Attorney: The chief prosecutors at the county or local level.

Police Investigation Report: The statement by the police of the details of the crime, including all the evidence needed to support each element of the offense.

Community Prosecution: The program that recognizes that crime reduction is built on community partnerships, so prosecutors become problem solvers looking to improve the overall safety and well-being in the communities over which they have jurisdiction.

Nolle Prosequi: the term used when a prosecutor decides to drop a case after a complaint has been made.

Discretion: The use of personal decision making and choice in carrying out operations in the criminal justice system.

Grand Jury: A group (usually comprised of 23 citizens) chosen to hear testimony in secret and to issue formal criminal accusations (indictments).

Pretrial Diversion: The system by which the prosecutor postpones or eliminates criminal prosecution in exchange for the alleged offender's participation in a rehabilitation program.

Convictability: A term describing the likelihood of gaining a guilty verdict at trial. Prosecutors assess the convictability of the accused when deciding to move forward with a prosecution.

Defense Attorney: The counterpart of the prosecuting attorney in the criminal process; the counsel for the defendant in a criminal trial who represents the individual from arrest to final appeal.

Model Rules of Professional Conduct: Guidelines set forth by the American Bar Association that defines the ethical standards of licensed attorneys.

Indigent Defendant: A person who is needy and poor or lacks the means to hire an attorney.

Gideon v. Wainwright: U.S. Supreme Court ruled that state courts must provide counsel to indigent defendants in felony prosecutions.

Argersinger v. Hamlin: Supreme Court extended the obligation to provide counsel to all criminal cases in which the penalty includes imprisonment regardless of the whether the offense is a felony or a misdemeanor.

Miranda v. Arizona: Procedural safeguards, including the right to counsel, must be followed at custodial interrogation to secure the privilege against self-incrimination.

Assigned Counsel: Public defendant services provided mainly by local private attorneys appointed and paid for by the court.

Public Defender: An attorney generally employed by the government to represent poor persons accused of a crime at no cost to the accused.

Recoupment: The requirement that the indigent offender repay the state for at least part of their legal services.

Ad Hoc Assigned Counsel System: The presiding judge appoints attorneys on a case-by-case basis.

Coordinated Assigned Counsel System: An administrator oversees the appointment of counsel and sets up guidelines for the administration of indigent legal services.

Contract System: A block grant is given to a lawyer or law firm to handle indigent defense cases; there are two types of contract system: (1) the attorney may be given a set amount of money and is required to handle all cases assigned, or (2) the lawyers agree to provide legal representation for a set number of cases for a fixed fee.

Mixed System: Uses both public defenders and private attorneys in an attempt to draw on the strengths of both; the public defender system operates simultaneously with the assigned counsel system or contract system to offer total coverage to the indigent defendant.

Pro Bono: The practice by private attorneys of taking without fee the cases of indigent offenders as a service to the profession and the community.

Reasonable Competence Standard: The standard by which legal representation is judged: did the defendant receive a reasonable level of legal aid?

***Strickland v. Washington*:** The Supreme Court ruled that a defendant's claim of attorney incompetence must have two components: the defendant must show that (1) the counsel's performance was deficient and that such errors were made as to eliminate the presence of counsel guaranteed by the Sixth Amendment, and (2) the deficient performance prejudiced the case to an extent that the defendant was deprived of a fair trial (that is, a trial with reliable results).

Subpoena: A court order requiring the recipient to appear in court at an indicated time and date.

Chapter Outline

I.   Introduction: Two legal adversaries in the criminal court process
      A.   The prosecutor
            1.   represents the state's interest
            2.   possesses great discretionary authority
      B.   The role of the defense
            1.   represents the legal interests of the accused
            2.   legal obligation to provide a competent and adequate defense
      C.   Judge serves as the intermediary

II.   The prosecutor
      A.   Afforded variouss titles
            1.   district attorney
            2.   county attorney
            3.   state's attorney
            4.   U.S. attorney

B.   Duties
       1.   primary duty is to enforce the criminal law
       2.   seek justice
       3.   convict the guilty
       4.   live up to ABA ethical standards
C.   Politics and prosecutors
       1.   elected or appointed
       2.   party affiliation
       3.   voter constituency
       4.   community pressures
       5.   interest groups
D.   Prosecutorial misconduct
       1.   pressure for guilty convictions v. justice
       2.   product of political pressure or notoriety
       3.   misconduct is rarely punished
       4.   may conceal or misrepresent evidence
       5.   influence juries
       6.   impugn witness testimony
       7.   refer to tainted evidence
       8.   factors linked to prosecutorial excesses
               a.   seeking highest charge
               b.   expansive interpretation of criminal law
               c.   winning attitude
               d.   obtains most severe penalties
E.   Profile of the state-level prosecutior's office
       1.   79,000 attorneys, investigators & support staff in 2,341 prosecutor offices nationwide
       2.   median budget of $318,000
       3.   median salary of chief prosecutor is $85,000
       4.   half employ less than 10 people
F.   The duties of the prosecutor
       1.   prosecutor is the chief law enforcement officer of the jurisdiction
       2.   general duties
               a.   enforcing the law
               b.   representing the government
               c.   maintaining proper standards of conduct
               d.   criminal justice reform
               e.   public spokesperson
       3.   specific duties
               a.   investigation
               b.   police cooperation
               c.   determining the charge
               d.   interviewing witnesses
               e.   review warrants
               f.   subpoena witnesses
               g.   pretrial hearings
               h.   plea bargaining
               i.   criminal trials
               j.   sentencing recommendations
               k.   appeals

G.   Priority prosecution – responding to specific crime problems
1.   major felonies
2.   drug offenses
3.   white collar crime
4.   high-tech crimes
5.   environmental crimes
6.   career criminals
7.   rape and sexual assault
8.   the role of protector of public health

H.   Types of prosecutors
1.   federal prosecutors – appointed by the President
      a.   U.S. Attorney General is chief prosecutor – administrator
      b.   U.S. Attorneys are the assistant prosecutors who try cases
2.   state and county prosecutors – mostly appointed by the Governor
      a.   attorney general – chief prosecutor of each state
      b.   district attorney – chief prosecutor at the county level
      c.   employ assistant attorneys assigned to various divisions
3.   urban prosecutor's offices
      a.   usually headed by a district attorney
      b.   divisions for felonies, misdemeanors, trial & appeals
4.   rural prosecutor's offices
      a.   chief prosecutor handles most of the work alone
      b.   sometimes afforded part-time assistant prosecutors

I.   The prosecutor within society
1.   criticized for bargaining justice away and for political aspirations
2.   often target particular crime problems
3.   working with law enforcement
      a.   involvement in the criminal investigation
      b.   collaborate on the police investigation report
      c.   prove legal advice
      d.   train police personnel
4.   working with the community
      a.   adopting a community prosecution philosophy that build on community partnerships
            i.   align resources with community needs
            ii.   problem solvers looking to improve safety
            iii.   community prosecutor positions
            iv.   meet with the police daily
            v.   difficult to evaluate
      b.   community prosecution programs link to community policing

III.   Prosecutorial discretion
A.   Prosecutorial options
1.   reject or dismiss case
      a.   insufficient evidence
      b.   witness problems
      c.   interest of justice
      d.   due process problems
      e.   received a plea on another case
      f.   pursue a pretrial diversion option
      g.   referral for prosecution in another jurisdiction

        2.   charges to file
        3.   grand jury
B.   Exercise of discretion
        1.   system factors
                a.   clogging the system
                b.   effectiveness
                c.   concentration on serious cases
        2.   case factors
                a.   attitude of the victim
                b.   cost
                c.   undue harm to suspect
                d.   alternative procedures
                e.   civil sanctions
                f.   suspect cooperation
                g.   victim/offender relationship
C.   Disposition factors
        1.   selecting alternative non-criminal actions
        2.   pretrial diversion to appropriate community social service agency
        3.   seek to rehabilitate the offender
D.   Political factors
        1.   elected status makes office susceptible to pressure
                a.   public outrage
                b.   media pressure
                c.   interest groups
        2.   can produce negative justice outcomes
E.   The role of prosecutorial discretion
        1.   proper usage can prevent rigid implementation of the law
        2.   can result in abuse and the abandonment of the law
                a.   political creatures
                b.   convictability worries

IV.   The defense attorney
A.   Accused has constitutional right to an attorney
        1.   may obtain private counsel
        2.   indigent may be assigned private counsel or a public defender
B.   Traditional treatment of defense attorneys
        1.   looked down upon
        2.   low pay
        3.   few law school courses
C.   The role of the criminal defense attorney
        1.   advocate attorney for his/her client
        2.   officer of the court
                a.   uncover basic facts
                b.   uncover elements of the criminal act
        3.   must uphold the integrity of the legal profession
        4.   observe fair play and professional ethics
D.   functions of criminal defense attorney
        1.   investigation
        2.   interview client, police and witnesses
        3.   discussions with prosecutor
        4.   represent client in pretrial procedures

        5.   plea negotiations
        6.   prepare for trial
        7.   file legal motions
        8.   represent defendant in trial
        9.   assist in sentencing decision
        10.   appeal
    E.   Ethical issues -- different dilemmas than the prosecutor
        1.   cross-examining to discredit truthful witnesses
        2.   put a witness on stand who will knowingly commit perjury
        3.   tempting or advising a client to commit perjury
        4.   ongoing criminal activities by the client
        5.   Danielle Van Dam case
    F.   Defense attorney should:
        1.   maintain client confidentiality
        2.   advise client to adhere to constitutional requirements
        3.   advise client of rights
        4.   provide a zealous defense
        5.   force the prosecutor to prove his/her case
        6.   cast doubt on client's guilt

V. The right to counsel – no one can be deprived of freedom without legal representation
    A.   Indigent defendants
        1.   federal courts provide counsel to indigent defendants under the
                Sixth Amendment
        2.   *Gideon v. Wainwright* held that state courts must provide counsel
                for indigent defendants
    B.   Right to counsel applies to:
        1.   during any police interrogation – *Escobedo v Illinois*
        2.   following a custodial interrogation – *Miranda v. Arizona*
        3.   during postconviction interrogation – *Massiah v. United States*
        4.   during arraignment – *Hamilton v. Alabama*
        5.   during pretrial hearing – *Coleman v. Alabama*
        6.   post-indictment lineup – *United States v. Wade*
        7.   when submitting a guilty plea – *Moore v. Michigan*
        8.   during the plea bargaining process – *Brady v. United States*
        9.   at trial in a state capital case – *Powell v. Alabama*
        10.   during any felony trial - *Gideon v. Wainwright*
        11.   where penalty includes imprisonment - *Argersinger v. Hamlin*
        12.   during adjudication that may lead to commitment - *In re Gault*
        13.   at the time of sentencing – *Townsend v. Burke*
        14.   during initial appeal – *Douglas v. California*
        15.   during probation revocation hearing - *Mempa v Rhay*
        16. during parole revocation hearings – *Morrisey v. Brewer*
    C.   Right to counsel does not apply to:
        1.   preindictment lineups
        2.   booking process
        3.   grand jury hearing
        4.   subsequent appeals
        5.   disciplinary proceedings in correctional facility
        6.   postrelease revocation hearings

D.   The private bar
     1.   nationally known defense attorneys are few in number
     2.   some serve as house counsel to ongoing criminal enterprises
     3.   more typical is the attorney who accepts many cases for small fees
E.   Legal services for the indigent
     1.   poor legal services stem from:
         a.   legal restrictions
         b.   not enough defense attorneys
         c.   indifference of the legal bar
         d.   large caseloads for public defenders
         e.   limited resources in defense programs
     2.   categories of indigent defense
         a.   public defender system
         b.   assigned counsel system
         c.   contract system
         d.   mixed system
     3.   costs of defending the poor
         1.   4.5 million indigent defendants at $1.5 billion annually
         2.   recoupment requires partial repayment for legal services
         3.   programs are overburdened and under funded
     4.   public defender offices cost $75-100 billion annually
     5.   NIJ's Neighborhood Defender Service
F.   Public versus private attorneys
     1.   conviction rates are about the same
     2.   public attorneys yield higher rate of incarceration for guilty clients
     3.   public attorneys yield shorter sentences for incarcerated clients

VI.   The defense lawyer as a professional advocate
     A.   Plea bargaining predominates because of the strain on time and resources
     B.   The adversary system reconsidered
         1.   plea bargaining is a major tool used by prosecution and defense
         2.   courtroom personnel form "working groups" which exclude the defendant

VII.   The informal justice system
     A.   Plea bargain dominates due to time and resource restraints
     B.   Formal justice system is eroding
     C.   Players share a common interest to move the case along or settle the matter

VIII.   Competency of defense attorneys
     A.   *Taylor v. Illinois* - affirmed conviction despite attorney's error
     B.   Reasonable competence standard
         1.   defendant must demonstrate that counsel substantially departed from the standard
         2.   may be necessary to prove prejudice to the defendant
     C.   Defining attorney competence
         1.   *Strickland v. Washington* - proof of incompetence rests on:
             a.   counsel's performance deficient and serious errors made as to eliminate the presence of counsel as guaranteed by the Sixth Amendment
             b.   deficient performance deprived defendant of a fair trial

2.   *Wiggins v. Smith, Warden et al.* - *Strickland* applies to capital cases
D.   Relations between the prosecutor and defense attorney
    1.   adversarial conflicts
        a.   prosecution subpoenas lawyers to testify
        b.   use of grand jury to question private defense investigators
        c.   defense ignores client who intends to commit perjury
        d.   goal ought always be to seek justice
    2.   relationships and images are often shaped by the media

Chapter Summary

Depending on the level of government and the jurisdiction, the **prosecutor** may be known as a **district attorney, county attorney, state's attorney** or **U.S. attorney**. The prosecutor is generally a member of the practicing bar, appointed or elected to the position. Although the primary duty of the prosecutor is the enforcement of criminal law, the prosecutor's fundamental obligation as an attorney is to seek justice as well as convict those who are guilty. When faced with public and media pressure, prosecutors often place priorities on certain types of cases, such as white-collar crime, high-tech crimes, environmental crimes, sex crimes, public health issues, or the prosecution of career criminals.

Prosecutorial misconduct is unethical behavior motivated by the desire to obtain a conviction. Appellate courts use the **harmless error doctrine** and generally uphold convictions where the misconduct is not considered serious. Prosecutors are not personally liable for such misconduct.

Just as police officers no longer simply make arrests, prosecutors need to do more than try cases. **Community prosecution** recognizes that crime reduction is built on community partnerships. This is accomplished by (1) placing prosecutors in selected communities to work at police stations, (2) increasing communication with police and community groups and organizations, and (3) using prosecutorial resources to solve community problems and not just prosecuting individual cases.

The prosecutor exercises a great deal of **discretion** in deciding whether or not to institute criminal proceedings, in selecting alternative dispositions, and in determining formal charges. The prosecutor can opt to not prosecute as case through the issuance of a **nolle prosequi** order, or he/she may seek and indictment through the **grand jury** or at a preliminary hearing. Among the variables that influence these prosecutorial decisions are system factors, case factors, and the convictability of the offender. Discretion has two effects because the proper exercise of discretion can improve the criminal justice system, while too much discretion can lead to abuses that result in abandonment of the law.

The **defense attorney** is the counterpart of the prosecuting attorney in the criminal process. The accused has a constitutional right to counsel, and when the defendant cannot afford an attorney, the state must provide one. The major functions of the defense attorney are to investigate the incident, represent the defendant at major pretrial procedures, plea bargain, prepare the case, represent the defendant at trial, and conduct the appeal.

In the landmark case *Gideon v. Wainwright*, the U.S. Supreme Court has judicially interpreted the **Sixth Amendment** to mean that counsel must be provided by the state to indigent defendants in all types of criminal proceedings where the penalty may be imprisonment. The Supreme Court has moved to extend the right to counsel to postconviction and other collateral proceedings in *Argersinger v. Hamlin*. In *Miranda v. Arizona*, the Court guaranteed the right to counsel during police interrogations. **Public defender** offices, organized at the state or county level, utilize public employees to provide legal services to indigent defendants. **Recoupment** is the process that allows states toi recover legal fees from indigent defendants after trial. In contrast, the **assigned counsel system** involves the use of private attorneys appointed by the court. A third program, the **contract system**, provides a block grant or fixed fee to a lawyer or law firm to handle indigent defense cases. In some areas, **mixed systems** exist, utilizing both public defenders and private attorneys.

The Supreme Court has also established a **reasonable competence standard** for defense attorneys. In *Strickland v. Washington*, the court set two criteria: (1) counsel's performance must be deficient enough to eliminate the Sixth Amendment guarantee the presence of counsel, and (2) the deficient performance prejudiced the case to an extent that the defendant was deprived of a fair trial. A **subpoena** is a court order requiring a witness to appear in court.

Fill-in-the-Blank Questions

1. The prosecutor participates with the _____ and the _____ _____ in the adversarial process and also is responsible for bringing the _____ case against the accused criminal.

2. When a prosecutor uses unethical behavior to gain a conviction, he/she is said to engage in _____ _____. When this occurs, appellate courts review the allegations and apply the _____ _____ doctrine to determine whether or not to overturn the conviction.

3. The prosecutor is either _____ or _____ to the office and is, consequently, a _____ figure in the criminal justice system.

4. The prosecutor normally has a _____ affiliation and needs to respond to community _____ and _____ _____.

5. A _____ _____ _____ program places a priority on the swift adjudication of those dangerous offenders who commit a high proportion of crime.

6. A _____ _____ is the chief legal officer and prosecutor of the state while a _____ _____ is the prosecutor at the county level.

7. Prosecutors have been criticized for bargaining _____ away, for using their positions as a stepping stone to higher _____ _____, and often simply _____ a criminal case.

8. The concept of community prosecution is not just a _____, but a new _____ for prosecutors to do their job.

9. A prosecutor may choose to drop a case using a _____ _____ order or may seek to pursue it through a preliminary hearing or by asking for a _____ _____ to be convened.

10. The key to the prosecutorial discretion is the power to _____ or _____ formal charges against a defendant.

11. In _____ _____, the prosecutor postpones or eliminates criminal prosecution in exchange for the alleged offender's participation in a rehabilitation program.

12. Diversion allows prosecutors to utilize the _____ _____ of justice because there is an offical _____ of the criminal process.

13. The _____ _____ is the counterpart of the prosecuting attorney in the criminal process.

14. The two main types of assigned counsel systems are the _____ _____ assigned counsel system, in which the presiding judge appoints attorneys on a case-by-case basis, and the _____ assigned counsel system, in which an administrator oversees the appointment of counsel and sets up guidelines for the administration of indigent legal services.

15. Under the contract system, a _____ _____ is given to a lawyer or law firm to handle indigent defense cases.

True/False Questions

T F 1. The prosecutor is ordinarily a member of the bar who appointed or elected to be a public prosecutor.

T F 2. The prosecutor's primary duty is to try cases.

T F 3. The prosecutor's fundamental obligation as an attorney is to convict those who are guilty, not to seek justice.

T F 4. The harmless error doctrine is used by appeals courts to rule on the issue of alleged prosecutorial misconduct.

T F 5. The prosecutor is not permitted to have contact with police officers prior to the officer's scheduled testimony in court.

T F 6. The local prosecutor is often the single most powerful individual in local government.

T F 7. Federal prosecutors are elected.

T F 8. Community prosecution models have little in common with community policing models.

T F 9. Nontraditional prosecutorial roles include such areas as prosecution of violence against the elderly and health care fraud cases.

T F 10. On the state and county levels, the chief prosecutorial officers are called the attorney general and the district attorney, respectively.

T F 11. The chief prosecutor (district attorney) rarely tries cases in rural jurisdictions.

T F 12. The prosecutor is generally the chief law enforcement official of the jurisdiction.

T F 13. The police and the prosecutor seldom compete with each other in seeking credit for the successful arrest, prosecution, and conviction of a criminal defendant.

T F 14. To align resources with community needs, some prosecutors need to work in the community daily.

T F 15. A grand jury proceeding accomplishes largely the same goals as a preliminary hearing.

T F 16. While determining which cases should be eliminated from the criminal process or brought to trial, the prosecutor has the opportunity to select alternative actions if they are more appropriate.

T F 17. The American Bar Association recommends against the use of social service programs as an alternative to prosecution.

T F 18. Political factors often sway a prosecutor's discretion to seek an indictment in a criminal case.

T F 19. *Gideon v. Wainwright* was a Supreme Court case focused on the issue of a defendant's right to counsel.

T F 20. The defense counsel is an officer of the court.

T F 21. Nowadays, the professional status of the criminal defense lawyer tends to be high.

T F 22. A mixed system of indigent counsel assignment uses both public defenders and private attorneys in an attempt to draw on the strengths of both.

Multiple Choice Questions

1. The prosecutor's primary duty is to _____.
   a. enforce the criminal law
   b. try cases
   c. seek justice
   d. convict those who are guilty

2. Unethical prosecutorial misconduct maybe fueled by which of the following?
   a. rarely seeks the highest charges
   b. interprets the criminal law narrowly
   c. attempts not to lose as many convictions as possible
   d. the desire to obtain convictions

3. Which of the following is **not** a reason why prosecutorial excesses occur?
    a. seeking the lowest charges
    b. interpreting the criminal law narrowly
    c. winning as many convictions as possible
    d. all of the above

4. More than _____ of the nation's prosecutor's offices have a prosecutor serving full time.
    a. one-third
    b. one-half
    c. two-thirds
    d. three-fourths

5. Which of the following problems is **not** among those being afforded priority prosecution lately?
    a. high-tech crimes
    b. environmental crimes
    c. public order crimes
    d. white-collar crimes

6. _____ is the most common environmental offense being prosecuted today at the local level.
    a. waste disposal
    b. water pollution
    c. air pollution
    d. toxic fumes

7. The two most important factors in deciding to prosecute environmental crimes at the local level are the:
    a. harm posed by the offense and the possibility of conviction
    b. harm posed by the offense and the criminal intent of the offender
    c. possibility of conviction and the criminal intent of the offender
    d. possibility of conviction and the prosecutor's political party

8. All of the following are characteristics of the chief prosecutor's office at the state and county level, **except** which?
    a. Full- and part-time attorneys perform the bulk of criminal prosecution.
    b. Most attorneys works for relatively high salaries.
    c. Most attorneys who work for the prosecutors are political appointees.
    d. Most attorneys take these positions to gain trial experience that qualify them for better jobs

9. The critical first step in developing the government's case against a suspect is the:
    a. decision to charge
    b. grand jury
    c. preliminary hearing
    d. police investigation report

10. Which of the following activities is **not** an area where police and prosecutors work together?
    a. providing legal advice
    b. training police personnel
    c. helping officers write their reports
    d. preparing the police officer's for trial

11. Which of the following is not a common reason for prosecutor's dismissing a case?
    a. insufficient evidence
    b. witness problems
    c. due process problems
    d. all of the above are common

12. _____ problems are the most common reasons prosecutors reject cases.
    a. Evidence
    b. Witness
    c. Due process
    d. Victim

13. _____ is the practice of dealing with an accused in a noncriminal fashion.
    a. Adversary process
    b. Community prosecution
    c. Discretion
    d. Pretrial diversion

14. The prosecutor may decide to seek a criminal complaint through grand jury or:
    a. information procedure
    b. judicial procedure
    c. chief prosecutor filings
    d. criminal courts process

15. Which of following is a core function of the defense attorney?
    a. investigating the incident
    b. entering into plea negotiations
    c. interviewing the police
    d. all of the above

16. In _____, the Supreme Court held that state courts must provide counsel to indigent defendants in felony prosecutions.
    a. *Miranda v. Arizona*
    b. *Argersinger v. Hamlin*
    c. *Gideon v. Wainwright*
    d. *Betts v. Brady*

17. In _____, the Supreme Court held that there is an obligation to provide counsel in all criminal cases in which the penalty includes imprisonment – regardless of whether the offense is a felony or a misdemeanor.
    a. *Miranda v. Arizona*
    b. *Argersinger v. Hamlin*
    c. *Gideon v. Wainwright*
    d. *Betts v. Brady*

18. _____ requires a state-appointed counsel for indigent offenders being interrogated by the police.
    a. *Miranda v. Arizona*
    b. *Argersinger v. Hamlin*
    c. *Gideon v. Wainwright*
    d. *Betts v. Brady*

19. Which of the following steps does require the assistance of counsel for the accused?
    a. booking procedures
    b. post-indictment lineups
    c. grand jury investigations
    d. appeals beyond the first review

20. A public defender gets assigned by which of the following?
    a. the prosecutor
    b. the jury
    c. the court
    d. the clerk of the court

21. Prior to the Supreme Court decision in *Gideon v. Wainwright*, public defendant services were provided mainly by:
    a. public defenders
    b. pro bono lawyers
    c. legal defense funds
    d. assigned counsels

22. Which amendment is the basis for providing counsel to the indigent offender?
    a. Fourth
    b. Fifth
    c. Sixth
    d. Fourteenth

23. Which of the following is the most popular form of indigent defense system?
    a. public defender
    b. assigned counsel
    c. contract
    d. law school

24. The first public defender program in the United States opened in 1913 in:
    a. Los Angeles
    b. New York
    c. Houston
    d. Atlanta

25. Ad hoc and coordinated counsel systems are associated with which of the following indigent defense systems?
    a. contract system
    b. court system
    c. assigned counsel system
    d. mixed system

26. What is the term for the process by which the state recovers some or all of the cost associated with providing legal defense to a indigent individual?
    a. nolle prosequi
    b. reimbursement
    c. pro bono
    d. recoupment

27. What is the legal standard that is used to assess the competency of a defense attorney?
    a. reasonable competence standard
    b. harmless error doctrine
    c. plain view doctrine
    d. *Gideon* standard

28. What landmark Supreme Court case applied professional competency standards for defense attorneys to death penalty cases?
    a. *Strickland v Washington*
    b. *Taylor v. Illinois*
    c. *Argersinger v. Hamlin*
    d. *Wiggins v. Smith, Warden et al.*

Essay Questions

1. Describe the ethical duties of a prosecutor.

2. Discuss the twelve major prosecutorial tasks of a prosecutor.

3. Explain the concept of community prosecution.

4. Discuss the seven most common reasons for rejection or dismissal of a criminal case.

5. Compare and contrast system factors, case factors, disposition factors, and political as they apply to prosecutorial discretion in charging decisions.

6. Discuss the major functions of a defense attorney.

7. Discuss the major ethical issues facing a defense attorney.

8. Compare and contrast the assigned counsel, contract, and mixed systems of indigent defense allocation.

9. Explain the problems of the criminal bar and their impact on defense lawyers as professional advocates.

10. Explain the reasonable competence standard for defense lawyers as outlined in *Strickland v. Washington*.

CHAPTER 10 ANSWER KEY

FILL-IN-THE-BLANK QUESTIONS

1. judge, defense attorney, state's
2. prosecutorial misconduct, harmless error
3. elected, appointed, political
4. party, voters, interest groups
5. criminal career prosecution
6. attorney general, district attorney
7. justice, political office, dismissing
8. program, strategy
9. nolle prosequi, grand jury
10. continue, discontinue
11. pretrial diversion
12. rehabilitative model, suspension
13. defense attorney
14. ad hoc, coordinated
15. block grant

TRUE/FALSE QUESTIONS

1.	T	12.	T
2.	F	13.	F
3.	F	14.	T
4.	T	15.	T
5.	F	16.	F
6.	T	17.	F
7.	F	18.	T
8.	F	19.	T
9.	T	20.	T
10.	T	21.	F
11.	F	22.	T

MULTIPLE CHOICE QUESTIONS

1.	A	15.	D
2.	D	16.	C
3.	C	17.	B
4.	D	18.	A
5.	C	19.	B
6.	A	20.	C
7.	B	21.	D
8.	B	22.	B
9.	D	23.	C
10.	C	24.	A
11.	A	25.	C
12.	A	26.	D
13.	D	27.	A
14.	A	28.	D

Chapter 11

Pretrial Procedures

Learning Objectives

At the conclusion of this chapter, the student should possess sufficient knowledge to achieve the following learning objectives:

1.   Provide a general description of the pretrial procedures that can occur between arrest and the formal criminal trial.

2.   Know the role and actions of pretrial services.

3.   Understands the concept of grand juries and preliminary hearings.

4.   Discuss the purpose and advantages of bail and constitutional limitations placed upon it

5.   Discuss the various types of bail systems.

6.   Recount the history of bail reform.

7.   Describe the difference between preventive detention and release on recognizance.

8.   Describe the arraignment and the plea options available to the defendant at the arraignment.

9.   Discuss the actors in plea bargaining, the legal issues raised, and the plea-bargaining decision making process.

10.   Explain the roles of the prosecutor, defense attorney, and judge in plea negotiations.

11.   Identify the different types of pleas and how they are used.

12.   Discuss pretrial diversion.

Keywords and Definitions

Pretrial Procedures: A series of events that are critical links in the chain of justice including arraignments, grand jury investigations, bail hearings, plea-bargaining negotiations, and predisposition treatment efforts.

Nolle prosequi: An order submitted by the prosecutor after criminal charges have been filed stating that the state will not proceed at this time with the case against the defendant.

Complaint: A sworn written statement to a court by the police, prosecutor, or individual alleging that an individual(s) has committed an offense and requesting indictment and prosecution.

Initial Appearance (Hearing): Appearance before a magistrate that occurs within twenty-four hours after a defendant's arrest; the purposes are to (1) inform the defendant of the charge, (2) take the plea, (3) set bail, and (4) appoint counsel.

Indictment: A formal written criminal accusation given by a grand jury setting out the crimes for which the defendant is to stand trial.

Information: The written accusation of the prosecutor setting out the charges against a defendant and used in place of the indictment in some jurisdictions.

Preliminary (Probable Cause) Hearing: A hearing before a magistrate to determine if the government has sufficient evidence to show probable cause that the defendant committed the crime.

Arraignment: The step at which the accused are read the charges against them, asked how they wish to plead, and advised of their rights.

Nolo Contendere: A plea meaning "I will not contest it," in which a defendant does not admit guilt but submits to sentencing; this plea cannot be used against the defendant in a subsequent civil suit.

Plea Bargaining: The decision reached between the prosecutor and the defense attorney to have the defendant plead guilty in exchange for some concession (a plea to a less serious charge).

Diversion: The use of a noncriminal alternative to trial such as referral to treatment or employment programs while suspending the criminal proceedings against the accused.

Bail: Money or some other security provided to the court to ensure the appearance of the defendant at every subsequent stage of the criminal justice process.

Pretrial Detention: The detention of the accused between the time of arrest and trial, usually in jail.

Stack v. Boyle: The Supreme Court found bail to be a traditional right to freedom before trial that permits unhampered preparation of a defense and prevents the criminal defendant from being punished prior to conviction.

Bail Bond: It is an instrument executed by a third party promising to forfeit money to the court if the defendant upon release does not appear for future criminal proceedings.

Bail Bonding: It is the business of providing bail by bail bondsmen to indigent offenders, usually at high rates of interest.

Release on Own Recognizance (ROR): A pretrial release procedure where the defendant does not post a bail bond or other security but promises to return to court.

Manhattan Bail Project: The project found that if the court had sufficient background information about the defendant, it could make a reasonably good judgment about whether the accused would return to court.

Bail Reform Act of 1984: Established that no defendants should be kept in pretrial detention simply because they could not afford money bail, established the presumption of ROR in all cases in which a person is bailable, and formalized restrictive preventive detention provisions to insure community safety.

Preventive Detention: The requirement that certain dangerous defendants be confined prior to trial for their own protection and that of the community.

Schall v. Martin: Supreme Court case upholding the application of preventive detention statutes to juvenile defendants.

United States v. Salerno: The Supreme Court ruled that the preventive detention act had a legitimate and compelling regulatory purpose and did not violate the due process clause.

Pretrial Detainee: An individual who is either denied bail or cannot afford to post bail and is thus held in secure confinement until trial.

Presentment: An accusation of a grand jury instructing the prosecutor to prepare an indictment against the accused.

Grand Jury: A group of citizens chosen to hear testimony in secret to determine if evidence exists for a person to stand trial on a criminal complaint.

True Bill: The action by a grand jury when it votes to indict an accused.

No Bill: The action by a grand jury when it votes against indicting an accused.

Exculpatory Evidence: Evidence favorable to the accused defendant.

Incriminating Evidence: Evidence unfavorable to the defendant's case.

United States v. Williams: Supreme Court rules that exculpatory evidence need not be presented to a grand jury.

Hill v. Lockhart: The Supreme Court ruling that to improve the effectiveness of defense counsel, the defendant needs to show a reasonable probability that, except for counsel's errors, the defendant would not have pleaded guilty.

Boykin v. Alabama: The Supreme Court ruled that the defendant must make an affirmative statement that the plea is voluntary before the judge can accept it.

Brady v. United States: The ruling of the Supreme Court that avoiding the possibility of the death penalty is not grounds to invalidate a guilty plea.

Bordenkirker v. Hayes: The Supreme Court ruling that a defendant's constitutional rights are not violated when a prosecutor threatens to reindict the accused on a more serious charge if he or she is not willing to plead guilty to the original offense.

Santobello v. New York: The Supreme Court decision that the promise of a prosecutor that rests on a guilty plea must be kept in a plea-bargaining agreement.

Ricketts v. Adamson: The Supreme Court decided the defendant is required to keep his or her side of the bargain to receive the promised offer of leniency, because plea bargaining rests on an agreement between parties.

North Carolina v. Alford: The Supreme Court decided that accepting a guilty plea from a defendant who maintains his or her innocence is valid.

United States v. Mezzanatto: The Supreme Court decision that a defendant who wants to plea bargain in federal court can be required to agree that if he testifies at trial, his statements during the plea-bargain negotiations can be used against him.

Chapter Outline

I.   Pretrial Procedures
      A.   critical steps between arrest and trial
            1.   booking
            2.   probable cause hearing
            3.   bail hearings
            4.   grand jury or preliminary hearing
            5.   arraignment
            6.   plea negotiations
            7.   pretrial diversion
      B.   The majority of cases are resolved in these stages
      C.   Many cases are dropped during these stages (nolle prosequi)
      D.   Must understand these steps if you want to understand the reality of justice process

II.   Procedures following arrest
      A.   Booking
            1.   police list possible charges against the suspect
            2.   fingerprinting and mugshots
            3.   participation in a lineup
            4.   complaint identifies formal charges and details of the crime and arrest
            5.   initial hearing
            6.   persons charged with a misdemeanor are usually released after booking
      B.   Felony procedures
            1.   preliminary hearing to establish probable cause that defendant committed crime
                  a.   some jurisdictions require an indictment from grand jury
                  b.   other jurisdictions file information document at preliminary hearing
            2.   formal arraignment; plead to charge

            a.   judge informs defendant of the charges, appoints counsel and sets bail

            b.   defendant pleads guilty, not guilty, or nolo contendere

III.   Pretrial services

    A.   Practices & programs that screen detained arrestees to provide the magistrate/judge with concise summaries of the arrestee's personal background as it relates to bail options

    B.   Pretrial service functions

        1.   seek to improve the release/detention decision

        2.   identify those for whom alternatives to incarceration are appropriate

        3.   monitor pretrial arrestees

        4.   magistrate/judge has an extensive list of pretrial release mechanisms

            a.   field citation release (police issue a ticket)

            b.   station house citation release (police verify information & release without booking

            c.   jail citation release (release deferred until arrival at jail and booking process completed

            d.   direct release authority by pretrial program (pretrial service makes bail release decision

            e.   bail schedule (post bail at jail based on schedule amounts)

            f.   judicial release (judge/magistrate or bail commissioner determines release options

IV.   Bail

    A.   Pretrial step that decides if defendant returns to the community until trial

    B.   Money or other security provided to the court to ensure the appearance of the defendant at every subsequent stage of the criminal justice process

        1.   bail decision and amount is set by the court

        2.   defendant must deposit all or some of the bail as a deposit

        3.   failure to appear at trial results in forfeiture of the deposit

        4.   denial of bail or failure to pay it results in jail stay until trial

    C.   Bail today

        1.   64% of defendants make bail

        2.   36% are detained until trial

            a.   29% can't afford it

            b.   7% denied bail (most serious crimes)

        3.   bonding agents lend money to people who can not make bail

        4.   numerous allegations of corruption

        5.   many states have abolished money practice and replaced it with a deposit bail system

    D.   Receiving bail

        1.   decision is based on the likelihood of defendant returning for trial

        2.   bail cannot be used to punish, coerce, or threaten the defendant

        3.   cannot be revoked by the court

        4.   critics charge that bail is unfair on the poor

            a.   poor can't afford to post bail

            b.   housing the poor costs taxpayers money

    E.   The legal right to bail

        1.   Eighth Amendment does not guarantee bail, prohibits excessive bail

        2.   bail may be financial discrimination

3.   in most cases, the defendant has a right to release on bail
4.   bail review hearings by a higher court serve as a check on judge
5.   *Stack v. Boyle*
      a.   U.S. Supreme Court case - bail permits unhampered preparation for trial
      b.   ruling prevents punishment prior to conviction
      c.   bail is excessive when it exceeds the amount calculated to ensure that the defendant will return for trial

F.   Making bail
    1.   bail is considered at a bail hearing shortly after arrest
    2.   court considers crime type, flight risk, and dangerousness of offender
    3.   powerful ties between bonding agents and the court
    4.   release on recognizance (ROR) option
      a.   no money required for release
      b.   successful option for low flight risks

G.   History of bail reform
    1.   Manhattan Bail Project
      a.   conducted by the Vera Institute of Justice
      b.   ROR program began in 1961
      c.   concluded that release based on verified information was more effective than money bail
      d.   pioneered use of release on recognizance
    2.   Bail Reform Act of 1966
      a.   first change in federal bail laws since 1789
      b.   stressed philosophy that release should be under the least restrictive method necessary to ensure court appearance
    3.   Bail Reform Act of 1984
      a.   established the presumption of ROR in the federal system
      b.   formalized restrictive preventive detention provisions
    4.   innovative bail systems now exist
      a.   ROR
      b.   conditional release
      c.   unsecured bail
      d.   privately secured bail
      e.   property bail
      f.   deposit bail
      g.   surety bail
      h.   cash bail

H.   Preventive detention
    1.   bail seeks to control serious offenders but release of non-dangerous offenders
    2.   1/3 of bailees fail to appear or commit a new crime while on release
    3.   preventive detention statutes require certain dangerous defendants to be confined until trial
    4.   Bail Reform Act of 1984 requires detention hearing
      a.   accused has right to counsel, to testify, & to call witnesses
      b.   government must present clear and convincing evidence of dangerousness
    5.   State provisions
      a.   exclusion of certain crimes

          b.   redefinition of bail

          c.   limited bail for recidivists

     6.   The legality of preventive detention

          a.   *Schall v. Martin* – upheld preventive detention of juveniles to protect the minor or society

          b.   *United States v. Salerno* - upheld preventive detention provision in Bail Reform Act as it applies to adults

I.   Pretrial detention

     1.   600,000 eople in one of 3,500 U.S. jails on any given day

     2.   over 50% of jail population is pretrial detention

     3.   jail overcrowding is increasing

     4.   jails are considered the weakest link in the justice process

     5. $100 a day or $36,000 annually to house a jail inmate

J.   The consequences of detention

     1.   more likely to be convicted

     2.   more likely to receive a prison sentence

V.   Charging the defendant

     A.   Proof of probable cause placed on the state

          1.   government's responsibility to prove probable cause

          2.   grand jury and preliminary hearing are procedures which evaluate evidence against the accused

     B.   The grand jury

          1.   history of the grand jury

               a.   early English common law

               b.   Magna Carta

               c.   group of freemen made up the grand jury

               d.   serve as a check on an arbitrary government

               e.   incorporated into the U.S. Constitution in the Fifth Amendment

          2.   use of grand jury is declining

               a.   in 1961, more than half of the states required grand jury indictments

               b.   most states give the prosecutor the option of a grand jury or proceeding directly to a preliminary hearing

          3.   two roles of the grand jury

               a.   independent investigating body

                    i.   examines the possibility that a crime occurred in the jurisdiction

                    ii.   a presentment with findings is issued at the end of investigation

               b.   accusatory role

                    i.   decides whether probable cause exists

                    ii.   witnesses called by prosecutor or via grand jury subpoenas

                    iii.   finds probable cause, a true bill is affirmed

                    iv.   no probable cause, a no bill is passed

          4.   logistics of the grand jury

               a.   16 to 23 members

               b.   chosen at random from the community

        c.   must be at least 18 years of age, be a U.S. citizen, a resident of the jurisdiction, and sufficient English
        d.   meets at the request of the prosecution
        e.   hearings are closed and secret
        f..   accused, defense, public not allowed to attend unless called to testify

    5.   criticisms of the grand jury
        a.   costly operation
        b.   a "rubber stamp" for the prosecution
        c.   delays the criminal justice process
        d.   *United States v. Williams* - exculpatory evidence need not be presented

    6.   suggested reforms
        a.   witnesses should have attorneys present
        b.   prosecutors should present exculpating evidence as well as incriminating evidence
        c.   witnesses should be granted 5th Amendment protection
        d.   grand jury should be informed of all the elements of the crime

C.   The preliminary hearing
    1.   establishes if probable cause for a trial exists; replaces grand jury in ½ states
    2.   general procedures
        a.   conducted before a magistrate or inferior court judge
        b.   proceedings are open to the public
        c.   prosecution, defendant and defense attorney present at hearing
        d.   may confront witnesses and challenge evidence
        e.   judge makes decision if probable cause exists
        f.   if so, defendant is bound over for trial
        g.   district attorney files an information with the court
    3.   waiving the preliminary hearing – defendant's choice
        a.   defendant has already decided to plead guilty
        b.   defendant wants to speed up the process
        c.   defendant hopes to avoid negative publicity

D.   Arraignment
    1.   judge informs defendant of charges and appoints counsel if not already retained
    2.   Sixth Amendment guarantees met
    3.   defendant is asked to enter a plea

E.   The plea
    1.   guilty
        a.   more than 90% of defendants plead guilty before reaching the trial stage
        b.   judge must inform defendant of consequences of plea and loss of constitutional guarantees
        c.   establish basis of plea and its voluntariness
        d.   inform defendant of right to counsel
        e.   inform defendant of possible sentencing outcomes
        f.   cannot be rescinded even if law is changed

            g.   sentencing hearing date is set

    2.   not guilty

           a.   verbally stated by defendant or counsel

           b.   automatically entered when defendant stands mute before the bench

           c.   trial date is then set

           d.   bail is reconsidered

    3.   Nolo Contendere

           a.   means "no contest"

           b.   essentially a guilty plea

           c.   may not be held against the defendant as proof in a subsequent civil matter

           d.   verbally and voluntarily stated by defendant and must be accepted by the judge

VI.   Plea bargaining

    A.   Estimated that more than 90% of convictions result from negotiated pleas

    B.   Avoiding trial benefits prosecutor, defense, and court

        1.   prosecutor gets a conviction

        2.   defense gets leniency

        3.   court saves time and resources

    C.   The nature of the bargain

        1.   concessions offered by the prosecution and accepted by judge

           a.   reduction of initial charges

           b.   reduce number of charges

           c.   recommend a lenient sentence

           d.   alter charge to a more socially acceptable one

           e.   judge shopping

        2.   complexities of plea bargaining

           a.   rarely a one-shot deal, rather negotiated over time

           b.   prosecutors seek connected or wired guilty pleas on multiple defendants

        3.   arguments for plea bargaining

           a.   reduced costs

           b.   improved court efficiency

           c.   can concentrate on serious cases

           d.   defendant avoids pretrial detention and delay

           e.   efficient allocation of resources

        4.   arguments against plea bargaining

           a.   encourages defendants to waive constitutional rights

           b.   results in lesser sentences and sentencing disparity

           c.   possibility of coercing innocent to plead guilty

    D.   Legal issues in plea bargaining

        1.   *Hill v. Lockhart* - defendant must prove reasonable probability that he would not have pleaded guilty if not for ineffectiveness of counsel to be satisfied

        2.   *Boykin v. Alabama* - an affirmative action must exist on the court record before judge can accept plea to establish voluntariness of the plea

        3.   *Brady v. United States* - guilty plea valid if entered to avoid possibility of death penalty

4.   *Bordenkircher v. Hayes* - rights are not violated if prosecutor threatens to reindict
5.   *Santobello v. New York* - prosecutor must keep promise or conviction may be reversed on appeal
6.   *Ricketts v. Adamson* - defendant must also keep his/her side of the agreement
7.   *People v Hicks* – violation of the agreement by defendant negates agreement
8.   *North Carolina v. Alford* - defendant could plead guilty without admitting guilt
9.   *U.S. v. Mezzanatto* - statements made by defendant during plea bargaining may be used at trial for impeachment purposes

E.   The role of the prosecutor in plea bargaining
    1.   few limits on discretion to plea bargain
    2.   pleas frequently sought after in weak cases
    3.   chief prosecutor may establish guidelines
    4.   concessions determined on a case-by-case basis
    5.   serves a leadership role as it indirectly sets policies

F.   The role of the defense counsel in plea bargaining
    1.   acts in an advisory role in negotiations
    2.   makes certain accused understands nature of plea bargaining process and the guilty plea
    3.   keeps defendant informed of developments

G.   The judge's role in plea bargaining
    1.   ABA argues that judge should not participate in negotiations
    2.   Federal Rules of Criminal Procedure prohibit federal judges from participating
    3.   ABA arguments against participation
        a.   creates impression defendant could not get a fair trial
        b.   lessens ability to determine voluntariness of the plea
        c.   inconsistent with use of PSI
        d.   may induce innocent to plead guilty
    4.   arguments for judicial intervention
        a.   make sentencing more uniform
        b.   process would be more fair and efficient

H.   Victim and plea bargaining
    1.   victim is not empowered at the pretrial stage and have no role in negotiations
    2.   no legal consequences for ignoring the victim during plea bargaining
    3.   ABA's Model Uniform Victims of Crime Act urges conference with victim

I.   Plea bargaining reform
    1.   develop uniform plea practices
    2.   restricted time periods for negotiations
    3.   defense counsel present during negotiations
    4.   open discussions
    5.   full information on offense and offender
    6.   judicial questioning of defendant before accepting the plea
    7.   judicial supervision of negotiation
    8.   ban or limit the use of plea bargaining

VII.   Pretrial diversion
   A.   Diversion programs were first established in the 1960's and 1970's
   B.   Diversion reduces stigma of conviction, reduces costs, and alleviates overcrowding
   C.   Factors in prosecutorial decision making
      1.   nature of crime
      2.   offender characteristics
      3.   first time offender
      4.   defendant cooperation
      5.   impact on community
      6.   opinion of the victim
   D.   Diversion programs take on various forms
      1.   separate, independent agencies
      2.   in-house programs
      3.   joint ventures
   E.   Criticisms of diversion
      1.   do not avoid stigmatism
      2.   do not reduce recidivism
      3.   may widen the net of control
      4.   federal funds are being cut

Chapter Summary

After arrest, the accused is ordinarily taken to the police station, where the police list the possible criminal charges against the accused and obtain other information for **booking** purposes. Once this is complete, the justice process begins **pretrial procedures**. The prosecutor must decide to pursue charges or issue a **nolle prosequi** order. In misdemeanor cases, the **complaint** is the formal written document identifying the criminal charge, the date and place of the crime, and the circumstances of the arrest. The complaint requests that the defendant be present at an **initial hearing** to be held soon after the arrest is made. Where a felony is involved, the formal charging process is ordinarily an **indictment** from a **grand jury** or an **information** through a **preliminary hearing**. The accused is then brought before the trial court for **arraignment**, during which the judge informs the defendant of the charge, ensures that the accused is properly represented by counsel, and determines whether the person should be released on bail or some other form of release pending a hearing or trial. At this point the defendant enters a plea of guilty, not guilty, or **nolo contendere** (no contest).

The use of money **bail** and other alternatives, such as **release on recognizance (ROR)**, allow most defendants to be free pending their return for trial. Today, **preventive detention** statutes are being used to hold **pretrial detainees** until trial. Since the Eighth Amendment to the U.S. Constitution prohibits the use of excessive bail, many challenge the use of preventive detention as unconstitutional. However, in *United States v. Salerno*, the Supreme Court upheld the use of preventive detention.

The prosecutor controls the proceedings of the grand jury and need only **incriminating evidence** against the defendant. **Exculpatory evidence** is not required. When a grand jury is done deliberation, it issues a **presentment** report that includes a recommendation on indictment. A decision to indict is called a **true bill** and a decision not to indict is termed a **no bill**.

One of the most common practices in the criminal justice system is the process of **plea bargaining**, or the exchange of legal concessions by the state for a plea of guilty by the defendant. More than 90 percent of criminal convictions result from negotiated pleas of guilty. Because of overcrowded criminal court caseloads and the needs of the prosecution and defense, plea bargaining has become an essential, yet controversial part of the administration of justice. Proponents contend that it actually benefits both the state and the defendant by trimming costs as well as time, and the defendant may receive a reduced sentence. Opponents, on the other hand, argue that plea bargaining is objectionable because it encourages a defendant to waive the constitutional right to trial. Guidelines and safeguards have been developed to make the process more visible and uniform.

Another important feature in the early court process is the placing of offenders into **pretrial diversion** programs prior to their formal trial or conviction. Diversion involves suspension of formal criminal proceedings against an accused while that person participates in a community treatment program under court supervision. These programs vary in size but generally possess the same goal of constructively bypassing criminal prosecution by providing a reasonable alternative in the form of treatment, counseling or employment.

Fill-in-the-Blank Questions

1. Pretrial procedures are important components of the criminal justice system because the great majority of all criminal cases are resolved _____ at this stage and never come before the _____ in the form of a trial.

2. When a misdemeanor arrest occurs, the officer will often issue a _____ that designates the offense that was committed, the circumstances surrounding the act, and the date and place where it occurred.

3. The _____ is the charging document issued by the prosecutor and brought before a lower court, while grand jury will issue an _____.

4. A plea of not guilty sets the stage for trial on the merits or for negotiations between the prosecutor and defense attorney, known as _____ _____.

5. At the pretrial stage, the criminal justice system is required to balance the often conflicting goals of ensuring _____ _____ and respecting the _____ of the arrestee.

6. At the _____ stage, the defendant is given a opportunity to enter a plea of guilty, not guilty, or _____ _____.

7. Bail is _____ or some other _____ provided to the court to ensure the _____ of the defendant at every subsequent stage of the criminal justice process.

8. _____ _____ _____ is a form of pretrial release in which the defendant is not required to post bail but promises to appear at trial.

9. _____ _____ statutes require that certain dangerous defendants be confined prior to trial for their own _____ and that of the community.

10. A _____ _____ requires the defendant to pay the entire amount of bail set by the _____ to secure release.

11. Pretrial detainees are individuals who either are _____ bail or cannot _____ to post bail before trial and are kept in _____.

12. A _____ is a report of a grand jury. A _____ _____ is issued if the grand jury votes to indict and a _____ _____ is issued if they vote not to indict.

13. The evidence suggests that, if convicted, people who do not receive _____ are much more likely to be sent to prison and to do more time than people who avoid _____ _____.

14. The grand jury was an early development of _____ _____ _____ and originates from the ancient document the _____ _____.

15. The grand jury has the power to act as an _____ _____ _____ by examining the _____ of criminal activity within its jurisdiction and these efforts are directed toward _____ rather than _____ criminal conduct.

True/False Questions

T F 1. The arraignment, grand jury investigation, and bail hearing are all parts of the pretrial procedures.

T F 2. During plea negotiations, the prosecutor and the defense seldom meet to try to arrange a non-judicial settlement for the case.

T F 3. Individuals arrested on a misdemeanor charge are ordinarily released from the police station on bail to answer the criminal charge before a court at a later date.

T F 4. A probable cause hearing is another name for the preliminary hearing.

T F 5. A plea of *nolo contendere* is the same as a not guilty plea.

T F 6. Pretrial services help courts deal with the problem of determining which arrestees can safely be released pending trial.

T F 7. Pretrial services are a form of diversion.

T F 8.   One of the advantages of pretrial programs is that they can operate at different stages of the judicial process, thereby increasing the number of release options available to the courts.

T F 9.   Once the amount of bail is set by the court, the defendant is required to deposit all or a percentage of the entire amount in cash or security.

T F 10. The Eighth Amendment guarantees a constitutional right to bail.

T F 11. Surety bail requires the defendant to pay only a percentage of his/her bail amount to gain pretrial release.

T F 12. The Manhattan Bail Project found release on recognizance programs to be an effective form of pretrial release.

T F 13. There are roughly half as many people in pretrial custody as people incarcerated in the United States.

T F 14. Jails are considered to be one of the strongest links in the criminal justice process.

T F 15. Detained defendants have a much higher probability of being imprisoned than those released into the community.

T F 16. It is likely that a judge's decision making is influenced by the pretrial behavior of bailees.

T F 17. The grand jury was created as a check against arbitrary prosecution by a judge who might be a puppet of the government.

T F 18. The concept of the grand jury was incorporated into the Fourth Amendment of the U.S. Constitution.

T F 19. An indictment is also called a "true bill" and the failure to indict is a "no bill."

T F 20. The grand jury hearing can be open and public upon the request of the defendant.

T F 21. A preliminary hearing is an alternative to the grand jury.

T F 22. A preliminary hearing is closed and secret.

T F 23. The defendant can waive his/her right to a preliminary hearing.

T F 24. Crime victims are empowered at the pretrial stage of the justice process and often are afforded mandated involvement in plea negotiations

Multiple Choice Questions

1. Obtaining information, listing the criminal charges, fingerprinting, and photographing are part of which stage in the justice process?
    a. arraignment
    b. preliminary hearing
    c. grand jury
    d. booking

2. The formal written document identifying the criminal charge, the date and place where the crime occurred, and the circumstances of the arrest is called the:
    a. complaint
    b. arrest
    c. booking
    d. presentment

3. At which stage in the justice process does a judge rule on whether or not the government has sufficient evidence to show probable cause that the accused has committed the crime?
    a. preliminary hearing
    b. arraignment
    c. grand jury
    d. booking

4. At the _____, the accused is informed of the charge, the judge ensures the defendant has counsel, the judge determines if bail is appropriate and/or should continue, the defendant enters the plea, and the stage is set for the trial, if the plea is not guilty or nolo contendere.
    a. initial appearance
    b. preliminary hearing
    c. arraignment
    d. booking

5. Which type of court procedure is sometimes called a probable cause hearing?
    a. the grand jury indictment
    b. the preliminary hearing
    c. the arraignment
    d. the bail hearing

6. What happens if the defendant is released on bail but fails to appear in court as ordered?
    a. the defendant is sentenced in absentia
    b. the plea of guilty is automatically entered
    c. the bail deposit is forfeited
    d. the right to pro bono representation is forfeited

7. Which Constitutional Amendment to the Constitution prohibits the imposition of "excessive bail?"
    a. Fourth
    b. Fifth
    c. Eighth
    d. Fourteenth

8. In _____, the Supreme Court ruled that bail is excessive when it exceeds an amount reasonably calculated to ensure that the defendant will return for trial.
    a. *Stack v. Boyle*
    b. *United States v. Salerno*
    c. *Hill v. Lockhart*
    d. *Boykin v. Alabama*

9. About _____ percent of those released on bail could be considered failures for one reason or another.
    a. 20
    b. 30
    c. 45
    d. 55

10. What pretrial release method was pioneered by the Vera Institute of Justice in the report on the Manhattan Bail Project?
    a. cash bail
    b. property bail
    c. surety bail
    d. release on own recognizance (ROR)

11. The Bail Reform Act of 1966 authorized the _____ percent deposit bail.
    a. 10
    b. 20
    c. 30
    d. 40

12. The Bail Reform Act of 1984 required that _____, as well as risk of flight, be considered in the release detention decision.
    a. seriousness of the offense
    b. ability to pay
    c. community safety
    d. all of the above

13. In _____, the Supreme Court upheld the provision on preventive detention in the Bail Reform Act of 1984.
    a. *Stack v. Boyle*
    b. *Boykin v. Alabama*
    c. *Hill v. Lockhart*
    d. *United States v. Salerno*

14. On any given day in the United States, over _____ people are held in more than 35,000 local jails.
    a. 110,000
    b. 220,000
    c. 300,000
    d. 600,000

15. More than _____ percent of those held in local jails have been accused of crimes, but not convicted.
    a. 20
    b. 30
    c. 50
    d. 75

16. It costs approximately _____ per year to hold a person in jail.
    a. $50,000
    b. $40,000
    c. $30,000
    d. $20,000

17. What procedure is often used as an alternative to the grand jury?
    a. the initial hearing
    b. the arraignment
    c. the preliminary hearing
    d. the criminal trial

18. A grand jury normally includes _____ people.
    a. 16 to 23
    b. 18 to 20
    c. 19 to 24
    d. 25 to 30

19. More than _____ percent of criminal convictions are estimated to result from negotiated pleas of guilty.
    a. 60
    b. 70
    c. 80
    d. 90

20. In _____ the Supreme Court ruled that to prove ineffectiveness, the defendant must show a "reasonable probability that, but for counsel's errors, he would not have pleaded guilty and would have insisted on going to trial.
    a. *Boykin v. Alabama*
    b. *Brady v. United States*
    c. *Hill v. Lockhart*
    d. *North Carolina v. Alford*

21. In _____ the Supreme Court ruled that an affirmative action that the pleas was made voluntarily must exist in the record before a trial judge can accept a guilty plea.
    a. *Boykin v. Alabama*
    b. *Brady v. United States*
    c. *Hill v. Lockhart*
    d. *North Carolina v. Alford*

22. In _____ the Supreme Court ruled that a guilty plea could be accepted from a defendant who was maintaining his or her innocence.
    a. *Boykin v. Alabama*
    b. *Brady v. United States*
    c. *Hill v. Lockhart*
    d. *North Carolina v. Alford*

23. In _____ the Supreme Court ruled that a guilty pleas is not invalid merely because it is entered to avoid the possibility of the death penalty.
    a. *Boykin v. Alabama*
    b. *Brady v. United States*
    c. *Hill v. Lockhart*
    d. *North Carolina v. Alford*

24. In _____ the Supreme Court ruled that the promise of the prosecutor must be kept and that the breaking of a plea-bargaining agreement by the prosecutor required a reversal for the defendant.
    a. *Bordenkircher v. Hayes*
    b. *Santobello v. New York*
    c. *Ricketts v. Adamson*
    d. *United States v. Mezzanatto*

25. In _____ the Supreme Court ruled that defendants must keep their side of a bargain to receive the promised offer of leniency.
    a. *Bordenkircher v. Hayes*
    b. *Santobello v. New York*
    c. *Ricketts v. Adamson*
    d. *United States v. Mezzanatto*

26. In _____ the Supreme Court ruled that a defendant's due rights process are not violated when a prosecutor threatens to reindict the accused on more serious charges if he or she does not plead guilty to the original offense.
    a. *Bordenkircher v. Hayes*
    b. *Santobello v. New York*
    c. *Ricketts v. Adamson*
    d. *United States v. Mezzanatto*

27. In _____ the Supreme Court ruled that statements made by the defendant during plea bargaining can be used at trial for impeachment purposes.
    a. *Bordenkircher v. Hayes*
    b. *Santobello v. New York*
    c. *Ricketts v. Adamson*
    d. *United States v. Mezzanatto*

28. Whose input is not legally required during the plea bargaining process?
    a. the prosecutor
    b. the defendant
    c. the defense attorney
    d. the victim

Essay Questions

1. Discuss the sequence of steps that make up the pretrial procedures and briefly describe the function and process of each.

2. Describe five different innovative bail systems that are in use in the United States.

3. Discuss the Manhattan Bail Project and its influence on the Bail Reform Act of 1966.

4. Discuss the requirements that are contained in the Bail Reform Act of 1984.

5. Discuss preventive detention and how states have incorporated the concept into their own bail systems.

6. Describe the recommendations contained in the American Bar Association's *Grand Jury Policy and Model Act*.

7.   Describe what takes place during the arraignment.

8.   Discuss the three possible pleas a defendant can make and the effects of each plea on the defendant.

9.   List the advantages and disadvantages of plea bargaining.

10. Discuss the role of the prosecutor, defense attorney, judge, defendant, and victim in plea negotiations.

CHAPTER 11 ANSWER KEY

FILL-IN-THE-BLANK QUESTIONS

1. informally, courts
2. complaint
3. information, indictment
4. plea bargaining
5. community safety, rights
6. arraignment, nolo contender (no contest)
7. money, security, appearance
8. release on recognizance
9. preventive detention, protection
10. cash bail, judge
11. denied, afford, jail
12. presentment, true bill, no bill
13. bail, pretrial detention
14. English common law, Magna Carta
15. independent investigating body, possibility, general, individual

TRUE/FALSE QUESTIONS

1.	T	13.	F
2.	F	14.	F
3.	F	15.	T
4.	T	16.	T
5.	F	17.	T
6.	T	18.	F
7.	F	19.	T
8.	T	20.	F
9.	T	21.	T
10.	F	22.	F
11.	T	23.	T
12.	T	24.	F

MULTIPLE CHOICE QUESTIONS

1.	D	15.	C
2.	A	16.	B
3.	B	17.	C
4.	C	18.	A
5.	B	19.	D
6.	C	20.	C
7.	C	21.	A
8.	A	22.	D
9.	B	23.	B
10.	D	24.	B
11.	A	25.	C
12.	C	26.	A
13.	D	27.	D
14.	D	28.	D

Chapter 12

The Criminal Trial

Learning Objectives

At the conclusion of this chapter, the student should possess sufficient knowledge to achieve the following learning objectives:

1.   Describe the process of adjudication and the criminal trial in a general context.

2.   Describe the conditions necessary for a fair and speedy trial.

3.   Know what it means to confront witnesses.

4.   Explain the process of the pro se defense.

5.   Discuss the issues surrounding the broadcast of criminal trials.

6.   Describe the process of *voir dire*, and the differences between challenges for cause and preemptory challenges.

7.   Discuss the different ways that evidence is presented in criminal trials.

8.   Discuss the different avenues of appeal which are open to the convicted individual.

9.   Differentiate between types of evidence and evidentiary standards.

Keywords and Definitions

Adjudication: The process through which a determination of guilt or innocence is reached in the adult criminal justice system.

Bench Trial: A form of criminal trial where the judge alone renders the verdict.

Riggins v. Nevada: Case in which the Supreme Court ruled that forced treatment of an incompetent defendant is permissible.

Sell v. United States: Case in which the Supreme Court set out four rules to guide the use of forced treatment on an incompetent defendant.

Confrontation Clause: The constitutional right of a criminal defendant to see and cross-examine all the witnesses against him or her.

Hearsay Evidence: Testimony that is not firsthand but relates information told by a second party.

Coy v. Iowa: The Supreme Court limited the protection available to child sex victims at the trial stage by ruling out the use of protective screens to separate the victim from the offender during cross-examination.

Maryland v. Craig: The Supreme Court decided that alleged child abuse victims could testify by closed-circuit television if face-to-face confrontation would cause them trauma.

Duncan v. Louisiana: The Supreme Court held that the Sixth Amendment right to enjoy a jury trial is applicable to all states, as well as to the federal government, and that it can be interpreted to apply to all defendants accused of serious crimes.

Baldwin v. New York: The Supreme Court decided that a defendant has a constitutional right to a jury trial when facing a prison sentence of six months or more, regardless of whether the crime committed was a felony or a misdemeanor; for sentences of less than six months, a jury trial is not required unless it is authorized by state statute.

Lewis v. United States: The Supreme Court said there was no Sixth Amendment right to a jury trial for a string of petty offenses tried together even where the potential total sentence could exceed six months.

Williams v. Florida: The United States Supreme Court held that a six-person jury in a criminal trial does not deprive a defendant of the constitutional right to a jury trial.

Six-Person Jury: The minimum size of a jury that is accepted by the Supreme Court.

Apodaca v. Oregon: The Supreme Court held that the Sixth and Fourteenth Amendments do not prohibit criminal convictions by less than unanimous jury verdicts in non-capital cases.

Powell v. Alabama: The Supreme Court concluded that the presence of a defense attorney is so vital to a fair trial that the failure to appoint counsel was a denial of due process under the Fourteenth Amendment.

Gideon v. Wainwright: The right to counsel is so fundamental and ethical to a fair trial that states are obligated to abide by it under the Fourteenth Amendment's due process clause.

Argersinger v. Hamlin: The Supreme Court extended the obligation to provide counsel to all criminal cases in which the penalty includes imprisonment regardless of whether the offense is a felony or a misdemeanor.

Alabama v. Sheldon: Case in which the Supreme Court extended the right of counsel a sentencing hearing in which the threat of imprisonment exists.

Faretta v. California: The Supreme Court recognized a defendant's pro se right to defend oneself on a constitutional basis, while making it conditional on a showing that the defendant could competently, knowingly, and intelligently waive one's right to counsel.

Pro se: The defense of self-representation; from the Latin "for himself."

Martinez v. Court of Appeals of California: The Supreme Court found that historical and practical differences between trials and appeals convinced them that due process does not require a recognition of the right to self representation in criminal appeals.

Klopfer v. North Carolina: The Supreme Court held that the effort by the government to postpone a person's trial indefinitely without reason denies that person the right to a speedy trial guaranteed by the Sixth and Fourteenth Amendments.

Doggett v. United States: The Supreme Court found that a delay of eight and one-half years between indictment and arrest was prejudicial to the defendant and required a dismissal of the charges against the defendant.

Nebraska Press Association v. Stuart: The Supreme Court ruled unconstitutional a judge's order prohibiting the press from reporting the confessions implicating the defendant in the crime.

Gannett Co. v. DePasquale: The Supreme Court held that the press has a right of access of constitutional dimensions, but that this right was outweighed by the defendant's right to a fair trial; therefore, the closing of a preliminary hearing to the press to protect a defendant's right to a fair trial was constitutional.

Press-Enterprise Co. v. Superior Court: The Supreme Court ruled that closure of a preliminary hearing is permissible under the First Amendment only if there is a substantial probability that the defendant's right to a fair trial would be prejudiced by publicity that closed proceedings would prevent; this case clearly established the First Amendment right of access to criminal trials.

Richmond Papers, Inc. v. Commonwealth of Virginia: The Supreme Court clearly established that criminal trials must remain public.

In re Oliver: The Supreme Court held that the secrecy of a criminal contempt trial violated the right of the defendant to a public trial under the Fourteenth Amendment.

Chandler v. Florida: The Supreme Court decided that subject to certain safeguards, a state may allow electronic media coverage by television stations and still photography of public criminal proceedings over the objection of the defendant in a criminal trial.

Venire (Jury Array): The list of jurors called for jury duty from which jury panels are chosen.

Voir Dire: The process of jury selection involving the questioning of prospective jurors to ascertain their prejudices; the objective is to select unbiased and objective jurors.

Challenge for Cause: the process of dismissing a prospective juror by either side during the voir dire because the juror has indicated a bias.

Peremptory Challenges: The process by which the prosecution and defense excuse prospective jurors even though they have not exhibited any bias.

Swain v. Alabama: The Supreme Court upheld the use of peremptory challenges in isolated cases to exclude jurors by reason of racial or other group affiliations.

Batson v. Kentucky: The Supreme Court struck down the ***Swain*** doctrine of excluding jurors by peremptory challenges for reasons of racial or other group affiliations.

Powers v. Ohio: The Supreme Court held that a defendant may object to the race-based removal of a juror even when the defendant is a member of a different racial group.

Georgia v. McCollum: The Supreme Court found that criminal defendants may not seek to exclude potential jurors strictly on the basis of race.

J. E. B. v. Alabama: The Supreme Court ruled that prosecutors and defense attorneys may not use peremptory challenges to strike men or women from juries solely on the basis of gender.

Ham v. South Carolina: The Supreme Court held that the defense counsel of a black civil leader was entitled to question each juror on the issue of racial prejudice.

Taylor v. Louisiana: The Supreme Court overturned the conviction of a man by an all-male jury because a Louisiana statute allowed women, but not men, to exempt themselves from jury duty.

Turner v. Murray: The Supreme Court ruled that a defendant accused of an interracial crime in which the death penalty is an option can insist that prospective jurors be informed of the victim's race and be questioned on the issue of their bias.

Lockhart v. McCree: The Supreme Court decided that jurors who strongly opposed capital punishment may be disqualified from determining a defendant's guilt or innocence in capital cases.

Direct Examination: Initial questioning of a witness by the party who called the witness to obtain testimony regarding the case.

Cross-Examination: The prosecution's questioning of a witness called by the defense, or visa versa.

Real Evidence: Any object or other form of physical evidence produced for inspection at the trial.

Circumstantial Evidence: Evidence that does not allow for the direct inference of fact.

Directed Verdict: A verdict in a case where the judge removes the decision from the jury by either telling them what to do or by actually making the decision. Tthis occurs when the state has not been able to prove the elements of the crime and the judge orders a directed verdict of acquittal.

Rebuttal Evidence: Evidence presented by the prosecution or defense to refute or disprove the evidence presented by the other party.

Surrebuttal Evidence: Evidence presented to refute the rebuttal evidence of the other party.

Sullivan v. Louisiana: Case in which the Supreme Court ruled unconstitutional jury instructions containing the words "substantial" basis for a declaration of reasonable doubt.

Sequestration: Keeping jurors apart from one another and from the outside world so their decisions are not influenced by outside events.

Verdict: A finding of a jury or judge on questions of fact at the trial.

Hung Jury: A jury where members cannot reach a verdict.

Sentence: The punishment or criminal sanction imposed by the court on a convicted defendant, usually in the form of a fine, incarceration, or probation.

Habeas Corpus: An important judicial writ requiring that a person claiming illegal detention be brought to court to determine the legality of the detention.

Collateral Attack: A legal petition requesting a postconviction remedy for a criminal conviction.

Douglas v. California: The Supreme Court held that an indigent defendant has a constitutional right to the assistance of counsel on a direct first appeal.

Combined DNA Index System (CODIS): The computerized database that allows DNA taken at a crime scene to be searched electronically to find matches against samples taken from convicted offenders and other crime scenes.

Beyond a Reasonable Doubt: Refers to the degree of certainty required for judge or juror to find a criminal defendant guilty.

Preponderance of the Evidence: Standard proof in civil cases where evidence is more convincing to the judge or jury than opposing evidence.

In Re Winship: The Supreme Court directed that proof beyond a reasonable doubt was the appropriate standard for proving each element of an offense.

Chapter Outline

I.   Introduction
- A.   Adjudication process
  1. an open hearing to determine the truth
  2. the trial is intended to be the symbol of objective and impartial justice
  3. majority of defendants do not go through the trial process for various reasons
- B.   Formal trial structure
  1. jury trial
     - a. constitutional right of all accused
     - b. defendant may choose to waive the right in favor of a bench trial
  2. bench trial
     - a. judge alone hears the case and renders the verdict
     - b. most common in lower courts
     - c. judge may continue or suspend the case without a hearing

II.   Legal rights during trial
- A.   The Right to be competent at trial
  1. defendant must be mentally competent to stand trial
  2. trial must be postponed for a mentally incompetent person

3.   *Riggins v. Nevada* – allowed medically appropriate treatment of a mentally incompetent defendant by force

4.   *Sell v. United States* – court set out rules for forced medication
   a. there must exist an important governmental interest at stake
   b. must establish that forced medication will significantly further process
   c. less intrusive treatments are unlikely to yield substantially similar results
   d. administering the drugs must be deemed medically appropriate

B. The right to confront witnesses
   1. guaranteed by the confrontation clause in the Sixth Amendment
   2. confrontation clause restricts the admissibility of hearsay evidence
   3. allows for face-to-face challenges to the witness's assertions
   4. *Coy v. Iowa* - the use of a screen to shield child witness from the defendant is unconstitutional
   5. *Maryland v. Craig* - allows use of closed-circuit television testimony in child abuse cases

C. The right to a jury trial
   1. guaranteed by the Sixth Amendment
   2. most defendants waive right to jury trial
   3. *Duncan v. Louisiana* - right to jury trial applicable in all state defendants charged with a serious offense
   4. *Baldwin v. New York* - right to jury trial when faced with prison sentence of six months or more
   5. *Lewis v. United States* - no constitutional guarantee of jury trial even where a string of petty offenses carry a potential aggregate sentence exceeding six months
   6. traditional number of jurors is twelve but *Williams v. Florida* held that a 6-person jury is legal
   7. *Apodica v. Oregon* - upheld 10 of 12 verdict in non-capital case
      a. unanimous verdicts are the rule in federal system and all but 2 states
      b. unanimity is required of six person juries

D. The right to counsel at trial
   1. right to counsel in state trial is a fundamental right in the criminal justice system
   2. applies also to indigent defendants
   3. rulings in this area are a good example of gradual decision making by the Court and the relationship between the Bill of Rights and the Fourteenth Amendment
   4. *Powell v. Alabama* - the Scottsboro Boys case held that failure to appoint counsel was a violation of due process
   5. *Gideon v. Wainwright* - right to counsel is fundamental and ethical to a fair trial
   6. *Argersinger v. Hamlin* - no imprisonment without representation
   7. *Alabama v. Shelton* – right to counsel for suspended sentence that can carry prison or jail time in the case of sentence violation

E. The right to self-representation
   1. Court grants constitutional right to self-representation in *Faretta v. California*
   2. defendant has the option to proceed *pro se* or for themselves
   3. *pro se* right has constitutional basis

4.   must competently, knowingly, and intelligently waive right to counsel

5.   court may terminate right to self-representation at any time during the trial

6.   suggested alternative is standby attorney

F.   The right to a speedy trial

     1.   Sixth Amendment guarantee

     2.   modern court system is congested

     3.   *Klopfer v. North Carolina*

          a.   extended right to state cases

          b.   a *nolle prosequi* with leave is a violation of constitutional rights

          c.   established reasons for a speedy trial

               i.   witness availability

               ii.   reduce defendant anxiety and pretrial detention

               iii.   avoid pretrial publicity that compromises fairness

               iv.   avoid delays that might compromise the defense

     4.   *Doggett v. United States* - eight and a half year delay is prejudicial

     5.   efforts to define a speedy trial:

          a.   1967 President's Commission on Law Enforcement and the Administration of Justice – 9 months to resolution is a reasonable time

          b.   1973 National Advisory Commission on Criminal Justice Standards and Goals – goal of 60 days to trial in felony case, 30 for misdemeanors

          c.   Federal Speedy Trial Act of 1974 sets 100 day requirement

               i.   information or indictment within 30 days of arrest

               ii.   arraignment within ten days of indictment

               iii.   trial within 60 days of arraignment

          d.   many states provide even shorter time periods

III. Fair trial versus free press

     A.   The right to a fair trial

          1.   a fair trial is held before an impartial judge and jury in an environment of judicial restraint and orderliness with fair decision making

          2.   guaranteed by due process clauses of Fifth and Fourteenth Amendments

          3.   violations of fair trial include hostile courtroom crowd, improper pressure on witnesses, prejudicial behavior toward defendant, the wearing of prison clothing, and adverse pretrial publicity

          4.   conflict between restraining media coverage to protect the defendant's right to a fair trial and the media's constitutional right to news coverage

     B.   The law of fair trial

          1.   *Nebraska Press Association v. Stuart* - order prohibiting publication of defendant's confession ruled unconstitutional

          2.   *Gannett Co. v. DePasquale* - public access denied to pretrial hearing on motion to suppress evidence

          3.   *Press-Enterprise Co. v. Superior Court* – preliminary hearing is open to public

     C.   The right to a public trial

          1.   *Richmond Newspapers Inc. v. Virginia* - criminal trials must remain public

          2.   even trials involving sexually sensitive matters with underage victims should be open to the public

3.   *In re Oliver* - secret trial violates Fourteenth Amendment
     D.   Televised criminal trials
         1.   televising trials have produced questionable outcomes
             a.   William Kennedy Smith's rape trial
             b.   Mike Tyson's rape trial
             c.   Timothy McVeigh
             d.   *People v. O.J. Simpson*
             e.   *State of Massachusetts v. Louise Woodward*
         2.   state courts often permit TV cameras or CCTV
         3.   use of TV cameras, video recorders and still photography is banned in federal court
         4.   *Chandler v. Florida* - electronic media and photography allowed in trial over the objections of the defendant

IV.   The trial process
     A.   The criminal trial
         1.   a formal process
         2.   conducted in a specific and orderly fashion
         3.   with rules of law, procedure and evidence
         4.   it is a structured adversarial proceeding
         5.   minor variations exist across jurisdictions but basic steps remain
     B.   Jury selection
         1.   jurors are selected randomly from tax assessment, drivers license, or voter registration lists
         2.   many states mandate a residency requirement but few impose qualifications
         3.   most prohibit convicted felons from serving as well as public officials
         4.   the *venire* or jury array is the term for the initial list of potential jurors
         5.   the clerk of court is responsible for compiling the *venire* and selecting names
         6.   *voir dire* – to tell the truth
             a.   process of determining the appropriateness of potential jurors
             b.   prosecution, defense, and sometimes the judge may question potential jurors about their background as well as knowledge and interests in case
             c.   jurors must be impartial and able to render a verdict based solely on the evidence presented
             d.   challenges for cause are unlimited in number
             e.   the juror is removed for cause if unable to render impartial verdict
             f.   preemptory challenges excuse jurors for undisclosed reasons and are limited in number by state statute
                 i.   *Swain v. Alabama* - upheld exclusion of jurors due to race
                 ii.   *Batson v. Kentucky* - struck down *Swain*; a peremptory challenge based on race is unconstitutional
                 iii..   *Powers v. Ohio* - prohibits exclusion of juror of opposite race
                 iv.   *Georgia v. McCollum* – prohibits exclusion based solely on race
                 v.   *J.E.B. v. Alabama* - bars gender-based challenges
                 vi.   some states forbid challenges based on religion

7.   impartial juries
       a.   Sixth Amendment right
       b.   studies show that pressure in the jury room exists
       c.   *Ham v. South Carolina* - jurors may be questioned about racial prejudice
       d.   *Taylor v. Louisiana* - conviction overturned where women but not men could exempt themselves from jury duty
       e.   *Turner v. Murray* - a defendant charged with a capital, interracial crime may inform prospective jurors of victim's race and question them on bias
       f.   *Lockhart v. McCree* - jurors who strongly oppose the death penalty may be disqualified from capital trials
       g.   sequestration is at the discretion of the judge
       h.   issues of race, gender and ethnicity in jury selection remain unresolved

C.   Opening statements
       1.   generally the prosecution goes first
       2.   provides a concise overview of evidence to follow
       3.   infrequently used in bench trials

D.   Presentation of the prosecutor's evidence
       1.   call witnesses for direct examination by prosecution
       2.   the defense conducts cross-examination
       3.   *Lee v. Illinois* - codefendant confession inadmissible unless the person is available for cross-examination

E.   Types of evidence at a criminal trial
       1.   testimonial evidence from witnesses
       2.   all evidence must have relevance to the proceeding
       3.   real or physical evidence
       4.   circumstantial or indirect evidence
       5.   modern importance of videotapes as real evidence

F.   Motion for a directed verdict
       1.   option for the defense once the prosecution rests its case
       2.   defense asks for a verdict of not guilty without presenting any evidence
       3.   alleges evidence is insufficient to prove guilt beyond a reasonable doubt
       4.   decided by a judge's ruling

G.   Presentation of evidence by the defense attorney
       1.   defense has the option to present some or no witnesses
       2.   defendant has option to take the stand
       a.   Fifth Amendment right not to self-incriminate
       b.   defendant is subject to cross-examination if he/she takes the stand
       3.   after defense rests the prosecution may present rebuttal evidence
       4.   this may be followed in turn with the defense presenting surrebuttal evidence
       5.   after all evidence is presented the defense may again ask for a directed verdict

H.   Closing arguments
       1.   both parties review facts and evidence in a most favorable manner
       2.   both parties are allowed to draw reasonable inferences
       3.   both parties have free hand in arguing about the facts, issues & evidence
       4.   cannot comment on new evidence or defendant's failure to testify

5.   normally the defense goes first followed by prosecution

I.   Instructions to the jury
    1.   the judge will instruct or charge the jury on:
         a.   pertinent principles of law
         b.   elements of the offense
         c.   evidence required for proof
         d.   burden of proof required for the verdict
    2.   judge may allow adversaries to suggest instruction but need not give them
    3.   improper instructions are often basis for appeal
    4.   *Sullivan v. Louisiana* – one word can constitute improper instructions

J.   The verdict
    1.   after being given their instructions, the jury retires to deliberate in private
    2.   usually required to be unanimous, not required by the Constitution but is the rule in federal and most state criminal trials
    2.   hung jury is unable to reach a verdict of guilty or not guilty
    3.   prosecutor has the option to retry the case after a hung jury
    4.   not guilty verdict yields defendant's release
    5.   guilty verdict usually leads to presentence investigation prior to sentencing
         a.   subsequent date for sentencing hearing
         b.   defense may motion for a new trial
         c.   defendant released on bail or held in custody until sentencing

K.   The sentence
    1.   normally the responsibility of the trial judge
    2.   often influenced by information contained in a presentence report prepared by probation department
    3.   sentencing options determined by legislative order
    4.   judge exercises discretion within mandates

L.   The appeal
    1.   3 appeal options for the defendant
         a.   direct appeal
         b.   post conviction remedy
         c.   federal court review
    2.   the direct appeal and federal court review focus on a higher court assessment of an alleged error that affected conviction
    3.   "plain error" rule v. "harmless error" direct extraordinary errors to federal review
    4.   the direct appeal exists as a matter of right in most jurisdictions
    5.   the post-conviction remedy is sometimes referred to as a collateral attack
         a.   primary means for state inmates to receive federal review
         b.   involves the use of a legal petition such as *habeas corpus*
    6.   the court transcript serves as the basis for any appellate review
    7.   appeals are time-consuming and complex
    8.   *Douglas v. California* - indigent have right to assistance of counsel on a direct first appeal
    9.   subsequent appeals may be made *in forma pauperis* at the court's discretion
    10.   prosecution does not usually have the right to appeal in criminal cases
         a.   some leeway exists in the case of constitutional issues

                b.   double jeopardy clause – no second prosecution on same charges in the case of an acquittal or conviction
11.   appellate court may reverse or uphold the lower court ruling
12.   criminal appeals are increasing in number in most jurisdictions

V.   Evidentiary standards
      A.   Proof beyond a reasonable doubt
          1.   required for a criminal conviction
          2.   dates back to early American history
          3.   *In re Winship* - beyond a reasonable doubt is a applied to juvenile trials
          4.   must be established for each element of the offense
          5.   second highest standard of proof available
      B.   Other evidentiary standards
          1.   absolute certainty – 100% certainty
          2.   beyond a reasonable doubt – criminal trials
          3.   clear and convincing evidence – civil commitments
          4.   preponderance of evidence – civil trial
          5.   probable cause – arrest, preliminary hearing, motions
          6.   reasonable suspicion – appellate review, police investigations
          7.   less than probable cause – police investigation where safety concern exists

VI.   Trial reform in the Twenty-First century
      A.   Criminal trial practices in the future
          1.   continue to be adversarial
          2.   use of DNA evidence will growl
          3.   communications technology
      B.   The jury system and jury service
          1.   scientific jury selection
          2.   refining peremptory challenges
          3.   should jury verdicts be unanimous?
          4.   should judges summarize the law for jurors?

Chapter Summary

The process through which a determination of guilt or innocence is reached in the adult criminal justice system is called the **adjudication** process. The trial remains a focal point in the adjudication process even though the classic jury trial of a criminal case is quite uncommon. The **confrontation clause** of the Sixth Amendment guarantees the defendant the right to a public trial by a jury of one's peers, although this right is frequently waived in favor of a **bench trial** where the judge alone hears the evidence and renders the verdict. The Court has ruled that a defendant must be mentally competent to stand trial but has set out criteria by which an incompetent defendant may be subject to involuntary treatment. The Sixth Amendment also provides the defendant the right to confront witnesses against him or her, and the defendant has a fundamental right to counsel, but may choose to exercise the right to self-representation and proceed *pro se*. A speedy and fair trial is also guaranteed by the U.S. Constitution and various amendments to it.

The right to a fair trial has often been balanced against the First Amendment free press protection. While the U.S. Supreme Court has firmly established that criminal trials must remain public, a major issue is the presence of electronic media in the courtroom. While federal courts do not permit the use of television cameras, video recorders, and still photography, in most jurisdictions such coverage is at the discretion of the judge.

The trial of a criminal case is a formal process conducted in a specific and orderly fashion in accordance with the rules of criminal law, procedure, and evidence. A key step in the criminal trial process is the jury selection. During the process of *voir dire*, the prosecution and the defense can eliminate prospective jurors by **challenges for cause** and by a limited number of **peremptory challenges**. The U.S. Supreme Court has ensured compliance with the constitutional mandate for an impartial jury by decisions such as ***Batson v. Kentucky*** which eliminates racial discrimination in jury selection.

After jury selection, the trial proceeds through **opening statements** by each side, presentation of the evidence by the prosecutor and the defense attorney, and closing arguments. **Real evidence**, **circumstantial evidence**, **rebuttal evidence** by the state and **surrebuttal evidence** by the defense are generally included in this process. Witnesses are subject to **direct** and **cross-examination** by attorneys. The judge may decide to render a **directed verdict** acquitting the defendant if the prosecution has not done a good job making their case. After closing arguments, the judge will instruct, or *charge*, the jury on the applicable principles of law. In reaching their **verdict**, the jury must bear in mind that the criminal process requires **proof beyond a reasonable doubt** for each element of the offense. If the jury reaches a guilty verdict, the **sentence** will normally be imposed by the trial judge. In most jurisdictions, the defendant has an automatic right to **appeal** a conviction. If a defendant loses a direct first appeal, he or she can seek a discretionary appeal to a higher court, but if indigent, does so without the benefit of provided counsel.

Fill-in-the-Blank Questions

1. _____ stage of the criminal justice process begins with a hearing that seeks to determine the _____ of regarding the facts of the case.

2. If a defendant waives his/her right to a jury trial, a _____ _____ will occur in which a _____ hears the evidence and renders the verdict.

3. The _____ _____ to the Constitution is essential to a fair criminal trial because it restricts and controls the admissibility of _____ _____ at trial.

4. A defendant has the right to proceed _____ _____ whereby he/she presents one's one defense at trial.

5. The right to a speedy trial in federal prosecutions is guaranteed by the _____ _____ to the Constitution, but the right was made applicable to the states by the _____ v. _____ _____ decision.

6. In total, a defendant must be brought to trial in the federal system within _____ days in order to comply with the Speedy Trial Act of 1974.

7. The main objection to the use of modern technology in the courtroom is the extent to which it might influence _____, _____, and the _____.

8. The trial of a criminal case is a formal process conducted in a specific and orderly fashion in accordance with the rules of _____ _____, _____, and _____.

9. The initial list of persons chosen to provide the state with a group of capable citizens able to serve on a jury is called _____ or _____ _____.

10. Peremptory challenges enable the defense and prosecution attorneys to excuse jurors for no _____ reason or for _____ reasons.

11. According to the _____ v. _____ decision, jurors who strongly oppose capital punishment may be disqualified from determining a defendant's guilt or innocence in capital cases.

12. Those called as witnesses begin by providing testimony via _____ _____ to the attorney who called them to the stand.

13. _____ evidence bearing on or establishing the facts in a crime is ordinarily admissible, but evidence that is _____, remote, or unrelated to the crime should be excluded by the court.

14. _____ _____ are used by the attorneys to review the facts and evidence of the case in a manner favorable to each of their positions.

15. Preventing the jury from having contact with the outside world is called _____.

True/False Questions

T F 1. The classic jury trial of a criminal case is a common occurrence.

T F 2. The defendant has the right to challenge not only the witness, but also the witness's assertions and perceptions.

T F 3. The Supreme Court has ruled that a jury of less than six people is constitutional, if the decision is unanimous.

T F 4. Defendants can be convicted by a jury of less than 12 persons.

T F 5. A pretrial hearing cannot be closed to the press except if prejudice will result to the accused.

T F 6. The right to self representation is not supported by the Sixth Amendment.

T F 7. The federal court system has banned the use of television cameras, video recorders, and still photography.

T F 8. Specialty courts (e.g., drug court) have not been successful in speeding up the adjudication process.

T F 9. Both the prosecution and the defense question all persons selected for the pool of jurors to determine their appropriateness to sit on the jury in a process called *venire*.

T F 10. If a juror admits that he is biased or prejudiced against the defendant; he will be removed from serving on the jury through the use of a peremptory challenge.

T F 11. Under certain circumstances the court may ask prospective jurors "content" questions.

T F 12. The number of peremptory challenges is fixed at two.

T F 13. Opening statements by the prosecutor are designed to outline the facts of the case.

T F 14. The defense attorney's opening statement indicates how the defense intends to show that the accused is innocent of the charge.

T F 15. Cross-examination comes right after direct examination.

T F 16. Criminal trials permit 3 different types of verdicts.

T F 17. Circumstantial evidence can be used in trial proceedings.

T F 18. After the defense concludes its case, the government then presents it surrebuttal evidence.

T F 19. Either party can forgo the right to make a final summation to the jury.

T F 20. The judge will instruct or charge the jury members on the principles of law that ought to guide and control the jury's decision on the defendant's innocence or guilt.

T F 21. In a criminal case, a preponderance of the evidence is sometimes enough to convict.

T F 22. If the defendant is convicted, the judge normally orders a presentence investigation.

T F 23. The judge always imposes the sentence.

T F 24. In most jurisdictions, direct criminal appeal is a matter of right.

Multiple Choice Questions

1. Which of the following rules guides the use of forced medication on a mentally ill individual who is deemed incompetent to stand trial?
    a.   the court must find that important governmental interests are at stake
    b.   the court must find that forced medication will significantly further the case
    c.   the court must conclude that administering the drugs is medically appropriate
    d.   all of the above are rules in this regard

2. The right to confront witnesses is found in the _____ Amendment.
    a.   Fourth
    b.   Fifth
    c.   Sixth
    d.   Fourteenth

3. _____ limited the protection available to child sex victims at the trial stage.
    a.   *Coy v. Iowa*
    b.   *Maryland v. Craig*
    c.   *Duncan v. Louisiana*
    d.   *Baldwin v. New York*

4. In _____, the Supreme Court decided that alleged child abuse victims could testify by closed-circuit television if face-to-face confrontation would cause them trauma.
    a.   *Coy v. Iowa*
    b.   *Maryland v. Craig*
    c.   *Duncan v. Louisiana*
    d.   *Baldwin v. New York*

5. _____ asserts that the Sixth Amendment right to enjoy a jury trial is applicable to all states, as well as the federal government, and that it can be interpreted to apply to all defendants accused of serious crimes.
    a.   *Coy v. Iowa*
    b.   *Maryland v. Craig*
    c.   *Duncan v. Louisiana*
    d.   *Baldwin v. New York*

6. In _____, the Supreme Court held that a defendant has a constitutional right to a jury trial when facing a prison sentence of six months or more, regardless of whether the crime committed was a felony or a misdemeanor.
    a.   *Coy v. Iowa*
    b.   *Maryland v. Craig*
    c.   *Duncan v. Louisiana*
    d.   *Baldwin v. New York*

7. The Supreme Court, in _____, ruled that a six-person jury in a criminal trial does not deprive a defendant of the constitutional right to a jury trial.
    a.   *Gideon v. Wainwright*
    b.   *Apodaca v. Oregon*
    c.   *Williams v. Florida*
    d.   *Powell v. Alabama*

8. In _____, the Supreme Court held that the Sixth and Fourteenth Amendments do not prohibit criminal convictions by less than unanimous jury verdicts in noncapital cases.
    a. *Gideon v. Wainwright*
    b. *Apodaca v. Oregon*
    c. *Williams v. Florida*
    d. *Powell v. Alabama*

9. The Supreme Court ruled in _____ that the presence of a defense attorney is so vital to a fair trial that the failure to appoint counsel is a denial of due process of law under the Fourteenth Amendment.
    a. *Gideon v. Wainwright*
    b. *Apodaca v. Oregon*
    c. *Williams v. Florida*
    d. *Powell v. Alabama*

10. The _____ case held that the right to counsel is so fundamental and ethical to a fair trial that the states are obligated to abide by it under the Fourteenth Amendment's due process clause.
    a. *Gideon v. Wainwright*
    b. *Apodaca v. Oregon*
    c. *Williams v. Florida*
    d. *Powell v. Alabama*

11. The ruling in _____ states that no person can be imprisoned for any offense – whether classified a petty offense, a misdemeanor, or a felony – unless he or she is offered representation by counsel.
    a. *Argersinger v. Hamlin*
    b. *Klopfer v. California*
    c. *Martinez v. Court of Appeals of California*
    d. *Faretta v. California*

12. The Supreme Court's ruling in _____ states that a defendant has a constitutional right to defend himself or herself if he or she can show they competently, knowingly, and intelligently waive the right to counsel.
    a. *Argersinger v. Hamlin*
    b. *Klopfer v. California*
    c. *Martinez v. Court of Appeals of California*
    d. *Faretta v. California*

13. Which of the following rules applies to a six-person jury in a serious felony case?
    a. they must be sequestered
    b. their verdict can always be overruled by the judge
    c. their verdict must be unanimous
    d. this format is not allowed in a felony case

14. The Supreme Court ruling that efforts to postpone a trial indefinitely without reason denies a defendant the right to a speedy trial is contained in
    a. *Argersinger v. Hamlin.*
    b. *Klopfer v. California.*
    c. *Martinez v. Court of Appeals of California.*
    d. *Faretta v. California.*

15. The _____ decision ruled unconstitutional a trial judge's order prohibiting the press from reporting confessions implicating the defendant in the crime.
    a. *Gannett Co. v. DePasquale*
    b. *Nebraska Press Association v. Stuart*
    c. *Richmond Newspapers, Inc. v. Commonwealth of Virginia*
    d. *Press-Enterprise Co. v. Superior Court*

16. The _____ decision held the press had a right of constitutional dimensions but that the defendant's right to a fair trial outweighed this right.
    a. *Gannett Co. v. DePasquale*
    b. *Nebraska Press Association v. Stuart*
    c. *Richmond Newspapers, Inc. v. Commonwealth of Virginia*
    d. *Press-Enterprise Co. v. Superior Court*

17. In _____ the Supreme Court clearly established the First Amendment right of access to criminal trials.
    a. *Gannett Co. v. DePasquale*
    b. *Nebraska Press Association v. Stuart*
    c. *Richmond Newspapers, Inc. v. Commonwealth of Virginia*
    d. *Press-Enterprise Co. v. Superior Court*

18. What crime were the Scottsboro boys charged with?
    a. murder
    b. robbery
    c. rape
    d. theft

19. Documentary evidence, such as writings and records, are examples of what type of evidence?
    a. testimonial
    b. real
    c. circumstantial
    d. direct

20. While not explicitly stated in the Constitution, the Court has found support for legal self-representation in which constitutional amendment?
    a. First Amendment
    b. Fourth Amendment
    c. Fifth Amendment
    d. Sixth Amendment

21. In _____ the Supreme Court said content questions are not constitutionally compelled in a voir dire hearing, unless the failure to ask them would result in an unfair trial.
    a.   *In re Oliver*
    b.   *Swain v. Alabama*
    c.   *Mu'Min v. Virginia*
    d.   *Chandler v. Florida*

22. Which of the following was the reason for the speedy trial guarantee according to the Court?
    a.   to improve the credibility of the trial
    b.   to avoid extensive pretrial publicity and questionable conduct of officials
    c.   to reduce the anxiety for the defendant awaiting trial
    d.   all of the above

23. What evidentiary standard is used for arrest and search warrants?
    a.   clear and convincing evidence
    b.   probable cause
    c.   preponderance of evidence
    d.   reasonable suspicion

24. What is the evidentiary standard required for a criminal conviction?
    a.   absolute certainty
    b.   probable cause
    c.   proof beyond a reasonable doubt
    d.   preponderance of evidence

Essay Questions

1.   Discuss the standards that the state must meet when using forced medication on an incompetent defendant.

2.   Discuss the reasons that the Supreme Court gave in *Klopfer v. North Carolina* for a speedy trial.

3. Explain the provisions of the federal Speedy Trial Act of 1974.

4. Discuss the arguments for and against the use of televisions in a courtroom.

5. List the basic steps of the criminal trial with a jury.

6. Discuss the use of peremptory challenges and the role that race, gender, and ethnicity play in these actions.

7.   Discuss the reasons why a defense counsel might ask for a directed verdict.

8.   Describe the criminal appeals process, including the three different appeal options that exist.

9.   Identify the seven evidentiary standards and their usage in the American justice system.

10. Describe the most likely trial reforms that will take place in the 21st Century.

CHAPTER 12 ANSWER KEY

FILL-IN-THE-BLANK QUESTIONS

1. adjudication, truth
2. bench trial, judge
3. confrontation clause, hearsay evidence
4. pro se
5. Sixth Amendment, Klopfer, North Carolina
6. 100
7. judges, witnesses, accused
8. criminal law, procedure, evidence
9. venire, jury array
10. particular, undisclosed
11. Lockhart, McCree
12. direct examination
13. circumstantial, prejudicial
14. closing arguments
15. sequestration

TRUE/FALSE QUESTIONS

1.	F	13.	T
2.	T	14.	T
3.	F	15.	T
4.	T	16.	F
5.	T	17.	T
6.	F	18.	F
7.	T	19.	T
8.	F	20.	T
9.	F	21.	F
10.	F	22.	T
11.	T	23.	F
12.	F	24.	T

MULTIPLE CHOICE QUESTIONS

1.	D	13.	C
2.	C	14.	B
3.	A	15.	B
4.	B	16.	A
5.	C	17.	D
6.	D	18.	C
7.	C	19.	B
8.	B	20.	D
9.	D	21.	C
10.	A	22.	B
11.	A	23.	B
12.	D	24.	C

Chapter 13

Punishment and Sentencing

Learning Objectives

At the conclusion of this chapter the student should possess sufficient knowledge to achieve the following learning objectives:

1.   Discuss the concept of criminal punishment

2.   Provide a succinct history of punishment practices.

3.   Discuss the difference between concurrent and consecutive sentences.

4.   Explain the various reasons for criminal sanctions.

5.   Compare and contrast the practices of determinate sentencing, structured sentencing, and mandatory sentencing.

6.   Describe the operation of sentencing guidelines and comment on the problems of guidelines.

7.   Describe the operation of "three strikes and you're out" laws and comment on the problems associated with these statutes.

8.   Provide details from research describing the effects of extralegal factors on sentencing.

8.   Provide a brief review of the practice of capital punishment in this country.

9.   Articulate numerous arguments for and against the death penalty.

10.   Describe the issues and research related to the deterrent effect of capital punishment.

Keywords and Definitions

Sanctions: Formal and informal social control mechanisms designed to enforce society's laws and standards.

Punishment: Any form of pain, suffering, loss, or sanction that is inflicted upon a person in response to their violation of a norm or law.

Poor Laws: Seventeenth-century English laws that were used to indenture poor vagrant children living on urban streets.

Penitentiary: A state or federal correctional institution used to house convicted felons, usually for a term of one year or more; Also known as a prison.

General Deterrence: A crime control policy that depends on the fear of criminal penalties gain compliance from others who are contemplating future criminal acts.

Incapacitation: The crime control policy of keeping dangerous criminals in confinement to eliminate the risk of their repeating their offense in society.

Specific Deterrence: A crime control policy that suggests that punishment should be severe enough to convince convicted offenders never to repeat their criminal activity.

Retribution: The element of criminal sanctioning that seeks to punish people for what they have done, because they deserve punishment for their misdeeds.

Blameworthy: Status of a person who has committed evil or injurious behavior and is due punishment.

Just Desert: The philosophy of justice that asserts that those who violate the rights of others deserve to be punished.

Rehabilitation: A model of criminal justice that views its primary purpose as helping to care for people who cannot manage themselves.

Felony: Any crime that carries a penalty of incarceration in a state or federal prison for a term of one year or more.

Wergild: Under medieval law, the money paid by the offender to compensate the victim and the state for a criminal offense.

Restitution/Equity: A type of criminal sanction that requires the offender to repay society or the victim of the crime for the trouble the offender caused.

Concurrent Sentence: Literally, running sentences together so that the sentences begin on the same day and are completed after the longest term has been served.

Consecutive Sentence: Prison sentences for two or more criminal acts that are served one after the other.

Indeterminate Sentence: Statutory provision for a type of sentence to imprisonment, in which after the court has determined that the convicted person should be imprisoned, the exact length of imprisonment and parole supervision is fixed within statutory limits by a parole authority.

Determinate Sentence: Statutory provision for a type of sentence to imprisonment, in which after the court has determined that the convicted person should be imprisoned, the exact length of imprisonment and parole supervision is fixed within statutory limits by the legislature.

Good Time: Time taken off a prison sentence in exchange for good behavior within the institution.

Sentencing Guidelines: Provide recommended sentences for offenders based on the seriousness of the offense and the offender's background.

Descriptive Sentencing Guidelines: Voluntary/advisory sentencing guidelines that merely suggest rather than mandate sentencing to a judge.

Prescriptive Sentencing Guidelines: Judges are required to use the guidelines to shape their sentencing decisions and their sentencing decisions may be open to appellate review if they stray from the mandated sentence; Also known as presumptive sentencing guidelines.

Mandatory Sentence: A statutory requirement that a certain penalty will be set and carried out in all cases on conviction for a specified offense or a series of offenses.

Truth-in-Sentencing: Sentencing reform movement sponsored by the federal government mandating that a convicted felon serve a minimum of 85% of their court-imposed sentence.

Three Strikes and You're Out: Type of criminal sentence that allows a life sentence to be given to any offender convicted of a third felony, even a relatively minor one.

Sentencing Disparity: Refers to the fact that people receive different criminal sentences for committing similar criminal acts.

Chivalry Hypothesis: View that low female crime and delinquency rates are a reflection of the leniency with which police treat female offenders.

Victim Impact Statement: A statement by a crime victim to the sentencing judge that allows the victim's experiences be taken into consideration when deciding the appropriate sentence.

Contextual Discrimination: Refers to the practices of judges in some jurisdictions who impose harsher sentences on African-American offenders who victimize whites, or impose prison sentences on racial minorities in "borderline" cases for which whites get probation.

Brutalization Effect: The belief that capital punishment creates an atmosphere of brutality that enhances rather than deters the level of violence in society.

Furman v. Georgia: A 1972 Supreme Court case that deemed the discretionary imposition of the death penalty to be cruel and unusual punishment in violation of the Eighth and Fourteenth Amendments. The decision led to a four year national moratorium on capital punishment.

Gregg v. Georgia: A 1976 Supreme Court case that deemed Georgia's revised two-phase capital punishment trial process (guilt phase and sentencing phase) constitutional.

McKleskey v. Kemp: Supreme Court case that deemed social science evidence of at-large racial bias in capital sentencing insufficient evidence of racial bias in a specific case. The Court ruled that bias must be established on a case by case basis.

Wilkins v. Missouri: Supreme Court set a limit of 16 years of age as the minimum age for a capital sentence. The decision was affirmed in *Stanford v. Kentucky*.

Atkins v. Virginia: Supreme Court deemed executions of mentally retarded criminals to be unconstitutional.

Death Qualified Jury: A jury in which any person opposed in concept to capital punishment has been removed during voir dire.

Witherspoon v. Illinois: The Supreme Court deemed it acceptable to excuse prospective capital jurors who are opposed to the death penalty.

Lockhart v. McCree: The Supreme Court ruled that the removal of an anti-death penalty juror is not a violation of the Sixth Amendment rights of the defendant.

Miller-El v. Cockrell: Supreme Court ruled that jury selection in a capital case cannot be tainted by racial bias.

Ring v. Arizona: Supreme Court ruled that juries, not judges, must preside over the sentencing phase of a capital case.

Chapter Outline

I.   Introduction
      A.   Samantha Runnion case
            1.   pretrial publicity
            2.   use of DNA evidence
            3.   use of the death penalty
      B.   Punishment used against criminals
            1.   criminal sanction or punishment
            2.   past punishments included physical torture, branding or whipping, and death
            3.   modern forms of punishment included fines, community sentences, incarceration, and capital punishment

II.   History of punishment
      A.   Considerable change in punishment and correction of criminals over the ages
            1.   changes reflect customs, economic conditions, and religious & political ideals
            2.   banishment and exile were most common state-administered punishments in Greek and Roman societies
            3.   interpersonal violence was considered to be a private matter by ancient peoples
            4   the Middle Ages saw private justice with offenses settled in blood feuds
            5.   Romans used fines or exchange of property
            6.   during the feudal period, the forfeiture of land and property was common
            7.   the term felony is a derivative of *felonia*--a breach of faith with one's feudal lord
            8.   development and use of the wergild developed in the twelfth century
            9.   common law developed during this time
            10.   the eleventh century saw the birth of common law but the use of fines and brutal physical punishment continued as common practices into the sixteen century

        a.   the criminal wealthy could buy their way out of punishment & into exile

        b.   the criminal poor faced increased use of capital & corporal punishment

        c.   gruesome physical tortures & punishment via a public spectacle used

B. Public work and transportation in the sixteen century
1. changing demands of social conditions cause changes in punishment
    a. urbanization
    b. colonization
2. poor laws enacted and Brideswell workhouse developed in 1557
3. Order in Council of 1617 granted a reprieve and stay of execution to allow transportation to the colonies to fill labor shortages
4. 1787 to 1875, over 135,000 felons were transported to Australia

C. The rise of the prison
1. transportation to colonies is limited and gulf between classes grows
2. as crime rate grows so does the barbarity of physical punishments
3. social philosophers argue for the use of confinement and incapacitation
4. incarceration in penitentiaries replaces physical punishment in 1800s

III. The goals of modern sentencing
  A. General deterrence
    1. control crime by deterring potential criminals in the community
    2. certainty, severity, and celerity of punishment
    3. may be wishful thinking
  B. Incapacitation
    1. inmate unable to repeat criminal act while incarcerated
    2. depends on prediction of future criminality
  C. Specific deterrence
    1. convince offenders that recidivism would not be in their own best interests
    2. current recidivism rates of over 68% shortly after release from prison
  D. Retribution/just desert
    1. criminals deserve punishment
    2. criminal sentencing must be fair, equitable, and commensurate to the harm done
    3. sentencing guidelines to control judicial decision making
  E. Rehabilitation
    1. treatment for readjustment to society
    2. based on prediction of future needs of the offender, not the gravity of the offense
    3. criticized because little evidence exists of its effectiveness
  F. Equity/Restitution
    1. pay back victims, the justice system, and society for losses and costs
    2. use of fines, forfeiture, community service, and restitution
  G. Imposing the sentence
    1. sentence is usually subject to judicial discretion
      a. starts with staturoty provisions
      b. shaped by presentence investigation
    2. some jurisdictions and circumstances call for jury sentencing or statutory sentencing without discretion

3. defendants convicted of two or more charges
    a. concurrent sentences are served at the same time
    b. consecutive sentences are served back-to-back

IV. Sentencing models
  A. The indeterminate sentence
    1. penal reform in late 1800's with Enoch Wines and Zebulon Brockway argue that treatment should fit the offender
    2. seeks to individualize the sentence and provide flexibility for judges
    3. the most widely used type of sentence in the U.S.
    4. terminology includes minimum and maximum sentence, parole, and time off for good behavior
    5. usually, the max sentence set by judge and min sentence by legislature
  B. Determinate sentences
    1. first kind used in the U.S.
    2. sentence the defendant to a fixed term of years
    3. no release on parole
    4. actual time can be reduced via good time rules
  C. Structured sentences
    1. written guidelines or standards
    2. guidelines classify seriousness of offense and background of the offender
    3. goals of sentencing guidelines
      a. no judicial discretion to reduce gender and race disparities
      b. more uniform and consistent sentencing
      c. allow for projection and prioritization of correctional resources
      d. allow severity to be driven by the offense
      e. truth-in-sentencing
      f. open, rational, and understandable sentencing process
      g. tailor particular sanctions to particular offenders
      h. encourage intermediate & community-based sanctions
      i. reduce prison overcrowding
      j. increase judicial accountability
    4. How are guidelines used?
      a. 18 states have some sort of structured sentencing
        i. 7 states use voluntary/advisory guidelines
        ii. 11 states use presumptive sentencing guidelines
      b. prescribed guidelines are established by sentencing commissions
      c. variations exist across jurisdictions
        i. coexisting with parole release or abolishing parole
        ii. narrow ranges or broad ranges
        iii. incarceration sentences or intermediate sentencing
        iv. appellate review or no appellate review
    5. Minnesota guidelines
      a. grid system of sentencing
        i. prior record
        ii. severity of offense
      b. judges retain some discretion
        i. deviate in the case of aggravating or mitigating circumstances
        ii. must provide written justification

                              iii.   prosecution or defense can appeal deviation
                      c.   term of imprisonment equals 2/3 of sentence
                      d.   supervised release equals remaining 1/3
                      e.   violation of prison rules can cut into supervised release portion
            6.   Federal guidelines
                      a.   U.S. Sentencing Guideline Commission sets down complex set
                            of rules and abolished parole in federal system
                      b.   guidelines are extensive and detailed
                      c.   magistrate/judge first determines base penalty
                              i.   may be adjusted upward for serious or violent crime
                              ii.   may be adjusted upward for criminal history
                      d.   convert penalty scores into months to be served using
                            sentencing table
                              i.   offense levels on vertical axis
                              ii.   criminal history on horizontal axis
            7.   How effective are guidelines?
                      a.   criticized as discriminatory against African Americans and
                            Hispanics
                      b.   criticized for the crack v. powder cocaine controversy
                      c.   inclusion of juvenile convictions hurts minorities
                      d.   require incarceration for petty offenses
                      e.   judges don't consider mitigating circumstances
                      d.   federal prison population is increasing
                      e.   little incentive to plea-bargain
      D.   Mandatory sentences
            1.   limit discretion and increase sanctions
            2.   require incarceration for specific crimes or recidivists
            3.   prescribe equal treatment for all offenders who commit the same crime
            4.   exclude possibility of probation
            5.   three strikes laws
      E.   Truth-in-sentencing
            1.   requires that a set percentage of sentence must be served
            2.   restricts parole and good-time credits
            3.   Violent Offender Incarceration and Truth-In-Sentencing Grants Program
                      a.   linked prison construction funds to 85% rule
                      b.   more than ½ of the states are now in compliance

V.   Sentencing practices
      A.   National trends
            1.   in 2000, 40% of felons sentenced to state prison, 28% to local jails
            2.   in 2000, the typical felon received a 4.5 year sentence, and served ½ of it
            3.   criminals are doing more time behind bars
                      a.   community sentences are used less often
                      b.   increases in the percent of sentence served
      B.   Factors in sentencing
            1.   social class
                      a.   lower social class gets longer sentences
                      b.   social class affects quality of legal representation
            2.   gender
                      a.   the chivalry hypothesis
                      b.   women are less likely to be incarcerated and receive

preferential court treatment
       c.   women are granted lenient pretrial release and lower bail
   3.   age
       a.   more lenient toward the elderly
       b.   harshest terms imposed on 21-29 year olds
   4.   victim characteristics
       a.   effect of victim impact statements
       b.   sentence may be reduced if victim has negative personal or social qualities
   5.   race
       a.   research fails to show a definitive pattern of racially
       b.   discriminatory sentencing
       c.   latest federal research shows that whites are les likely than blacks to go to prison
       d.   disproportionate number of African Americans in prison
       e.   prejudice manifested in indirect fashion
       f.   discrimination effects may be indirectly measured in plea bargaining, pre-sentence reports, bail, or quality of legal representation

VI.   Capital punishment
   A.   History of capital punishment
      1.   more than 14,500 U.S. executions since 1608
      2.   most executions have been for murder and rape
      3.   Supreme Court recently condoned its usage to first degree murder cases
      4.   death penalty currently used in 38 states and by the federal government
      5.   more than 3,500 people sit on death row
         a.   between 70 and 100 are executed each year
         b.   most serve 10 years on death row awaiting their fate
      6.   issues of wrongful conviction have been raised lately
      7.   lethal injection has become the predominate method of execution
   B.   International use of the death penalty
      1.   83 countries still have the death penalty, 36 have it on the books but don't use it
      2.   during 2002 - 1,526 prisoners were executed in 31 countries, 3,248 people were sentenced to death in 67 countries
         a.   China executed 2,500 in its Strike Hard campaign in 2001
         b.   Saudi Arabia, Iran, and English-speaking Caribbean counties are active
      3.   International law precludes executing juveniles
         a.   seven countries have executed juveniles since 1990
         b.   a total of 20 juveniles have been executed during the decade, 13 in US
   C.   Arguments for the death penalty
      1.   incapacitation – rid society of killers
      2.   deterrent – send a message
      3.   morally correct – biblical references
      4.   proportional sanction – an eye for an eye
      5.   reflects public opinion - 67% of American favor usage
      6.   unlikely chance of error – legal controls and appeals

D.   Arguments against the death penalty
         1.   possibility of error – can't undo it
         2.   unfair use of discretion – arbitrary and capricious
         3.   the most serious criminals escape death – medical technology sets charge
         4.   misplaced vengeance – emotional response
         5.   no deterrence – crimes of passion
         6.   hope of rehabilitation – murders are good release risks
         7.   racial, gender, and other bias – offender/victim relationships
         8.   causes crime – killers won't give up
         9.   brutalization effect – sends the wrong message about killing
         10.   expense – capital cases costs more

D.   Legal issues in the death penalty
         1.   *Furman v. Georgia* (1972) - discretionary imposition of the death penalty in an arbitrary and capricious manner unconstitutional
         2.   *Gregg v. Georgia* (1976) - reinstated use of death penalty with the use of guided discretion
         3.   *McClesky v. Kemp* - ruled that scientific evidence is not conclusive proof of racial bias in a specific case
         4.   *Wilkins v. Missouri and Stanford v. Kentucky* set a court limit of 16 on the age a defendant could be sentenced to death
         5.   *Atkins v. Virginia* – execution of mentally retarded is unconstitutional

E.   Death-qualified juries
         1.   *Witherspoon v. Illinois* - upheld practice of excluding jurors who are opposed to the death penalty
         2.   *Lockhart v. McCree* - death qualified juries do not violate Sixth Amendment
         3.   *Ring v. Arizona* – juries, not judges, must preside over sentencing phase
         4.   *Miller-El v. Cockrell* – jury selection cannot be tainted by racial bias
         5.   capital jury project
             a.   research teams interview capital jurors
             b.   decision making often strays from legal and moral guidelines
             c.   jurors do not accept responsibility for their decisions
             d.   extralegal factors shape decisions

F.   Does the death penalty deter murder?
         1.   immediate impact studies measure effect immediately after a well publicized execution
         2.   time-series analysis compare long term trends
         3.   contiguous state analysis compare murder rates in states with death penalty against rates in states without death penalty
         4.   less than conclusive evidence emerges from the research

Chapter Summary

Punishment and sentencing has changed considerably though the ages. In early Greek and Roman civilizations, the most common state-administered punishment was banishment or exile. During the feudal period, the main emphasis of criminal law and punishment was on maintaining public order. The Middle Ages saw the birth of the **wergild** conce4pt, requiring compensation be paid by offenders to victims. The development of the common law in the eleventh century led to standardization of penal punishments. However, the sixteenth century brought hard labor, indentured servitude via **poor laws**, and overseas transportation to the colonies. The American Revolution ended transportation overseas, and the eighteenth century brought the rise of prisons.

Today, after a defendant has been found guilty of a crime, the state has the right to impose a **criminal sanction**. The **punishment** refers to any pain, suffering, loss, or sanction inflicted upon a convicted criminal. The objectives of criminal punishment today can usually be grouped into several distinct areas: **general deterrence**, **incapacitation**, **specific deterrence**, **retribution/just desert**, **rehabilitation** and **restitution/equity**.

There are numerous sentencing models in use today. **Indeterminate** models allow the judge wide discretion in setting a sentence. **Determinate** sentencing models allow no discretion and impose fixed sentences for a particular crime. The only way for a sentence to be reduced is through the inmate accumulating **good time** for obeying the rules of the institution. **Sentencing guidelines** were recently introduced to reduce judicial discretion and impose standardization to sentencing practices. **Descriptive sentencing guidelines** are voluntary guidelines that allow the judge some discretion in setting sentences, **Prescriptive sentencing guidelines** are rigid rules handed down by a sentencing commission that severely limit the judges discretion. **Mandatory sentencing** models provide equal treatment for all offenders who commit the same crime, regardless of age, sex, or other variables. Recent **truth-in-sentencing** laws require convicted felons to serve a set proportion, usually 85% of their court imposed sentences. Each of these sentencing models is based on philosophical differences about punishment, rehabilitation, and justice. Because a wide variety of sentencing practices are utilized, concern has developed regarding judicial discretion and the degree to which disparity exists in the sentencing process. When convicted of multiple crimes, an offender may serve the sentences back-to-back (**consecutively**), or overlapping (**concurrently**).

Several legal factors such as severity of the offense, the offender's prior criminal record, and use of violence affect the judge's sentencing decision. Research has also shown a correlation between sentencing and social class, race, gender, age, and victim characteristics.

The most severe sentence used in our nation is capital punishment. The use of capital punishment has been hotly debated, with many common arguments given for the retention as well as the abolition of its use. In 1972, the U.S. Supreme Court in *Furman v. Georgia* decided that the discretionary imposition of the death penalty was cruel and unusual punishment under the Eighth and Fourteenth Amendments of the Constitution. Then, in 1976, the U.S. Supreme Court, in *Gregg v. Georgia*, found valid the new Georgia statute which held that a finding by the jury of at least one "aggravating circumstance" out of ten was required before pronouncing the death penalty in murder cases. In *McLesky v. Kemp*, the U.S. Supreme Court ruled that the evidence of racial patterns in capital sentencing was not persuasive, absent a finding of racial bias in the immediate case. **Death-qualified juries** are required in capital cases and numerous Supreme Court rulings have outlined the constitutionality of capital jury issues. Considerable empirical research has been carried out on the effectiveness of capital punishment as a deterrent, almost all of which confirms that there is no deterrent effect. In fact, some research points to a **brutalizing effect**, suggesting that executions actually increase murder rates by raising the general violence level in society.

Fill-in-the-Blank Questions

1. The complexity of punishing criminals stems from the wide variety of
    _____ available and the _____ judges have in applying
    them.

2. _____ _____ were sixteenth century English laws that were used to put
    vagrants and abandoned children to work.

3. _____ _____ involves punishing the offender to serve as an example
    for others.

4. _____ _____ is the view that those who violate the rights of
    others deserve a punishment that fits the seriousness of the crime.

5. According to _____, the essential purpose of the criminal process is to punish
    deserving offenders fairly and justly in a manner that is proportionate to the gravity of their
    crimes.

6. Because criminals gain from their misdeeds, it seems both _____ and
    _____ to demand they reimburse society for its loss caused by their crimes.

7. Three strikes and you're out laws are an example of a _____ sentence.

8. _____ sentences are tailored to fit individual needs.

9. Sentencing guidelines are usually based on the _____ of a crime and the
    _____ of an offender.

10. The effort to limit judicial discretion and at the same time "get tough" on crime has been the
    development of the _____ _____.

11. Judges may be more lenient with _____ defendants and punitive toward
    _____ ones.

12. The death penalty may be the ultimate form of _____.

13. The _____ effect argues that the _____ of the death penalty
    may actually produce more violence than it prevents.

14. The landmark 1972 case _____ v. _____ decided that the
    discretionary use of the death penalty was unconstitutional and began a national moratorium
    on its use.

15. Research has shown that murder rates do not seem to _____ when a state
    abolishes capital punishment any more so than they _____ when the death
    penalty is adopted.

True/False Questions

T F 1. General deterrence argues that crime rates should fall as the chance of getting punished rises.

T F 2. The American Revolution marked the end of transporting criminals to America.

T F 3. Corporal punishment in the middle ages came from the philosophy of contrition.

T F 4. Penitentiaries are used at the federal level while prisons exist at the state level.

T F 5. Chronic offender research indicates that arrest and punishment seem to have little effect on experienced criminals and may even increase recidivism chance of first-time offenders.

T F 6. According to retribution, the punishment should fit the crime.

T F 7. Concurrent sentences run back-to-back.

T F 8. A sentencing target of 8 to 25 years in prison is an example of a determinate sentence.

T F 9. Most judges give the pre-sentence investigation report great weight.

T F 10. The most widely used type of sentence in the United States is the determinate sentence.

T F 11. Indeterminate sentences produce great disparity in the way people are treated in the correctional system.

T F 12. Although determinate sentences provide a single term of years to be served without benefit of parole, the actual time spent in prison is reduced by implementation of "good time."

T F 13. Sentencing guidelines are used to control sentencing discretion.

T F 14. Evidence supports an association between social class and sentencing outcomes.

T F 15. Research has found a consistent class-crime relationship.

T F 16. Victim personal characteristics have little influence on sentencing.

T F 17. Those who receive the harshest sentences are in the age group 21 to 29.

T F 18. The disproportionate number of African-American inmates in state prisons and on death row demonstrates the possibility of racial disparity in sentencing.

T F 19. More than two-thirds of all convicted felons are sentenced to time behind bars.

T F 20. Most studies on the death penalty have found that it reduces the murder rate.

Multiple Choice Questions

1. Of the following, which influence punishment and correction of criminals?
   a. customs
   b. economic conditions
   c. religion
   d. all of the above

2. What was the most common state imposed punishment in fifth century Roman civilization?
   a. mutilation
   b. burning at the stake
   c. fine or exchange of property
   d. flogging

3. The rise of the city and overseas colonization provided tremendous markets for manufactured goods which eventually led to offenders receiving _____ for their crimes.
   a. hard labor
   b. torture
   c. execution
   d. whipping

4. What was a common punishment during the feudal period, after the eleventh century?
   a. banishment and exile
   b. flogging and branding
   c. slavery
   d. forfeiture of land and property

5. Jails and workhouses were commonly used to hold all of the following offenders except:
   a. petty offenders
   b. felons
   c. homeless
   d. debtors

6. _____, the sheriff of Bedfordshire, inspired Parliament to pass legislation mandating the construction of secure and sanitary structures to house prisoners.
   a. Cesare Beccaria
   b. John Howard
   c. Alexander Maconochie
   d. Walter Crofton

7. _____ has (have) remained the primary mode of punishment for serious offenses in the United States.
   a. Incarceration
   b. Probation
   c. Fines
   d. a and b

8. Which of the following sentencing goals is designed to give a signal to the community at large that crime does not pay.
    a. Incapacitation
    b. Rehabilitation
    c. General deterrence
    d. Specific deterrence

9. The purpose of _____ is to insure that criminals will not be able to repeat their offenses while they are under state control.
    a. incapacitation
    b. rehabilitation
    c. general deterrence
    d. specific deterrence

10. The goal of _____ is to convince convicted offenders that crime does not pay and that recidivism is not in their best interests.
    a. incapacitation
    b. rehabilitation
    c. general deterrence
    d. specific deterrence

11. Which of the following punishment models relies on the prediction of future behavior?
    a. incapacitation
    b. rehabilitation
    c. specific deterrence
    d. all of the above

12. What fundamental emotion in would-be offenders that is targeted in deterrence theory?
    a. anger
    b. fear
    c. greed
    d. envy

13. The _____ sentence is the heart of the rehabilitation model of justice.
    a. indeterminate
    b. determinate
    c. mandatory
    d. presumptive

14. In a certain state, the maximum sentence is set by the legislature and cannot be changed, but the minimum sentence is determined by the judge. The state is using the _____ sentence.
    a. indeterminate
    b. determinate
    c. mandatory
    d. presumptive

15. The earliest kind of sentencing model used in the United States was the
    _____ sentence.
    a. indeterminate
    b. determinate
    c. structured
    d. mandatory

16. The failure to prevent future criminality is often a criticism of which punishment goal?
    a. specific deterrence
    b. retribution
    c. general deterrence
    d. just deserts

17. What is another term that retribution advocates use to describe the concept of blameworthiness?
    a. recidivism
    b. just deserts
    c. specific deterrence
    d. severity

18. Which of the following is correct concerning gender and sentencing?
    a. Women receive more favorable treatment early in the criminal justice system.
    b. Favoritism is greatest for white women.
    c. Judges may perceive women as better risks than men.
    d. Women spend more time in pretrial detention than men.

19. More than _____ confirmed executions have been carried out in America under civil authority.
    a. 11,000
    b. 14,500
    c. 20,000
    d. 22,500

20. Restitution is best exemplified by which early common law concept?
    a. deterrence
    b. wergild
    c. lex talionis
    d. rehabilitation

21. In _____ the Supreme Court ruled that the discretionary imposition of the death penalty was cruel and unusual punishment.
    a. *Jurek v. Texas*
    b. *Gregg v. Georgia*
    c. *Furman v. Georgia*
    d. *McLesky v. Kemp*

22. The Supreme Court, in _____, decided that a convicted offender can be sentenced to death when one or more "aggravating circumstances" are involved.
   a. *Jurek v. Texas*
   b. *Gregg v. Georgia*
   c. *Furman v. Georgia*
   d. *McLesky v. Kemp*

23. The Supreme Court decision in _____ stated that racial bias must be found in the immediate case before racial pattern evidence in capital sentencing can be considered persuasive.
   a. *Jurek v. Texas*
   b. *Gregg v. Georgia*
   c. *Furman v. Georgia*
   d. *McLesky v. Kemp*

24. In _____ the Supreme Court set the age limit of 16 for which defendants could be sentenced to death.
   a. *Witherspoon v. Illinois*
   b. *McLesky v. Kemp*
   c. *Wilkins v. Missouri*
   d. *Lockhart v. McCree*

25. How many states currently have the death penalty?
   a. 13
   b. 28
   c. 38
   d. 49

26. What is the most common method of execution in use today in America?
   a. hanging
   b. lethal injection
   c. electrocution
   d. lethal gas

Essay Questions

1. Distinguish between general and specific deterrence.

254

2. Explain the concept of incapacitation and the justification for it.

3. Distinguish between a concurrent and a consecutive sentence, giving examples of each.

4. Discuss the criticisms of the indeterminate sentence.

5. Discuss the structure and effectiveness of sentencing guidelines.

6. Discuss the structure and effectiveness of "three strikes and you're out" laws.

7. List the factors that affect sentencing and discuss how each factor does so.

8. Argue in favor of the death penalty.

9. Argue against the death penalty.

10. Describe what researchers have found concerning the death penalty as a deterrent.

CHAPTER 13 ANSWER KEY

FILL-IN-THE-BLANK QUESTIONS

1. sentences, discretion
2. poor laws
3. general deterrence
4. just desert
5. retribution
6. fair, just
7. mandatory
8. indeterminate
9. seriousness, background
10. mandatory sentence
11. elderly, younger
12. incapacitation
13. brutalization, brutality
14. Furman, Georgia
15. decrease, rise

TRUE/FALSE QUESTIONS

1.	T	11.	T
2.	T	12.	T
3.	F	13.	T
4.	F	14.	T
5.	T	15.	F
6.	T	16.	F
7.	F	17.	T
8.	T	18.	T
9.	F	19.	T
10.	F	20.	F

MULTIPLE CHOICE QUESTIONS

1.	D	14.	A
2.	C	15.	B
3.	A	16.	A
4.	D	17.	B
5.	B	18.	C
6.	B	19.	B
7.	A	20.	B
8.	C	21.	C
9.	A	22.	B
10.	D	23.	D
11.	D	24.	C
12.	B	25.	C
13.	A	26.	B

Chapter 14

Community Sentences: Probation, Intermediate Sanctions, and Restorative Justice

Learning Objectives

At the conclusion of the chapter the student should possess sufficient knowledge to achieve the following learning objectives:

1.   Understand the concept of community sentencing.

2.   Know the history of probation.

3.   Discuss the different kinds of probation sentences.

4.   Discuss the rules or terms of probation.

5.   Discuss the issue of probation revocation.

6.   Describe the effectiveness of probation.

7.   Discuss the concept of alternative sanctions and the forms that they take from fines to community incarceration.

8.   Describe the concept of the punishment ladder.

9.   Discuss the principles of restorative justice and the programs currently in use.

10.   Discuss the concept of reintegrative shaming.

Keywords and Definitions

Alternative (Intermediate) Sanctions: A group of community-based punishment options that fall between probation and prison on the punishment ladder.

Judicial Reprieve: A judge's suspension of sentence in medieval England, it allowed the defendant to seek a pardon, gather new evidence, or demonstrate reformed behavior.

Recognizance: A medieval practice that allowed convicted offenders to go free in the community if they agreed to enter a debt relation with the state.

Sureties: During the Middle Ages, people who made themselves responsible for people given release or a reprieve.

Probation: A sentence entailing the conditional release of a convicted offender into the community under the supervision of the court (in the form of a probation officer), subject to certain conditions for specified time.

John Augustus: The individual credited with pioneering the concept of probation.

Revocation: The termination of probation, parole, or other community-based sanction that leads to the imposition of the original term of incarceration.

Suspended Sentence: A prison term that is delayed while the defendant undergoes a period of community treatment; if the treatment is successful, the prison sentence is terminated.

Presentence Investigation: An investigation performed by a probation officer attached to a trial court after the conviction of a defendant. The report contains information about the defendant's background, education, previous employment, and family; his or her own statement concerning the offense; prior record; interviews with neighbors or acquaintances; and his or her mental and physical condition.

Intake: The process by which a probation officer settles a case at the initial appearance before the onset of formal proceedings.

Diagnosis: The analysis of the probationer's personality and the subsequent development of a personality profile that may be helpful in treating the offender.

Risk Classification: The process of classifying and assigning of cases to a level and type of supervision on the basis of the client's particular needs and the risks that the offender presents to the community.

Treatment Supervision: Based on knowledge of psychology, social work, or counseling and the diagnosis of the offender, the treatment program that will, it is hoped, allow the probationer to fulfill the probation contract and make a reasonable adjustment to the community.

Avertable Recidivists: Those offenders in the community whose crimes could have been avoided if they had been sent to prison in the first place.

Minnesota v. Murphy: The Supreme Court ruled that the probation officer-client relationship is not confidential like doctor-patient or attorney-client relationships.

Griffin v. Wisconsin: The Supreme Court held that a probationer's home may be searched without a warrant on the grounds that probation departments "have in mind the welfare of the probationer" and must "respond quickly to evidence of misconduct."

Mempa v. Rhay: The Supreme Court held that a probationer was constitutionally entitled to counsel in a revocation-of-probation proceeding where the imposition of sentence had been suspended.

Morrissey v. Brewer: The Supreme Court ruled that parolees were entitled to an informal inquiry to determine whether there was probable cause to revoke their parole; the same standard has been applied to probationers.

Gagnon v. Scarpelli: The Supreme Court held that both probationers and parolees have a constitutionally limited right to counsel in revocation proceedings.

United States v. Granderson: The Supreme Court found that it would be unfair to force a probationer to serve more time in prison than he would have if originally incarcerated.

Day fees: Fees imposed on probationers to offset the costs of their sanction.

HotSpot Probation: A program that uses community supervision, involving teams of police officers, probation officers, and citizens to provide increased monitoring of probationers in a small geographic area.

Tate v. Short: The Supreme Court recognized that incarcerating a person who is financially unable to pay a fine discriminates against the poor.

Day Fine: A fine geared to the average daily income of the convicted offender in an effort to bring equity to the sentencing process.

Forfeiture: The seizure of personal property by the state as a civil or criminal penalty.

Zero Tolerance: A forfeiture policy whereby defendants lose their homes, cars and other valuables for the slightest law violation.

Restitution: A typical criminal sanction that requires the offender to repay society or the victim of the crime for the trouble the offender caused.

Monetary Restitution: Involves a direct payment to the victim as a form of compensation.

Community Service Restitution: May be used in victimless crimes and involves work in the community in lieu of more severe criminal penalties.

Split Sentencing: A sentence that includes a jail term as a condition of probation.

Shock Probation: A sentence in which offenders serve a short prison term to impress them with the pains of imprisonment before they begin probation.

Shock Incarceration: A short prison sentence served in boot-camp facilities.

Intensive Probation Supervision: A type of intermediate sanction involving small probation caseloads and strict daily or weekly monitoring.

House Arrest: Requires convicted offenders to spend extended periods of time in their own homes as an alternative to an incarceration sentence.

Electronic Monitoring: Devices designed to manage offender obedience to home confinement orders.

Residential Community Corrections: A nonsecure facility that is not part of a prison or jail, but houses offenders, from which the offenders depart to work, attend school, and/or participate in treatment activities and programs.

Day Reporting Centers: Non-residential, community-based treatment programs.

Restorative Justice: A perspective on justice that replaces punishment goals with healing, accountability, and restoring the social damages cause by criminal acts.

Reintegrative Shaming: Restorative justice practice that involves the use disapproval of deeds and internal shaming to informally control wrongdoing in the community.

Sentencing Circle: A practice in Native American communities where a group of tribal leaders meet to informally deal with conflicts between group members.

Chapter Outline

I.   Community sentencing
      A.   Criminals sentences mandating that a convicted offender be placed and maintained in the community under special guidelines
      B.   Non-punitive approach targeting first time, non-violent offenders
            1.   deserve a second chance
            2.   pose little threat to society
      C.   Popular options in alternative or intermediate sanctions
            1.   at an all-time high in terms of usage
            2.   numerous programs alternatives
      D.   Usually less costly than jail or prison
      E.   Allow the offender to remain in community, avoid stigma & trauma of prison
      F.   Scaling of severity and security to protect public safety
      G.   Growth area in criminal justice

II.   History of probation
      A.   Roots in English common law
            1.   judges in Middle Ages granted clemency and stays of execution
            2.   also used judicial reprieves to suspend punishment
            3.   recognizance allowed people to remain free to repay debt to society
                 a.   repay debt through work
                 b.   surety made themselves responsible for the releasee
      B.   Early American efforts
            1.   John Augustus credited with originating idea of modern probation
            2.   Massachusetts authorizes probation officer for the city of Boston in 1878
            3   federal government established probation system for U.S. courts in1925

III.   Probation today
      A.   Basics
            1.   convicted offender is placed & maintained in community with court supervision
            2.   based on premise that average offender is not a danger to society

3. can control the prisonization process and give offenders a second chance
4. involves a suspension of sentence with a promise of good behavior in return for community supervision
5. contract between court and offender
6. the rules or conditions of probation must be obeyed or probation may be revoked
7. the sentence is for a fixed period of time

B. Awarding probation
1. probation may be granted by state and federal courts
2. granted to adult felons and misdemeanants and juvenile delinquents
3. it is granted by the judge but can be based on jury recommendations
4. statutes may prohibit probation for adults convicted of specific crimes
5. most probationary sentences are suspended sentences of time behind bars
6. some probation is based on a deferred sentence

C. Extent of probation
1. 2,000 probation agencies in the United States
2. 4 million adults under federal or state probation
3. number of people on probation has quadrupled since 1980
4. 30 states combine probation and parole supervision in one agency
5. 1/3 of all felony cases

D. Who is on probation?
1. 77% male with female representation is on the rise
2. 1/2 white, 1/3 black
3. ½ felons
4. 60% direct sentence, 22% suspended
5. 75% required to regularly report to probation officer
6. mostly public order and property offenses

E. Eligibility for probation
1. may be determined by state statute with judge discretion
2. some states have guidelines for granting probation to control judge discretion

F. Probation conditions
1. court has broad discretion in establishing conditions 2. may not impose capricious or cruel conditions
2. base conditions can be supplemented by special conditions
   a. drug treatment and testing conditions
   b. cooperation with legal authorities (e.g. testify against others)
   c. mental health services
   d. exotic conditions for sex offenders
      i. must register
      ii. cease contact in class of victims
      iii. internet restrictions
      iv. polygraph

G. Administration of probation services
1. varied models
   a. organized with state or local control, combined adult and juvenile
   b. the typical department is situated in a single court district
   c. the chief probation officer is responsible for hiring, supervision and training
   d. large departments have assistant chiefs

2. major functions of probation officers
   a. supervise cases
   b. rehabilitate
   c investigate
   d. collect fines and restitution
   e intake - interview complainants and defendants on future actions
3. Probation officer style vary
   a. social worker model
   b. law enforcement model

H. Duties of probation officers
1. intake
2. pre-sentence investigation
3. diagnosis and risk classification
4. treatment supervision

I. How successful is probation?
1. probation is humane, maintains community and family ties, and is cost effective
   a. $2,000 annual cost of probation vs. $20,000 for prison
   b. community and family ties can be maintained
2. most probation orders are successful
   a. about 61% success rate
   b. serious offenders most likely to recidivate
3. Rand Corporation study finds most common federal sentencing alternative
4. factors related to probation failure
   a. young unemployed males
   b. social and psychological disabilities
   c. habitual offenders
   d. recidivism rates still lower recidivism than for prisoners

J. Civil rights of probationers
1. Supreme Court has ruled that probationers have a unique status, and have fewer constitutional guarantees
2. *Minnesota v. Murhpy* self incrimination protections do not apply at a probation appointment, probation officer client relationship is not confidential.
3. *Griffin v. Wisconsin* – probationers home may be searched without a warrant
4. United States v. Knights – warrantless searches of probationer's house is constitutional

K. Revocation rights of probationers
1. *Mempha v. Rhay*- probationers have a right to counsel at a revocation hearing
2. *Morrissey v. Brewer* - parolees who violate conditions of parole entitled to a formal revocation hearing with minimum due process requirements
3. *Gagnon v. Scarpelli* - probationers and parolees have a constitutionally limited right to counsel in revocation proceedings
4. *U.S. v. Granderson* - upon revocation, original sentence stands as though no probation granted

L. Probation's future
1. most popular alternative sentence
   a. flexibility

     b. alleviates prison overcrowding

     c. cost effective

     d. pressure to expand its usage to other crimes

   2. future trends

     a. imposition of probation day fees

     b. hotspot probation

     c. use as a correctional alternative with other intermediate sanctions

IV. Intermediate sanctions

  A. Community corrections that emphasize rehabilitation with added control function

  B. Probation plus alternatives

   1. intensive probation supervision

   2. house arrest

   3. shock probation/split sentences

   4. electronic monitoring

   5. residential community corrections

   6. restitution orders

  C. Community corrections abroad

   1. Western European countries have similar crime rates to the United States but a much lower incarceration rate

   2. as crime rose in Europe, law makers looked to make sentencing more fair rather than harsh

  D. Advantages of intermediate sanctions

   1. cost effectiveness

   2. alleviate prison overcrowding

   3. fair, equitable and proportional

   4. part of the ladder of scaled punishment

  E. Fines

   1. financial penalties have negative impact on success rates

   2. day fines originated in Europe

   3. severity of punishment often geared to the offender's ability to pay

   4. *Tate v. Short* – cannot incarcerate those who cannot pay for other alternatives

  F. Forfeiture

   1. criminal forfeiture (in personam) and civil forfeiture (in rem)

   2. seizure of goods and instrumentalities related to the commission or outcome of a criminal act

   3. dates back to Middle Ages where forfeiture of estate was mandatory for felons

   4. Racketeer Influenced and Corrupt Organizations Act (RICO) and Continuing Criminal Enterprises Act (CCE) laws

   5. criticism of zero tolerance practices

  G. Restitution

   1. pay back victims of the crime or serve community to compensate for act

   2. community service to public institutions guidelines discussed

   3. monetary restitution to the victim

   4. has been embraced by courts given its victim focus

   5. critics argue that it widens the net of social control

  H. Shock probation and split sentencing

   1. both programs grant community release after taste of prison life

   2. prison is meant to shock them into law-abiding behavior

3. 30% of probationers receive a split sentence
    a. split sentencing programs make jail term a condition of probation
    b. serve the jail time then released for probation re-sentencing
4. shock incarceration may link a boot camp experience to short prison stay
5. criticisms and praise for each program
    a. reintegrate offender quickly back into community
    b. reduces prison populations
    c. even short prison term stigmatizes the offender

I. Intensive probation supervision
1. implemented in about 40 states with more than 100,000 clients
2. small, 15-40 client caseloads
3. goals are diversion, control, and reintegration
4. admissions criteria vary
5. how effective is IPS?
    a. evaluations indicate programs are generally successful
    b. failure rates may be quite high
    c. may be no better than traditional probation

J. House arrest
1. offender required to spend extended periods of time in their own home as an alternative to incarceration
2. 10,000 people under house arrest
2. administration varies greatly
3. surveillance by probation department or court appointed surveillance officers
4. little available research on effectiveness
5. criticized for having little deterrent effect

K. Electronic monitoring
1. often used to insure compliance with house arrest
2. programs have been around since 1964 - 150,000 offenders monitored today
3. types of technology
    a. remote alcohol detection devices
    b. ignition interlock devises
    c. programmed contact systems
    d. continuous signal devices
    e. victim notification systems
    f. field monitoring devices
    g. group monitoring units
    h. location tracking systems (GPS)
4. public supports EM as cost effective alternative
5. the limits of EM
    a. current technology is limited
    b. four times the initial cost and expenses of traditional probation
    c. lack rehabilitation effect
    d. lack deterrence
    e. widens the net of justice
    f. out of step with values on privacy and liberty

L. Residential community corrections (RCC)
1. the most secure of the intermediate sanction alternatives
2. non-secure building that houses pre-trial and adjudicated adult residents who work, attend school, participate in corrections programs

3. provide intermediate sanctions or as a prerelease center for parolees
4. operated by probation departments or private, nonprofit groups
   a. 2,000 state run facilities
   b. 2,500 privately run facilities
   c. 400 federally funded programs
5. used as pretrial release centers and as half-way back alternatives for probation and parole violators
6. day reporting centers (DRCs)
7. Drug treatment alternative-to prison (DTAP)

M. Can alternative sanctions work?
1. hold promise of being cost effective and controlling crime
2. some say it's a myth that they will reduce prison overcrowding
3. probation becoming more punitive than prison?
   a. given the choice between jail and probation, many choose jail
   b. probation has become much tougher over the last decade

V. Restorative justice
A. Based on the belief that traditional punishment produces more crime
1. destroys offender dignity
2. ineffective on recidivism
B. Resolution of conflict between the offender and victim should be resolved in the community
C. Goal is to mediate conflict and restore damage
D. John Braithwaite on shaming
1. stigmatization is degrading
2. reintegrative shaming is effective
E. Offender must accept accountability and responsibility
F. Restoration redefines crime as conflict, seeks to heal rifts between offender and victim
1. understanding must be mediated
2. offender accepts responsibility
3. offender commits to material and symbolic reparations
4. community support and assistance
G. Restoration programs
1. sentencing circles in Native American communities
2. school-based programs
3. first encounters by police
4. diversion from traditional court
5. innovative programs in the community
   a. Minnesota
   b. Vermont
   c. Travis County, Texas
H. Challenges of restorative justice
1. respect cultural and social differences
2. balancing the needs of the offender and victim
3. popular alternative at present

Chapter Summary

Judges often seek to impose **alternative sanction** to incarceration. The most common of these is **probation**, the practice of maintaining offenders in the community under supervision of court authority, can be traced historically to the traditions of **judicial reprieves, recognizance, and sureties** that existed under English common law. The modern concept of probation was pioneered by **John Augustus**, and has remained the sentence of choice in American courts. The philosophy behind probation is that the average offender is not actually a dangerous criminal or a menace to society. Probation is a contract between the offender and the judge that involves suspension of the offender's sentence in return for the promise of good behavior in the community and/or the fulfillment of other conditions determined by the sentencing judge. If the contract is not fulfilled, probation is **revoked** and the offender must serve out the original sentence.

Probation officers are normally charged with four primary tasks: **investigation, intake, diagnosis,** and **treatment supervision**. The investigation and **risk assessment** of defendants coming before the court for sentencing is a key responsibility, as are the recommendations in the probation officer's **presentence investigation**. Numerous factors influence the probation officer's investigation report, especially the nature of the current offense and the offender's criminal history.

Probationers enjoy few constitutional protections in that the probation officer can search the probationer's home without a search warrant and the probation officer-client relationship is not confidential like doctor-patient or attorney-client relationships. Probationers have been granted the right to counsel at probation revocation proceedings and the right to a formal revocation hearing after an informal hearing to determine whether probable cause for revocation exists.

The current trend in the United States is "probation plus," the addition of restrictive penalties and/or conditions to community service orders. These programs are known as **intermediate sanctions** and include programs that are typically administered by probation departments such as: **intensive probation supervision; house arrest; electronic monitoring; restitution; shock probation/split sentences;** and **residential community corrections**. While it is too soon to determine whether these programs are successful, they provide the hope of being low cost, high security alternatives to traditional corrections.

Restorative justice is a recent movement that seeks to replace punishment goals with informal efforts aimed at repairing the damages caused by crime. Building on Native American traditions such as the tribal **sentencing circle**, concepts such as **reintegrative shaming** are used to get the offender to accept responsibility for their actions, reintegrate them into the community, and get them to make amends with their victims.

Fill-in-the Blank Questions

1. Probation is a criminal sentence mandating that a convicted offender be placed and maintained in the _____ under the _____ of a duly authorized agent of the _____.

2. The common law practice of _____ _____ allowed judges to _____ punishment so that convicted offenders could seek a pardon, gather new evidence, or demonstrate that they had reformed their behavior.

3. Probation usually involves suspension of the offender's sentence in return for the promise of _____ _____ in the community under the supervision of the probation department. A violation of that contract leads to _____.

4. Probation may be revoked simply because the _____ and _____ of probation have not been met.

5. Some states have attempted to control _____ _____ by creating _____ for granting probation.

6. An important task of a probation officer is the investigation and evaluation of defendants in what is known as a _____ _____. Next, during the diagnosis stage, the offender is subject to a _____ _____ to determine their threat to the community.

7. A _____ _____ is a sentence of incarceration that is not carried out unless the offender disobeys the rules of probation while in the community.

8. Courts have _____ the use of probation conditions as long as they are _____ related to the _____ of probation.

9. In the investigative state of probation, the probation officer conducts and inquiry within the _____ to discover the factors related to the _____ of the offender.

10. The presentence investigation is conducted primarily to gain information for _____ _____, but in the event the offender is placed on probation, the investigation becomes a useful testimony on which to base _____ and _____.

11. Intake is a process by which probation officers interview cases that have been summoned to the court for _____ _____.

12. Diagnosis is the analysis of the probationer's _____ and the subsequent development of a _____ _____ that may be helpful in treating the offender.

13. House arrest programs are designed to be more _____ than intensive probation supervision or any other community supervision alternative and are considered a "_____ _____" before prison.

14. _____ _____ involves resentencing an offender to probation after a short prison stay.

15. Programs such as fines, forfeiture, and house arrest are examples of _____ _____.

True/False Questions

T F 1.   Probation typically involves the suspension of an offender's sentence for promise of good behavior in the community.

T F 2.   Probation assumes that the average offender is not actually a dangerous criminal or a menace to society.

T F 3.   The roots of probation can be traced back to Australian common law.

T F 4.   The most widely used correctional mechanism in the United States is the county jail.

T F 5.   Probation implies a contract between the court and the offender.

T F 6.   The probation officer has little say in the planning of a probationer's treatment program.

T F 7.   The granting of probation to serious felons is quite common.

T F 8.   Judges may legally impose restrictions tailored both to fit the probationer's individual needs and/or to protect society from additional harm.

T F 9.   Judges may not require a probationer to cooperate with legal authorities as a condition of probation.

T F 10.   Probationers have a right to challenge rules imposed at the time of sentencing or others imposed later by the court.

T F 11.   The typical probation department is situated in a multiple court district.

T F 12.   Probation officers are sometimes asked to collect fines due to the court by a probationer.

T F 13.   A convicted state felon is more likely to get a probation sentence than a prison sentence.

T F 14.   Research shows that classification has a substantial impact on reducing recidivism.

T F 15.   Prior record is related to probation success.

T F 16.   Forfeiture is a recently developed sanction.

T F 17.   Restitution ranks above probation on the punishment ladder.

T F 18.   The primary goal of intensive probation supervision is to reduce prison crowding.

T F 19.   Intensive probation supervision has been proven effective at reducing reoffending rates.

T F 20.   Day reporting centers are basically residential community corrections.

T F 21.   Restorative justice seeks to include all parties - the offender, victim, and community –
          in the justice process.

Multiple Choice Questions

1.   Common law sometimes required _____, people who made themselves
     responsible for the behavior of an offender after he was released.
          a.   bondsmen
          b.   sureties
          c.   probation officers
          d.   parole officers

2.   _____ of Boston is credited with originating the modern probation concept.
          a.   John Augustus
          b.   Alexander Maconochie
          c.   Emile Durkheim
          d.   Samuel Adams

3.   Probation is practiced in _____ states and by the federal government.
          a.   37
          b.   40
          c.   45
          d.   50

4.   Revocation means that the contract is terminated and the original sentence is:
          a.   reconsidered
          b.   enforced
          c.   recalculated
          d.   commuted

5.   Each probationary sentence is for a(n) _____ period of time, depending on
     the seriousness of the offense and the statutory law.
          a.   obligatory
          b.   indeterminate
          c.   fixed
          d.   minimum

6.   What entity usually maintains authority over probationers?
          a.   the court
          b.   the correctional authority
          c.   the victim's assistance office
          d.   a private, third party contractor

7.   The most common manner in which a probationary sentence is imposed is a
     _____ to probation which is used in about half the cases.
          a.   split sentence
          b.   suspended sentence
          c.   direct sentence
          d.   quick shock incarceration and then movement

8. The number of people on probation has done what in the last 20 years?
   a. decreased slightly
   b. remained the same
   c. doubled
   d. quadrupled

9. What is the primary purpose of the presentence investigation?
   a. to gather knowledge about the causal factors relating to criminality
   b. to gain information for judicial sentences
   c. to develop a rehabilitation treatment program
   d. to classify the probationer in a risk-need assessment scheme

10. What style of probation officer is most concerned with supervision, control, and public safety?
   a. social worker style
   b. law enforcers
   c. rookies
   d. risk classifiers

11. Which duty involves evaluating the probationer based on information from the initial intake or presentence investigation?
   a. investigation
   b. intake
   c. diagnosis
   d. treatment supervision

12. The greatest amount of discretion is found in a _____ controlled probation department.
   a. statewide
   b. judge
   c. centrally
   d. locally

13. Classification schemes are in synch with _____ sentencing models.
   a. desert-based
   b. rehabilitation-based
   c. deterrence-based
   d. restitution-based

14. What percent of adults leaving probation successfully complete their sentences?
   a. 45%
   b. 60%
   c. 75%
   d. 95%

15. A Rand Corporation study on probation found that percent of probationers were rearrested?
    a. 13%
    b. 35%
    c. 43%
    d. 65%

16. The _____ Supreme Court case holds that the probation officer-client relationship is not confidential.
    a. *Mempa v. Rhay*
    b. *Morrissey v. Brewer*
    c. *Griffin v. Wisconsin*
    d. *Minnesota v. Murphy*

17. The Supreme Court ruled in _____ that a probationer's home may be searched without a warrant.
    a. *Mempa v. Rhay*
    b. *Morrissey v. Brewer*
    c. *Griffin v. Wisconsin*
    d. *Minnesota v. Murphy*

18. The Supreme Court unanimously held in _____ that a probationer was constitutionally entitled to counsel in a revocation-of-probation hearing where the imposition of sentence had been suspended.
    a. *Mempa v. Rhay*
    b. *Morrissey v. Brewer*
    c. *Griffin v. Wisconsin*
    d. *Minnesota v. Murphy*

19. Probationers have the same right to an informal inquiry to determine whether there was probable cause to revoke their probation because the Supreme Court said in _____ that parolees had the right to a parole revocation.
    a. *Mempa v. Rhay*
    b. *Morrissey v. Brewer*
    c. *Griffin v. Wisconsin*
    d. *Minnesota v. Murphy*

20. The Supreme Court's _____ decision held that both probationers and parolees have a constitutionally limited right to counsel in revocation proceedings.
    a. *Gagnon v. Scarpelli*
    b. *Tate v. Short*
    c. *United States v. Granderson*
    d. *United States v. Ursery*

21. Intensive probation supervision, house arrest, electronic monitoring, and restitution orders fall under which of the following headings?
    a. corporal punishment
    b. probation
    c. intermediate sanctions
    d. restorative justice

22. What is the least punitive alternative on the punishment ladder?
    a. forfeiture
    b. pretrial release
    c. fines
    d. restitution

23. Day fines are geared to the offender's _____ to pay.
    a. cooperating
    b. wanting
    c. willingness
    d. ability

24. Electronic monitoring devices are primarily used in conjunction with what other sanction?
    a. residential community corrections facilities
    b. intensive probation supervision
    c. house arrest
    d. shock probation

25. What is the legal term for criminal forfeiture?
    a. in personam
    b. in rem
    c. in quidro
    d. in corpus delicti

26. Which of the following electronic monitoring systems utilizes global positioning systems?
    a. ignition interlock devices
    b. field monitoring devices
    c. group monitoring units
    d. location tracking systems

27. What percent of probationers receive split sentences?
    a. 10%
    b. 25%
    c. 40%
    d. 55%

28. _____ refers to having a jail term as a condition of probation.
    a. shock probation
    b. split-sentencing
    c. shock incarceration
    d. intensive probation supervision

29. Which of the following factors is not associated with the restorative justice movement?
    a. a philosophical framework that emphasizes community harm over punishment
    b. active involvement of the victim and community members in the justice process
    c. a return to intermediate sanctions
    d. the offender's participation in culture-based cleansing ceremonies

Essay Questions

1. Discuss the major functions that probation officers perform.

2. Discuss the factors that contribute to a persons failure on probation.

3. Discuss the factors that shape an individual's eligibility for a probation sentence.

4. Discuss the RICO act and this intermediate sanction's role in the war on drugs.

5. Describe the strengths and weaknesses of shock probation and split sentencing.

6. Describe the several ways in which intensive probation supervision is used.

7. Discuss the various technological variations of electronic monitoring systems currently in use.

8. Discuss structure and the effectiveness of residential community corrections programs.

9. Compare and contrast two intermediate sanctions in terms of their structure and effectiveness.

10. Describe the principles and practices that guide the reintegrative shaming model.

CHAPTER 14 ANSWER KEY

FILL-IN-THE-BLANK QUESTIONS

1. community, supervision, court
2. judicial reprieve, suspend
3. good behavior, revocation
4. rules, conditions
5. judicial discretion, guidelines
6. presentence investigation, risk assessment
7. suspended sentence
8. upheld, reasonably, purposes
9. community, criminality
10. judicial sentence, treatment, supervision
11. initial appearances
12. personality, personality profile
13. punitive, last chance
14. shock probation
15. intermediate sanctions

TRUE/FALSE QUESTIONS

1.	T	12.	T
2.	T	13.	F
3.	F	14.	F
4.	F	15.	T
5.	T	16.	F
6.	F	17.	T
7.	T	18.	T
8.	T	19.	F
9.	F	20.	T
10.	T	21.	T
11.	F		

MULTIPLE CHOICE QUESTIONS

1.	B	16.	D
2.	A	17.	C
3.	D	18.	A
4.	B	19.	B
5.	C	20.	A
6.	A	21.	C
7.	C	22.	B
8.	D	23.	D
9.	B	24.	C
10.	B	25.	A
11.	C	26.	D
12.	D	27.	A
13.	A	28.	B
14.	B	29.	C
15.	D		

Chapter 15

Corrections: History, Institutions, and Populations

Learning Objectives

At the conclusion of this chapter, the student should possess sufficient knowledge to achieve the following learning objectives:

1.   Describe the history of penal institutions.

2.   Discuss the differences between the Auburn (congregate) and Pennsylvania (isolation) prison systems.

3.   Discuss the history of penal reform

4.   Describe jail system operations in this country.

5.   Describe the structure and function of the new generation jails.

6.   Differentiate between maximum, medium and minimum security prisons.

7.   Discuss the super-maximum-security prison.

8.   Discuss the concept of penal harm.

9.   Discuss the benefits and drawbacks of boot camps.

10.   Explain the current trends in the U.S. prison population.

Keywords and Definitions

Corrections: The agencies of justice that take custody of offenders after their conviction and are entrusted with their treatment and control.

Prisons: State or federal correctional institution for incarceration of felony offenders for terms of one year or more.

Jails: A place to detain people awaiting trial, hold drunks and disorderly individuals, and confine convicted misdemeanants serving sentences of less than one year.

Hulks: Mothballed ships that were used to house prisoners in eighteenth-century England.

John Howard: An eighteenth-century British penal reformer who wrote *The State of Prisons*.

Walnut Street Jail: A wing of the Walnut Street Jail became the prison for convicted felons as a result of pressure from the Quakers on the Pennsylvania State Legislature.

Penitentiary House: Prisoner quarters in the Walnut Street Jail that contained the solitary or separate cells, as was the custom in England.

Tier System: Cells built vertically on five floors of the structure under the Auburn System.

Congregate System: The system under which prisoners eat and work in groups.

Auburn System: The prison system developed in New York during the nineteenth century that stressed congregate working conditions.

Pennsylvania System: The prison system developed in Pennsylvania during the nineteenth century that stressed total isolation and individual penitence as a means of reform.

Contract System: The system used earlier in the 20th century in which inmates were leased out to private industry to work.

Convict-Lease System: The system used earlier in the century in which the state leased inmates to a business for a fixed annual fee and the state gave up supervision and control.

Property in Service: The system in which control of prisoners transferred to the contractor or shipmaster until the expiration of the prisoners' sentences.

Ticket of Leave: A form of conditional release permitted former prisoners to be at large in specified areas; the conditions of their release were written on a license which former inmates were required to carry with them at all times.

Mark System: Inmates could earn their ticket-of-leave by accumulating credits for good conduct and hard work in prison.

Sumners-Ashurst Act: The 1940 act that makes it a federal offense to transport in interstate commerce goods made in prison for private use, regardless of the laws of the state receiving the goods

Prisoners' Rights Movement: After many years of indifference, state and federal courts ruled in case after case that institutionalized inmates had rights to freedom of religion and speech, medical care, procedural due process, and proper living conditions.

Medical Model: Views inmates as "sick people" who are suffering from some social malady that prevents them from adjusting to society.

Maximum Security Prisons: Correctional institutions that house dangerous felons and maintain strict security measures, high walls, and limited contact with the outside world.

Medium Security Prisons: Less secure institutions that house nonviolent offenders and provide more opportunities for contact with the outside world.

Minimum Security Prisons: The least secure institutions that house white-collar and nonviolent offenders, maintain a few security measures, and have liberal furlough and visitation policies.

Shock Incarceration: A short prison sentence served in boot-camp type facilities.

Boot Camps: A short term militaristic correctional facility in which inmates undergo intensive physical conditioning and discipline.

Community Corrections: Those state and federal correctional systems created as an alternative to closed institutions.

Halfway Houses: A community-based correctional facility that houses inmates before their outright release so that they can become acclimated to conventional society.

Chapter Outline

I.   Introduction
     A.   Correctional systems
          1.   federal, state, county, and local level jurisdictions
          2.   felons go to prison or penitentiaries, misdemeanors to jail & juveniles to homes
     B.   Conflict in penal philosophy
          1.   correctional institutions do not correct
          2.   rehabilitation, retribution, or incapacitation as guiding philosophy?
          3.   dominance of conservative philosophy demonstrated by presumptive and mandatory sentencing, increased inmate populations, and political rhetoric
     C.   Prisonization of the past 20 years
          1.   number of state/federal prison inmates has quadrupled from 400,000 to 1.2 million
          2.   650 new state/federal prison facilities built
          3.   number of local jails have tripled from 200,000 to 600,000
          4.   number of community-corrections sentences up from 1.3 million to 4 million
          5.   number of correctional employees more than doubled from 300,000 to 716,000

II.   History of correctional institutions
     A.   Early European history
          1.   original punishments were banishment, slavery, restitution, corporal punishment, and execution

2. 10th century English institutions were used to hold pre-trial detainees and persons awaiting execution of sentence
3. 12th century construction of English jails to hold thieves and vagrants prior to disposition of sentence
4. 16th century construction of Brideswell work houses
5. Le Stinche, an early Italian prison with separate cells opened in 1301
6. early English penal institutions were foul places that operated on the fee system
7. jails were run for personal gain by the shire reeve (sheriff)
8. growing inmate population from 1776-1785 forced use of prison hulks (ships)

B. Origins of corrections in the U.S.
1. correctional reform was first instituted in America
2. first American jail built in James City, VA in the 17th century
3. American correctional system originated in Pennsylvania under William Penn
   a. revised the criminal code to forbid torture
   b. emphasized hard labor, moderate flogging, fines, forfeiture of property
   c. began construction of county house of corrections
4. first American prison likely the Newgate Prison in 1773 or Castle Island in 1785

C. Pennsylvania system
1. modern system traced to Pennsylvania and the Philadelphia Society for Alleviating the Miseries of Public Prisons in 1787
2. creation of the Walnut Street Jail in 1790
   a. solitary confinement wing known as the penitentiary house
   b. similar institutions at Newgate, NY in 1791 and Trenton, NJ in 1798
3. Hallmarks of the Pennsylvania system
   a. single inmate to a cell
   b. cell designed as a miniature prison
   c. the Western Penitentiary built on a semi-circle design
   d. constant solitary confinement
4. the Eastern Penitentiary in Philadelphia

D. Auburn system
   1. response to overcrowding inherent in the Pennsylvania model
2. Auburn prison built in 1816
3. known as the tier or congregate system
   a. philosophy based on fear of punishment
   b. silence for all, solitude for only the worst offenders
   c. general population in separate cells by night, worked together by day

E. Developing prisons
1. Michel Foucault's theory of development
   a. punishment evolves with society
   b. complex societies seek complex forms of punishment
   c. punishment evolved from physical to psychological
2. regimentation becomes the norm (lockstep)
3. the Auburn system prevails with congregate working conditions, solitary confinement as a form of punishment, military regimentation

4.   religion permeates Pennsylvania system stresses penitence

5.   Auburn system won out over Pennsylvania system

F.   Prisons of the late 19th century

    1.   remarkably similar to today's prisons

    2.   Auburn system in place, except in PA

    3.   overcrowding leads to double cell format

    4.   prison industry is dominant theme

    5.   the contract system, the convict-lease system, or the state account system

    6.   National Congress of Penitentiary and Reformatory Discipline of 1870

         a.   forum to discuss inmate education, treatment and training

         b.   Organized by Enoch Wines and Theodore Dwight

         c.   Zebulon Brockway, warden of Elmira Reformatory attends

    7.   Broadway implements reforms at Elmira

         a.   education

         b.   library hours

         c.   lectures by Elmira College faculty

         d.   vocational training shops

         e.   parole - conditional release from prison

G.   Prisons in the early 20th century

    1.   time of contrast in U.S. prison system (reform vs. punish)

    2.   reforms of Mutual Welfare League led by Thomas Mott Osbourne

         a.   better treatment

         b.   end corporal punishment

         c.   provide an education

         d.   meaningful prison industry

         e.   bring society to the prison

    3.   conservative prison and state officials sought to maintain status quo

    4.   by the mid-1930's there was a change in inmate uniforms, abolish the whip and lash, the code of silence ended, and prisoners mingle on the yard

    5.   development of specialized prisons

    6.   prison industry comes under union pressure

         a.   Sumners-Ashurst Act limits interstate transport of prison-made goods

         b.   private investors back out due to lack of profits

    7.   inmate idleness becomes the order of the day

H.   Prisons of the modern era

    1.   three eras of change, 1960-1980

         a.   prisoner's rights movement

             i.   demise of the hands-off-doctrine

             ii.   freedom of religion, medical, due process, living conditions

         b.   violence and rioting

             i.   national concern due to riots at Attica & New Mexico

             ii.   tighter discipline and birth of super-max

         c.   rehabilitation and use of the medical model

             i.   individualized correctional treatment over generic punishment

             ii.   focus on reintegration into society

             iii.   furloughs and work release

             iv.   lack of results and high costs leads to reforms

2.   modern prisons as places for control, incapacitation and punishment
        a.   penal harm, no-frills movement
        b.   implement cheap, severe conditions

III.   Jails
        A.   Purposes
                1.   pretrial detention
                2.   detention of offenders awaiting sentencing
                3.   confinement of misdemeanants
                4.   probation and parole violators
                5.   relieve prison overcrowding
        B.   Jail demographics
                1.   15,000 local or municipal lockups hold for 48 hours
                2.   county jails hold inmates for up to one year
                3.   665,000 inmates, half are pretrial detainees
                4.   4-5% increase in annual population
        C.   Jail inmate characteristics
                1.   50,000 youths admitted to jail each year
                2.   90% male but female population on the rise
                3.   majority are minorities (40% black, 15% Hispanic)
                4.   history of physical or sexual abuse
        D.   Jail conditions
                1.   low priority item in the system -   oldest, most deteriorated institutions
                        a.   county-level authority with small tax base
                        b.   rule of custodial convenience
                        c.   under paid employees
                2.   overcrowded and ineffective
                        a.   targeted enforcement efforts
                        b.   mandatory jail time for certain offenses
        E.   New generation jails
                1.   modern design to improve effectiveness
                2.   allow for continuous observations of inmates
                3.   inmates live in pods
                        a.   single guard observation outside of pod
                        b.   dayroom
                        c.   clusters of cells
                        d.   video surveillance and panic button to other officers
                4.   indirect supervision jails
                        a.   correctional officer station inside secure room
                        b.   microphones and speakers allow for communication

IV.   Prisons
        A.   The prison system
                1.   federal and state governments run closed correctional facilities
                2.   vast and costly
                        a. $49 million per year
                        b.   946% increase in cost since 1977
        B.   Types of prisons
                1.   Maximum security prisons
                        a.   fortress-like with 25 foot high walls
                        b.   cells/blocks/wings surrounding courtyards

          c.   inmate numbers and uniform dress codes
          d.   close supervision by day, confinement by night
          e.   byword is security
          f.   ultra or supermax prisons as a new trend
              i.   house the most predatory criminals
              ii.   often exist as a wing or stand alone unit in max prison
              iii   cement, video cameras and guard towers
              iv.   isolation (22-24 hours in cells) & sensory deprivation
              v.   ultimate control mechanism for problem inmates
              vi.   42 states operate a ultra-max prison or unit
              vii.   20,000 beds nationwide
      2.   Medium security prisons
          a.   similar in appearance to max-security
          b.   security is less intense
          c.   more visitor privileges
          d.   greater treatment efforts
      3.   Minimum security prisons
          a.   no armed guards or walls
          b.   most trustworthy and least violent inmates
          c.   dormitories or small private rooms

V.   Prison inmate characteristics
    A.   Gender
        1.   women underrepresented in prison
        2.   male to female arrest ratio 3.5:1 overall, 6:1 violent offenders
        3.   most female inmates committed less serious offenses
    B.   Minorities
        1.   prison system is predominately minority
        2.   black males outnumber white males
        3.   10% of black males, 25-29 are in prison
    C.   Type of offense
        1.   roughly half of inmates are serving time for a violent crime
        2.   inmates doing time for drug offenses up more than 100,000 over last
             decade
    D.   Substance abuse
        1.   strong association between substance abuse and inmate status
        2.   survey of 400 Texas inmates fond 75% suffered from lifetime
             substance abuse
        3.   50% under the influence at the time of arrest
             many die from HIV related diseases
    E.   Physical abuse
        1.   prison inmates report a long history of physical abuse (19%)
        2.   history of mental health problems
        3.   only a few members of the educated, middle class end up in prison

VI.   Alternative correctional institutions
    A.   Farms and camps
        1.   primarily located in the South and West
        2.   farms
          a.   agricultural emphasize
          b.   40 in operation nationwide

3.   forestry camps
        a.   maintain state parks, fight fires or do reforestation
        b.   40 in operation nationwide
4.   ranches
        a.   raise cattle, breed horses
        b.   60 in operation, modstly in the west
5.   road camps
        a.   repair roads and highways
        b.   80 in operation nationwide

B.   Shock incarceration/boot camps
    1.   aimed at youthful, first-time offenders
    2.   military discipline, strict daily schedule, and physical training
    3.   short term (90-180 days)
    4.   common program goals
        a.   promote responsibility
        b.   improve decision-making skills
        c.   build self-confidence
        d.   teach socialization skills
    5.   common programs
        a.   education and training
        b.   vocational opportunities
        c.   counseling and treatment
    6.   wide variation in 75 programs across the country
    7.   evaluations show mixed results
    8.   programs are cheaper than overcrowded prisons
    9.   evaluations
        a.   lower recidivism than traditional prisons
        b   no evidence of lowered recidivism rates over probationers and parolees
    10.   inmates and staff feel is it a "valuable experience"

C.   Community corrections facilities
    1.   community treatment programs began in the 1960's
        a.   the goal was reintegration
        b.   commonly known as half-way houses
        c.   intended to bridge the gap between institutional and community life
        d.   special programs seek to cushion the shock of reintegration
    2.   recent programs have used facilities as stand alone sanction
        a.   target drug addicts and nonviolent offenders
        b.   cheap state or privately run facilities with treatment focus
    3.   converted residential homes or apartment buildings
    4.   use of ex-offenders as staff members
    5.   evaluations show a lack of support from the community
    6.   the climate of control in most houses caused problems

D.   Private institutions
    1.   prisons as money-making business opportunities
    2.   U.S. Corrections Corporations opened first private state prison in Marion, KY in 1986
        a.   264 facilities in operation at state and federal level
        b.   93,077 inmates in 2000

3.   models of operation
        a.   private corporation finances and builds prison, then runs it
        b.   private corporation finances and builds prison, then leases it back
        c.   private corporation provides a task=specific fee-for-services model

4.   some evidence that they reduce recidivism and are better run than public prisons

5.   potential problem areas
        a.   biased evaluations of effectiveness
        b.   cut corners to save costs
        c.   leave hard-core inmate for state care
        d.   widening the social control net
        e.   maintenance of liability insurance
        f.   loss of existing state correctional jobs
        g.   quality control
        h.   moral considerations
        i.   legal issues
        j.   deadly force by private guards?
        k.   inmate can't sue private prison under federal statutes

VII.   Correctional population
    A.   Historical overview
        1.   system currently holds over 2 million people
        2.   increased by 5% each year between 1925 and 1939
        3.   declined by 50,000 during World War II due to draft
        4.   steady increase in postwar era until 1961
        5.   declined about 30,000 during Vietnam era
        6.   dramatic rise till the present began in 1974
        7.   476 per 100,000 US residents are in prison, up from 411 in 1995
        8.   some evidence of recent stabilization
    B.   Chances of serving time
        1.   5.6 million adult residents have served time (1 in every 37)
        2.   blacks more likely to do time than whites or Hispanics
    C.   Why is the prison population rising?
        1.   growth linked to punitive public opinion, get tough approach
        2.   reduced judicial discretion and "truth in sentencing"
        3.   amount of time served is increasing
        4.   juveniles being tried as adults

Chapter Summary

When a person is convicted for a criminal offense, state and federal governments through their sentencing authority reserve the right to institutionally confine the offender for an extended period of time. The system of secure corrections comprises the entire range of treatment and/or punishment options available to the government, including **penitentiaries (prisons)**, **jails**, and **community corrections**. Adult felons may be placed in state or federal penitentiaries (prisons), which are usually isolated, fortress-like structures and misdemeanants are housed in county jails, sometimes called reformatories or houses of correction.

Today's correctional institutions can trace their development from European origins. In early England, the **shire reeve** or forerunner of the sheriff, served as the head jailer. Criminals were also often kept in mothballed ships called **hulks**. Punishment methods developed in Europe were modified and improved by American colonists, most notably **William Penn**. He replaced torture and mutilation with imprisonment at hard labor, fines and forfeiture. The modern correctional system has its roots in18th century Pennsylvania. Using a section of the **Walnut Street Jail**, authorities housed convicted felons in solitary cells within the **penitentiary house** or in isolation. In 1816, New York developed an alternative to the **Pennsylvania System** in the **Auburn Prison**, where prisoners ate and worked in groups during the day and were separated at night, an approach known as the **congregate system**. The prisons were built using the **tier system** of architecture.

With the rise in prison population came the development of **prison industry**. Under **contract systems** prison officials sold inmate labor to private businesses. Under **convict-lease systems** the state leased prisoners to businesses for a fixed annual fee and relinquished supervision and control. Another system allowed prisoners to produce goods for the state's use.

Many abuses occurred in prisons leading to calls for reform. Z.R. Brockway, warden of the Elmira Reformatory, advocated a "new penology" including: individualized treatment, indeterminate sentencing, **parole**, elementary education and vocational training. Until the 1960s, the courts exercised the **hands-off doctrine** toward prisons and abuses mounted. In the 1960s and 1970, the **medial model** was popular, and rehabilitation became the central focus. Since then, we have shifted to a no-frills approach known as the **penal harm movement**.

There are approximately 3,500 **jails** in the United States. These jails serve many purposes including: detaining accused offenders who cannot make or are not eligible for bail prior to trial; confining convicted offenders awaiting sentence and those convicted of misdemeanors; holding probationer and parolee violators who are awaiting a hearing; and housing felons when state prisons are overcrowded.

Closed correctional facilities, also known as **prisons**, are usually classified on three levels: **maximum**, **medium**, and **minimum security**; each with distinct characteristics. The significant rise in the prison population can be explained by the use of mandatory and determinate sentencing laws, increased eligibility for incarceration, and the limit on the availability for early release via parole. A recent shift in policy and architecture has led to the birth of the **super-maximum-security prison** for the most dangerous offenders.

Recent developments seeking to reduce **recidivism** rates, cost and alleviate overcrowding include **shock incarceration** in **boot camps**, community correctional facilities such as **halfway houses**, and **private prisons**. Privately run correctional institutions are jails and prisons operated by private companies which receive a fee for their services. There are some concerns about such institutions related to effectiveness, liability and service.

Fill-in-the-Blank Questions

1. In eighteenth century England, prisoners were often housed in mothballed ships called _____.

2. The first jails were deplorable because the jailers called _____ _____ ran them for _____ _____.

3. Under pressure from the famous Quaker reformer _____ _____, the modern prison was born in Philadelphia in 1790 when the _____ _____ Jail was opened.

4. The Auburn Prison system was known as the _____ system because most prisoners ate and worked in _____.

5. The philosophy of the Auburn system was _____ _____ through fear of punishment and _____ confinement.

6. Pennsylvania took the radical step of establishing a prison that placed each inmate in a _____ _____ located in a building called a _____ _____ for the duration of his sentence.

7. The supporters of the Pennsylvania system believed that the penitentiary was truly a place to do _____.

8. Under the _____-_____ system, the state _____ its prisoners to a business for a fixed annual fee and gave up supervision and control.

9. The _____ _____ doctrine was the judicial policy of not interfering in the administrative affairs of prisons.

10. _____ _____ jails allow for continuous observation of inmates as well as living area known as a pod.

11. Jail populations have been steadily rising, due in part to the _____ use of _____ jail sentences for common crimes such as drunk driving and to house inmates for whom there is no room in state _____.

12. A typical maximum-security facility is _____, surrounded by _____ _____ with guard towers at strategic places.

13. The byword of the maximum-security prison is _____.

14. Minimum-security prisons usually house the most _____ and the least _____ offenders.

15. Boot camps are an example of _____ incarceration whereby first-time offenders are sentenced to a sentence ranging from _____ to _____ days.

True/False Questions

T F 1.   The practice of incarcerating offenders for a long period of time as a punishment for their misdeeds did not become the norm of corrections until the 20th century.

T F 2.   The original legal punishments were typically banishment or slavery.

T F 3.   The Pennsylvania prison system took credit for the rapid decrease in the Pennsylvania crime rate that occurred between 1789 and 1793.

T F 4.   The "modern" American correctional system had its origins in New York.

T F 5.   The concept of parole was developed in America.

T F 6.   Rehabilitation was a central focus of the early American parole system.

T F 7.   Inmates at the Pennsylvania's Western Penitentiary were kept in solitary confinement almost constantly, being allowed out only for about an hour a day for exercise.

T F 8.   The Pennsylvania system reflected the influence of religion and religious philosophy on corrections.

T F 9.   The Pennsylvania system eliminated the need for large numbers of guards or disciplinary measures.

T F 10. The prisons of the late 19th century were totally dissimilar to the prisons of today.

T F 11. The development of the prison industry quickly led to the abuse of inmates.

T F 12. The rehabilitation movement of the 1960s was guided by the medical model.

T F 13. Half of jail detainees have not been convicted and are awaiting their trial.

T F 14. Alcatraz is classified as a super-maximum-security prison.

T F 15. About three-fourths of all inmates are serving time for violent offenses.

T F 16. A weak association exists between substance abuse and inmate status.

T F 17. About 80% of inmates report using drugs sometime during their life.

T F 18. There is little variation in the more than 75 shock incarceration/boot camp programs operating around the United States.

T F 19. Approximately 50,000 juveniles are admitted to adult jails each year.

T F 20. Mandatory sentencing laws have contributed to the increase in the numbers of inmates in America's prisons.

Multiple Choice Questions

1. In the first penal institutions, inmates had to pay for:
   a. food
   b. shelter
   c. services
   d. a and c

2. It was _____ whose efforts to create humane standards in the British penal system resulted in the Penitentiary Act, by which Parliament established a more orderly penal system.
   a. Alex Durham
   b. Thomas Mott Osborne
   c. John Howard
   d. William Penn

3. The first American jail was built in the _____ colonies.
   a. Virginia
   b. Massachusetts
   c. Georgia
   d. New York

4. The "modern" American correctional system has its origins in Pennsylvania under the leadership of:
   a. Alex Durham
   b. Thomas Mott Osborne
   c. John Howard
   d. William Penn

5. In 1787, the _____ formed the "Philadelphia Society for Alleviating the Miseries of Public Prison."
   a. Mormons
   b. Quakers
   c. Mennonites
   d. Moonies

6. In what state was Auburn prison located?
   a. Massachusetts
   b. Connecticut
   c. New York
   d. Alabama

7. The Auburn Prison design became known as the _____ system.
   a. tier
   b. hierarchal
   c. semicircular
   d. Quaker

8. Which prison system was known as the congregate system?
    a. the New Jersey system
    b. the Auburn system
    c. the Pennsylvania system
    d. the Newbern system

9. What was the key to discipline in the Auburn system?
    a. flogging
    b. branding
    c. prayer
    d. silence

10. The Western Penitentiary in Pennsylvania had an unusual architectural design; it had a
    _____ design.
    a. tier
    b. hierarchal
    c. semicircular
    d. Walnut Street

11. Today's American prisons are most similar to the _____ system.
    a. Auburn
    b. Western
    c. Walnut
    d. Pennsylvania

12. In a procedure known as the _____, prison officials sold the labor of
    inmates to private businesses.
    a. state account system
    b. contract system
    c. convict-lease system
    d. remuneration system

13. What was the term under the early British parole system for a conditional release that
    would permit a former prisoner to be at large in certain areas?
    a. property in service
    b. guardian system
    c. ticket-if-leave
    d. convict-lease

14. What was the underlying philosophy behind the rehabilitation movement in the 1960s?
    a. penal harm movement
    b. hands-off doctrine
    c. medical model
    d. contract system

15. The no-frills approach to prison administration is advocated by some advocates of the:
    a. penal harm movement
    b. contract system
    c. hands-off doctrine
    d. convict-lease system

16. Sing Sing, Joliet and the "The Rock" are examples of what type of prison?
    a. maximum security
    b. medium security
    c. minimum security
    d. a prison farm

17. Opposition by _____ put an end to the convict-lease system and forced inmate labor.
    a. Quakers
    b. organized labor
    c. Democrats
    d. the Bureau of Prisons

18. The byword of a maximum-security prison is what?
    a. rehabilitation
    b. security
    c. deterrence
    d. silence

19. According to the most recent statistics, about _____ of jailed inmates are not yet convicted.
    a. 25%
    b. 33%
    c. 40%
    d. 50%

20. What is the term for detaining an accused offender who cannot make bail prior to trial?
    a. post-conviction relief
    b. pretrial detention
    c. non-bail incarceration
    d. internment

21. According to the text, the purpose of jail is to _____ the mentally ill inmates and keep them separate from the rest of society.
    a. medicate
    b. manage
    c. rehabilitate
    d. incapacitate

22. There are approximately _____ inmates in the Nation's local jails and the jail population has been increasing about 5% per year.
    a. 350,000
    b. 500,000
    c. 600,000
    d. 750,000

23. Male inmates make up about _____ percent of the local jail population.
    a. 40
    b. 60
    c. 75
    d. 90

24. What is the name for a device that is used to screen inmate mail for forbidden substances?
    a. trace detector
    b. hulking device
    c. prepaid envelopes
    d. contract system

25. Which of the following is **not** a common criticism of private prisons?
    a. they cost more than state run facilities
    b. they take jobs away from state employees
    c. private companies will cut corners if left unchecked
    d. it is difficult to determine accountability for problems and mishaps

26. Which of the following is an example of a community correctional facility?
    a. hulks
    b. halfway house
    c. work camp
    d. drunk tank

Essay Questions

1. Distinguish between the Pennsylvania and Auburn systems.

2. Explain the influence of Quakers on the development of America's prisons.

3. Describe the evolution of parole from its roots in France to its early American usages at the Elmira Reformatory.

4. Discuss the three trends that shaped the direction of prisons in the era of the 1960s-1980s.

5. List the five primary purposes of the nation's jails.

6. Distinguish between the three levels of prison security.

7. Discuss the changes in design and treatment that go along with super-maximum-security prisons.

8. Discuss the benefits and shortcomings of shock incarceration programs.

9. Discuss the results of evaluation research on shock incarceration programs.

10. Discuss the pros and cons of private prisons.

CHAPTER 15 ANSWER KEY

FILL-IN-THE-BLANK QUESTIONS

1.   hulks
2.   shire reeves, personal gain
3.   William Penn, Walnut Street
4.   congregate, groups
5.   crime prevention, silent
6.   single cell, penitentiary house
7.   penance
8.   convict, lease, leased
9.   hands off
10. new generation
11. increased, mandatory, prisons
12. fortresslike, stone walls
13. security
14. trustworthy, violent
15. shock, 90, 180

TRUE/FALSE QUESTIONS

1.	F	11.	T
2.	T	12.	T
3.	T	13.	T
4.	F	14.	F
5.	F	15.	F
6.	T	16.	F
7.	T	17.	T
8.	T	18.	F
9.	T	19.	T
10.	F	20.	T

MULTIPLE CHOICE QUESTIONS

1.	D	14.	C
2.	C	15.	A
3.	A	16.	A
4.	D	17.	B
5.	B	18.	B
6.	C	19.	D
7.	A	20.	B
8.	B	21.	B
9.	D	22.	C
10.	C	23.	D
11.	A	24.	A
12.	B	25.	A
13.	D	26.	B

Chapter 16

Prison Life: Living in and Leaving Prison

Learning Objectives

At the conclusion of this chapter, the student should possess sufficient knowledge to achieve the following learning objectives:

1. Describe the total prison experience and adjustment process for inmates.

2. Describe the various elements of the inmate code.

3. Discuss the differences between prison culture today and earlier in the 20th century.

4. Compare and contrast female and male inmate cultures.

5. Discuss court rulings on inmate rights and the changes in correctional law that have occurred.

6. Describe the role of prison rehabilitation efforts.

7. Describe typical patterns of violence in prison and provide and explanation for prison violence.

8. Discuss the job roles and job stresses of the correctional officer.

9. Describe the process of parole from discretionary granting to revocation

10. Discuss how the problem of reentry has influenced the correction system.

Keywords and Definitions

Total Institutions: Inmates locked within their walls are segregated from the outside world, kept under constant scrutiny and surveillance, and forced to obey strict official rules to avoid facing formal sanctions.

Punk: Slang term for a weak inmate who is unable to protect himself form physical or sexual attacks.

Snitch: Slang term for an inmate who asks a guard for help or tells on another inmate.

Hustling: The sales of illegal commodities as drugs (uppers, downers, pot), alcohol, weapons, or illegally obtained food and supplies within the walls of a prison.

Niche: A kind of insulation from the pains of imprisonment, enabling the offender to cope and providing him or her with a sense of autonomy and freedom.

Inmate Subculture: The loosely defined culture that pervades prisons that has its own norms, rules, and language.

Inmate Social Code: Represents the values of interpersonal relations within the prison.

Argot: The unique language that influences the prison culture.

Prisonization: Assimilation into the separate culture in the prison that has its own set of rewards and behaviors.

Right Guy: Someone who uses the inmate social code as his personal behavior guide.

Deprivation Model: The view that the pains of imprisonment transform people and force them to adapt to the inmate subculture.

Importation Model: The view that the violent prison culture reflects the criminal culture of the outside world and is neither developed in nor unique to prisons.

Administrative Control Model: The view that inmate subculture is a product of the management style of the prison administration.

New Inmate Subculture: Recent development where African American and Latino inmates are much more organized along political and or religious lines, thus control the inmate subculture.

Make-Believe Family: Peer units formed by women in prison to compensate for the loss of family and loved ones that contain mother and father figures.

Therapeutic Community: Drug treatment model that uses positive peer pressure from fellow users and counselors who used to be inmates or drug abusers to combat drug use.

Less Eligibility: The idea that prisoners should always be treated less well than the most underprivileged law-abiding citizen.

Special-Needs Inmates: Those individuals who have a variety of social problems including the mentally retarded, the mentally ill, other disturbed inmates and the elderly.

Work (Furlough) Release: A prison treatment program that allows inmates to be released during the day to work in the community and returned to prison at night.

Percy Amendment: Federal legislation that allowed prison-made goods to be sold across state lines if the projects compiled with strict rules, such as making sure unions were consulted and preventing manufacturers from undercutting the existing wage structure.

Conjugal Visit: A prison program that allows inmates to receive private visits from their spouses for the purpose of maintaining normal interpersonal relationships.

Newjack: Slang term for a newly hired correctional officer.

Dothard v. Rawlinson: The Supreme Court upheld Alabama's refusal to hire female correctional officers on the grounds that it would put them in significant danger from the male inmates.

Inmate-Balance Theory: The theory that states that riots and other forms of collective action occur when prison officials make an abrupt effort to take control of the prison and limit freedoms.

Administrative-Control Theory: The theory that states that collective prison violence may also be caused by prison mismanagement, lack of strong security, and inadequate control by prison officials.

Civil Death: The custom of terminating the civil rights of convicted felons; for example, forbidding them the right to vote and marry. No state uses civil death today.

Hands-Off Doctrine: The judicial policy of not interfering in the administrative affairs of a prison.

Cooper v. Pate: The Supreme Court ruled that inmates who were being denied the right to practice their religion were entitled to redress under 42 U.S.C. 1983.

DeMallory v. Cullen: The Supreme Court said an untrained paralegal is not a constitutionally acceptable alternative to law library access.

Lindquist v. Idaho State Board of Corrections: The Supreme Court ruled that seven inmate law clerks for a prison population of 950 were sufficient legal representation since they had a great deal of experience.

Smith v. Wade: The Supreme Court decision that an inmate who has been raped can have access to the state court to sue a correctional officer for failing to protect the inmate from aggressive inmates.

Bounds v. Smith: The Supreme Court held that state correctional systems are obligated to provide inmates with either adequate law libraries or the help of people trained in the law.

Shaw v. Murphy: Case in which the Supreme Court ruled that an inmate does not have a right to correspond via mail with other inmates, even if the inmate is requesting legal advise.

Turner v. Safley: The Supreme Court ruling that prisoners do not have a right to receive mail from one another; inmate mail can be banned if the reason is "related to legitimate penological interests.

Ramos v. Lamm: The Supreme Court held that the institutional policy of refusing to deliver mail in a language other than English is unconstitutional.

Procunier v. Martinez: The Supreme Court decision that censorship of a prisoner's mail is justified only when (a) there exists substantial government interest in maintaining the censorship to further prison security, order, and rehabilitation, and (b) the restrictions are not greater or more stringent than is demanded by security precautions.

Nolan v. Fitzpatrick: The Supreme Court decision that prisoners may correspond with newspapers unless their letters discuss escape plans or contain contraband or otherwise objectionable material.

Mumin v. Phelps: The Supreme Court decision that if there is a legitimate penological interest, inmates can be denied special privileges to attend religious services.

O'Lone v, Estate of Shabazz: The Supreme Court held that prison officials can assign inmates work schedules that make it impossible for them to attend religious services as long as no reasonable alternative exists.

Rahman v. Stephenson: The Supreme Court stated that a prisoner's rights are not violated if the administration refuses to use the prisoner's religious name on official records.

Exceptional Circumstances Doctrine: Using this policy, the courts would only hear those cases involving the right to medical treatment in which circumstances totally disregarded human dignity, while denying hearings to less serious cases.

Newman v. Alabama: The Supreme Court decision that the entire Alabama prison system's medical facilities were declared inadequate due to factors such as insufficient physician and nurse resources; reliance on untrained inmates for paramedical work; intentional failure in treating the sick and injured; and failure to conform to proper medical standards.

Estelle v. Gamble: The Supreme Court mandated an inmates right to medical care stating "deliberate indifference to serious medical needs of prisoners constitutes the 'unnecessary and wanton infliction of pain,' proscribed by the Eighth Amendment."

Cruel and Unusual Punishment: Physical punishment that is far in excess of that given to people under similar circumstances and is therefore banned by the Eighth Amendment.

Jackson v. Bishop: Supreme Court case condemning corporal punishment in prison

Hope v. Pelzer et al.: The Supreme Court ruled that a correctional officer who knowingly violates the Eighth Amendment rights of an inmate can be held liable for damages.

Farmer v. Brennan: The Supreme Court ruling that prison officials are legally liable if knowing that an inmate faces a serious risk of harm disregards that risk by failing to take measures to avoid it or reduce it and that prison officials should be able to infer the risk from the evidence at hand; they need not be warned or told.

Estelle v. Ruiz: The Supreme Court ordered the Texas Department of Corrections to provide new facilities to alleviate overcrowding, to abolish the practice of using trustees, to lower the staff-to-inmate ratio, and to improve treatment services, and to adhere to the principles of procedural due process in dealing with inmates.

The Prison Litigation Reform Act of 1996: Limited the number of prison cases in federal court by providing that "no action shall be brought with respect to prison conditions" by an inmate in either federal or state prison "until such administrative remedies as are available are exhausted."

Parole: The early release of a prisoner from imprisonment subject to conditions set by a parole board.

Mandatory Parole Release: System whereby an inmate's release date is established at the beginning of the confinement period based on a percentage of time to be served. Rule violations can result in delays in the release.

Pennsylvania Bd. Of Probation and Parole v. Scott: The Supreme Court held that the exclusionary rule for illegally-obtained evidence did not apply to revocation proceedings.

Technical Parole Violation: Revocation of parole because conditions set by correctional authorities have been violated.

Intensive Supervision Parole: The program that uses limited caseload sizes, treatment facilities, the matching of parolee and supervisor by personality, and shock parole.

Chapter Outline

I.   Introduction
     A.   Prison system in crisis
          1.   high recidivism rates
          2.   failed rehabilitation
          3.   old, decrepit prisons
              a.   25 built before 1875
              b.   79 built between 1875 and 1924
              c.   141 built between 1925 and 1949
          4.   inmates resent conditions
          5.   correctional officers are fearful and tense
     B.   Overcrowded correctional system
          1.   most prisons are medium security but the majority of inmates are in maximum
          2.   large prisons with 1,000+ capacity arte the norm
          3.   operating above stated capacity
          4.   program space has been converted to living space

II.   Men imprisoned
     A.   The total institution
          1.   inmates locked away from outside world
          2.   forced to obey strict rules and schedules
          3.   personal property confiscated
          4.   human functions are curtailed
     B.   Living in prison
          1.   classification/ reception center
               a.   stripped, searched, shorn, and assigned living quarters upon arrival
              b.   tests to evaluate personality, background, offending, and needs follow
              c.   short-term stay to determine appropriate security level and institution
          2.   permanent assignment
              a.   effectiveness of placement
              b.   assigned a cell in general population
          3.   loss of liberty and privacy

C. Adjusting to prison
   1. learning the ins and outs of prison
      a. adjusting to boredom and loneliness
      b. gauging fellow inmates
      c. protecting themselves from victimization
      d. repeat customers have less to learn
   2. prison cliques
      a. groups based background or personal or political interest
      b. predatory personal and economic offenders
      c. snitches seek protection and segregation
   3. coping behavior
      a. each inmate has their own method and style of coping
      b. trial and error
      c. must learn to deal with correctional officers
      d. decide on hard time or easy time
      e. forced ideleness
      f. find a niche for themselves
      g. learning the black market and hustlers
         i. contraband suppliers
         ii. control of the market sparks violence
      h. developing social support network of peers
      i. difficult to predict who will adjust well and who will not
D. Prison culture
   1. inmate subculture made of unique set of norms and rules
   2. inmate social code
      a. passed on from generation to generation of inmates
      b. do not interfere with other inmates' interests
      c. handle grievances personally not via snitching
      d. limit emotional displays
      f. don't exploit fellow inmates
      g. be tough and be a man
      h. don't be a sucker to other inmates or administration
      i. keep your word
   3. Donald Clemmer's concept of prisonization
      a. learning the prison language
      b. learning sex roles
      c. learning norms
   4. development of the prison culture
      a. deprivation model
         i. product of prison life
         ii. pains of imprisonment cause changes in behaviour and attitude
      b. importation model
         i. inmates bring the culture into prison with them
         ii. culture shaped by newcomers and outside events
      c. administrative control model
         i. shaped by management style of administration
         ii. formal vs. informal structure shape inmate behaviors and attitudes
      d. the "new" inmate culture
         i. precipitated by Black Power movement
         ii. black and Latin inmates more organized than white inmates

              iii.   groups form along religious or political lines
              iv.   ethnic street gangs
              v.   racial polarity and tension is predominate force in prison
              vi.   rape is a common problem
       5.   long term prisonization can be destructive

III.   Women imprisoned
    A.   History
         1.   small female inmate populations prior to 1960's
         2.   4 female prisons built between 1930 and 1950
         3.   34 built during the 1980s
         4.   female inmates were traditionally viewed as morally depraved people
         5.   racial differences in treatment
    B.   Female population boom
         1.   increase of 100% since 1986
         2.   accelerated crime rates for women exceed those of men
         3.   get tough crime policies and sentencing add to growth
    C.   Female institutions
         1.   smaller than male prisons
         2.   many are minimum security institutions
         3.   some similar to college dorms
         4.   lack treatment programs
         5.   few vocational programs
         6.   genedered training
    D.   The female inmate
         1.   young
         2.   minority group member
         3.   unmarried
         4.   undereducated
         5.   underemployed
         6.   had a troubled family life
         7.   has children
         8.   substance abuse problems
         9.   high risk of exposure to HIV
    E.   Sexual exploitation
         1.   reports of sexual abuse of female inmates by staff
              a.   lewd remarks
              b.   voyeurism
              c.   rape
         2.   new laws and training seek to curb the abuses
         3.   a lack of reporting and follow up
    F.   Adapting to prison
         1.   experience and perpetrate less violence than men
         2.   confinement produces anxiety
         3.   less rigid inmate code
         4.   women experience anxiety and may commit self destructive acts
         5.   make believe families
              a.   mothers and fathers
              b.   formalized marriages and divorces
              c.   multiple roles
              d.   primary roles are sister-sister or mother-daughter

IV.   Correctional treatment methods
    A.   rehabilitation is hard to achieve
        1.   expensive providers
        2.   understaffing
        3.   philosophy of less eligibility
        4.   ignorance regarding effectiveness
    B.   Counselling programs
        1.   individual or group programs aimed at cognitive or psychosocial deficits
        2.   therapeutic communities
            a.   drug treatment model
            b.   experiential learning based on peer pressure and mutual self-help
            c.   structured social environment including staff and participants
            d.   staff are often recovering addicts or ex-cons
            e.   provides a transition from institutional to community existencxe
        3.   stimulate inmate self-awareness
        4.   utilize any number of techniques
    C.   Treating the special-needs inmate
        1.   may suffer physical and mental problems
        2.   the elderly inmate
            a.   longer sentences produce greying population
            b.   loners who experience depression and anxiety
            c.   chronic illnesses
            d.   may require special treatment or facilities
        3.   the drug-dependant inmate
            a.   lack of funding and inadequate programs
            b.   experimental efforts underway
        4.   the AIDS-infected inmate
            a.   prison life-style creates high risk situation
            b.   estimated at 362 in every 100,000 inmates
            c.   25,000 HIV infected inmates
            d.   inmates have a rate 5 times that of the total U.S. population
            e.   proper treatment difficult and costly
        5.   inmates with families
            a.   conjugal visits with spouse
            b.   private visits for the entire family
            c.   keeping inmate parents connected to children
    D.   Educational and vocational programs
        1.   educational programs
            a.   first treatment programs were educational at Walnut Street Jail
            b.   opportunity to obtain GED or high school diploma
               i.   41% of inmates lack high school degree
               ii.   26% get GED while in prison
            c.   opportunity to obtain college degree
            d.   innovative responses to inadequate funding for education programs
               i.   volunteers
               ii.   flex schedules
               iii.   statewide prison school districts
        2.   vocational services
            a.   basic prison industries
               i.   food services

      ii.   maintenance

      iii.. laundry

      iv. agriculture

   b. vocational training

      i.   most institutions provide vocational training

      ii.   training for carpentry, textile, service sector

   c. work release

      i.   supplement training or education programs

      ii.   live in institution at night, work in community during the day

      iii. may operate a community-based prerelease center

   d. vocational training for female offenders

      i.   especially deficient

      ii.   stress traditional women's work

      iii. sewing is most common vocational program

      iv. plans to expand programs

   e. private prison enterprises

      i.   Free Venture program

      ii.   Prison Industry Enhancement projects

      iii. Percy Amendment

      iv. state-use model

      v.   free enterprise model

   f. post-release programs

      i.   employment services that ease transition into community

      ii.   job counselling

      iii. skills assessment

E.   Inmate self-help

   1.   inmates organize themselves to help each other out

   2.   national chapters such as Alcoholics Anonymous

   3.   groups organized along racial and ethnic lines

   4.   groups to aid transition into society such as Fortune Society

F.   Can rehabilitation work?

   1.   Martinson report finds that "nothing works"

   2.   follow up research finds evidence that treatment may increase recidivism

   3.   conservative response- no frills movement

   4.   many still believe in rehabilitation and keep programs alive

G.   Treatment problems

   1.   lack of funds and facilities

   2.   low levels of participation

   3.   lack of diagnosis

V.   Guarding the institution

A. Correctional officers

   1.   play a number of roles and face complex task

   2.   duality of expectations

      a. maintain order and security

      b. advocate treatment and rehabilitation

   3.   increased emphasis on training and education

   4.   less tight knit than police officers

   5.   danger, tension and opposition from inmates

   6.   newjack- becoming a correctional officer

      a. cannot show fear

           b.   deviant side of being guard

           c.   violent side of himself

           d.   boredom interrupted by adrenaline rush

    B.   Female correctional officers

        1.   5,000 assigned to male institutions

        2.   *Dothard v. Rawlinson* - refusal to hire females if it places them in danger from male inmates is upheld by the Court

        3.   sexual assaults on female officers are rare

        4.   more negative attitudes from male peers than inmates

VI.   Prison violence

    A.   Types of violence

        1.   individual violence

           a.   sexual or physical assault on another inmate

               i.   20% claim to be raped during prison term

               ii.   Prison Rape Reduction Act of 2003

           b.   various explanations of inmate violence

               i.   violent problem-solvers

               ii.   prison environment breeds violence

               iii.   lack of conflict resolution options in prison

               iv.   code of silence

        2.   collective violence

           a.   riots or gang violence

           b.   possible explanations

               i.   inmate balance

               ii.   administrative control theory

               iii.   overcrowding

        3.   Inmate on staff violence

        4.   Staff on inmate violence

    B.   Reducing violence and disturbances through technology

        1.   ground penetrating radar

        2.   heartbeat monitoring

        3.   satellite monitoring

        4.   pulsed radar

        5.   sticky shocker

        6.   back-scatter imaging system for concealed weapons

        7.   body scanning screening system

        8.   transmitter wristbands

        9.   personal health status monitor

        10.   all-in-one drug detection spray

        11.   radar vital signs monitor, radar flashlight

        12.   personal alarm location system

        13.   angel chip

        14.   non-invasive body cavity scanner

        15.   non-invasive drug detection

VII.   Prisoners rights

    A.   Prior to 1960s

        1.   inmates had no civil rights – civilly dead

        2.   the "hands off" doctrine – only intervene for serious breach of 8th Amendment

3. justifications for Court's avoidance
   a. technical matter best left to experts
   b. apathetic society
   c. complaints involved privileges not rights
B. Prisoners' rights crusade from 1960 to 1980
   1. civil rights movement accelerated court intervention in prison administration
   2. use of Federal Civil Rights Act, 42 U.S.C. 1983
   3. *Cooper v. Pate*- recognized the right of prisoners to sue for civil rights violations
      a. focused narrowly on religious rights
      b. opened the door for subsequent suits
C. Substantive rights
   1. access to courts, legal services, and materials
      a. *DeMallory v. Cullen* – inmate paralegal is not acceptable representation
      b. *Lindquist v. Idaho State Board of Corrections* – inmate law clerks with experience are acceptable representation
      c. *Smith v. Wade* – rape victims can sue guard for lack of protection
      d. *Bounds v. Smith* – law libraries and trained representation reuired
   2. freedom of the press and expression
      a. traditionally censored mail and restricted reading material
      b. compelling state interest must now be demonstrated when modifying inmates' First Amendment rights
      c. *Turner v. Safley* – can limit inmate mail in case of penological interests
      d. *Ramos v. Lamm* – cannot limit the delivery of non-English mail
      e. *Pecunier v. Martinez* – compelling state interest needed to limit mail
      f. *Nolan v. Fitzgerald* – inmate can correspond with newspapers in limited fashion
      g. *Shaw v. Murphy* – no right to inmate-to-inmate correspondence
   3. freedom of religion
      a. guaranteed under the First Amendment
      b. right to assemble and pray in the religion of choice
      c. symbols and practices may be restricted if interfere with security
      d. special privileges can be applied
      e. *Mumin v. Phelps* – legitimate penal interest may limit religious services
      f. *O'Leone v. Estate of Shabazz* – inmate work schedule need not be altered for religious services
      g. *Rahman v. Stephenson* – Prison need not acknowledge inmate's religious name on prison records
   4. medical rights
      a. past policy was to restrict medical rights through the exceptional circumstances doctrine
      b. inmates generally use class action suits in these cases
      c. *Newman v. Alabama* - entire Alabama medical system declared inadequate
      d. *Estelle v. Gamble* – used deliberate indifference standard to mandate inmate's right to medical care
   5. cruel and unusual punishment
      a. Eighth Amendment protections
      b. cannot degrade human dignity
      c. cannot apply disproportional punishment

          d.   cannot use punishment that shocks the conscience or is
                 fundamentally unfair
          e.   cannot punish on the basis of status (race, religion, mental state)
          f.   cannot apply capricious punishment in flagrant disregard of due
                 process
          g.   *Jackson v. Bishop* - outlaws corporal punishment
          h.   Hope v. Pelzer et al. – prison officials are liable for abuses
      6.   overall prison conditions
          a.   inmates have a right to minimum standards for survival
          b.   *Farrmer v. Brennan* – officials liable for not reducing possible harm
          c.   *Estelle v. Ruiz* – mandated total overhaul of the Texas prison system
      7.   prisoners' rights today
          a.   more conservative court has curtailed some substantive rights
          b.   Prison Litigation Reform Act of 1996 – no inmate suits move
                 forward until all administrative remedied have been exhausted

VIII.   Leaving prison
     A.   Release mechanisms
          1.   parole
          2.   determinate release
          3.   commutation
          4.   mandatory release
     B.   Parole
          1.   determined by statutory requirement
          2.   granted by parole board and supervised by parole agent in community
             a.   discretionary parole allows boards discretion on release date and
                 terms
             b.   mandatory parole release specifies release point barring infractions
             c.   good time models allow time to be reduced by inmate compliance
          3.   650,000 people on parole
     C.   The parole board
          1.   four primary functions
             a.   select and place inmates on parole
             b.   aid, supervise, and control parolees in community
             c.   discharge parolee when parole function is deemed complete
             d.   revocation decisions
          2.   usually independent agencies of government
          3.   board usually number less than ten members
     D.   Parole hearings
        1.   full board or subcommittee reviews
        2.   may or may not meet with applicant
        3.   hearing involves review of pertinent information
        4.   inmate rights at hearing vary by jurisdiction
        5.   *Pennsylvania Bd of Probation & Parole v. Scott* –exclusionary rule does not
             apply to evidence used in parole revocation hearings
    E.   Parolees in the community
        1.   failure to comply may result in revocation
        2.   parole is a privilege for deserving inmates
        3.   conflict exists between treatment and supervision functions
        4.   Parole supervision is similar to probation supervision

F. Intensive supervision parole
   1. use of salient factor score or a point/guideline system to classify parole risk
   2. officers supervise smaller caseloads with more attention for each
G. The effectiveness of parole
   1. 68% rearrested within 3 years of release
      a. 47% reconvicted
      b. 25% return to prison
   2. murder, rape, and sexual assault have lowest recidivism rates
   3. one quarter of a million persons victimized annually by parolees
   4. parolees destabilize the community upon their return
H. Problems of parole
   1. prison stay does not resolve psychological and economic problems of offender
   2. social and economic consequences of imprisonization
   3. problems of reentry
      a. mandatory release stunts interest in rehabilitation efforts of inmate
      b. seek to make up for lost time on the streets
      c. prison produces medical and mental health problems
      d. fear of prison is lessened
      e. substance abuse
   4. parolees lose rights
      a. forbid from certain types of employment
      b. licensure limitations
      c. restricted movement
      d. no voting rights
      e. no parental rights
      f. grounds for divorce
      g. no jury duty
      h. no more public service
      i. no gun ownership
      j. registration and notice of residence
      k. civil death maintained

Chapter Summary

The average male inmate in American prisons is young, male, minority, poor, drug/alcohol abuser, and undereducated. American prisons are **total institutions**, with inmates completely segregated from the outside world, so inmates must learn to adjust to prison life. Some turn to the black market, or the hustle, selling illegal commodities. Many, finding themselves confronted by racial conflict, resort to segregation. Some seek to find their **niche** in the institution. **Punks** are inmates that cannot protect themselves from physical or sexual victimization. **Snitches** are inmates who turn to guars for help. Most inmates have a tendency to adhere to the unwritten rules of the **inmate subculture**. Those inmates who live by **the inmate social codes** are deemed **"right guys"** by fellow inmates. **Prisonization** is the process by which inmates assimilate into prison culture. Scholars have formulated the **deprivation model**, the **importation model**, or the **administrative control model** to explain this process. A **new inmate culture** has emerged that is divided along racial and ethnic lines.

The female crime rate is rising at a rate much faster than the male crime rate. The number of female prisoners has increased due to mandatory and determinate sentencing. Women's institutions tend to be less secure and smaller than men's institutions. Female inmates, like their male counterparts, have a tendency to be young, single, minority and undereducated. While the typical male inmate was a violent offender, female inmates have committed drug offenses. One problem associated especially with female incarceration is the disruption of family life. As a result, they often form **make-believe families** with other inmates to cope with the stress and loneliness.

Almost every prison facility employs some mode of treatment for inmates. This may come in the form of group counseling, educational, or vocational training. Substance abuse programs are often organized around the **therapeutic community** model stressing positive peer support. To supplement programs stressing rehabilitation, a number of states have implemented **work-release** or furlough programs, where the deserving inmates leave the institution and hold regular jobs in the community. **Conjugal visits** are another form of treatment where prisoners are able to have private meetings with their wives and family on a regular basis. Finally, prisoners are normally expected to work within the institution as part of their treatment program in areas such as food services, maintenance, laundry, and agriculture. Problems with such programs include inadequate funding and administration as well as the growing number of **special-needs inmates** such as mentally ill, elderly, drug-dependent, and AIDS-infected prisoners.

Guarding the institution is often very stressful and involves considerable role conflict. Female correctional officers are especially susceptible to abuse and ridicule from inmates and male peers. *Dothard v. Rawlingson* upheld Alabama's refusal to hire female guards for male facilities on the basis of security concerns.

Prisons are violent places with high levels of physical and sexual victimization. There exists individual violence and collective violence in the form of riots. Riots are explained using either the **inmate-balance theory** or the **administrative control theory**.

Prior to 1960, it was accepted that upon conviction an incarcerated individual forfeited all rights not expressly granted by statutory law or correctional policy. State and federal courts were reluctant to intervene in the administration of prisons unless the circumstances of a case clearly indicated a serious breach of the Eighth Amendment's protection against cruel and unusual punishment; this judicial policy is referred to as the **hands-off doctrine**. Inmates were often declared **civilly dead**, having all of their civil rights stripped from them for life. As the 1960's drew to a close, however, the hands-off doctrine underwent a process of erosion when activist groups began to utilize the courts. In the 1964 case of *Cooper v. Pate*, the Supreme Court recognized the right of prisoners to sue for civil rights violations in cases involving religious freedom. While this case applied to a narrow issue, it opened the door to providing other rights for inmates.

A major concern for the prisoners' rights movement was to increase the **substantive rights** of inmates. These rights include: access to courts, legal services and materials; freedom of the press and expression; freedom of religion; medical rights; freedom from **cruel and unusual punishment**; and the right to minimum conditions necessary for survival. Since 1980, a more conservative Court has curtailed some rights of prisoners, reverting to the hands-off doctrine.

Parole is the planned community release and supervision of incarcerated offenders prior to the actual expiration of their prison sentences. It is usually considered a way of completing a prison sentence in the community. The decision to parole is determined by statutory requirement and usually involves completion of a minimum sentence, less any good-time or special release credits. Newly devised **mandatory parole release** works in conjunction with conservative sentencing models to identify, at the start of confinement, a predetermined release date based on a set proportion of time served. Before being released into the community, a parolee is supplied with a set of parole rules that guide their behavior and sets limits on their activities. If, at any time, these rules are violated, the offender can be returned to the institution to serve the remainder of the sentence; this is known as a **technical parole violation**. The offender's parole can also be revoked by committing a new offense while in the community. **Intensive supervision parole (ISP)** is a form of parole characterized by smaller caseloads and more intense supervision for serious offenders. **Reentry** into free society is often a problem for inmates, causing high rates of recidivism.

Fill-in-the-Blank Questions

1. The inmate _____ _____ is a set of values and norms passed from generation to generation. Clemmer coined the term _____ process to refer to an inmate's adjustment to the norms of prison life.

2. Total institutions means that inmates locked within their walls are _____ from the outside world, kept under constant _____ and _____, and forced to obey the strict rules to avoid facing _____ sanctions.

3. Personal losses in prison include the deprivation of _____, goods and services, _____ relationships, autonomy, and _____.

4. Inmates may go through a variety of _____ and _____ _____, or cycles, as their sentences unfold.

5. _____ is the sale of such illegal commodities as drugs, alcohol, weapons, or illegally obtained food and supplies.

6. Inmates develop their own language or _____ to communicate. For example, a _____ is a term for an inmate who is unable to protect one's self and a _____ is a term to describe an inmate who turns to guards for help.

7. Women's prisons tend to be _____ in size than those housing male inmates and the majority of female prisons tend to be _____ institutions.

8. There is actually _____ _____ in major drug use between male and female offenders when measured over their _____ _____.

9. A _____-_____ family in a women's prison contains masculine and feminine figures acting as _____ and _____; some even act as _____ and take on the role of brother or sister.

10. The _____ model attributes inmate subculture to the pains of imprisonment that exist inside the walls of the institution while the _____ model suggests that the culture is shaped from the outside by the values and norms of incoming inmates.

11. Traditionally, the four basic prison industries have been food service, _____, _____, and _____.

12. Alcoholics Anonymous or the Fortune Society are examples of inmate _____-_____ programs

13. The greatest problem faced by prison guards is the _____ of their role as _____ of order and security and _____ of treatment and rehabilitation.

14. In _____ the Supreme Court ordered the Texas Department of Corrections to provide new facilities to alleviate overcrowding, to abolish the practice of using trustees, to lower the staff-to-inmate ratio, and to improve treatment services, and to adhere to the principles of procedural due process in dealing with inmates.

15. Once released into the community, the offender normally comes under the control of a _____ _____.

True/False Questions

T F 1. Prison overcrowding does not usually pose a threat to meaningful treatment efforts.

T F 2. Some state prison systems have banned cigarettes.

T F 3. Part of living in prison involves learning to protect oneself and developing survival instincts.

T F 4. Research has shown that heterosexual male inmates often turn to homosexual sex in prison.

T F 5. Argot refers to the unique set of norms and rules that the inmates form.

T F 6. Minority inmates are more tightly organized than whites in the new inmate culture of today.

T F 7. The importation model is the most likely explanation for defining the way inmates adopt to the prison culture.

T F 8. Rape as a means of expressing dominance, power, and anger is now an accepted prison norm.

T F 9. Before 1960, women were overrepresented in prison.

T F 10. Since many female inmates are parents and had custody of their children before their incarceration, a great deal of effort has been made to help them develop parenting skills.

T F 11. Female inmates usually have access to more meaningful prison work opportunities than male inmates.

T F 12. Female inmates tend to be older, white, unmarried, undereducated, and unemployed.

T F 13. The rigid, antiauthority inmate social code found in many male institutions also exists in female institutions.

T F 14. Despite good intentions, rehabilitative treatment within prison walls is extremely difficult to achieve.

T F 15. At the turn of the twentieth century, black female inmates were often housed in male prisons.

T F 16. The two groups of inmates at high risk for contracting the HIV virus are intravenous drug users who share needles and males who engage in homosexual acts.

T F 17. Under the Prison Litigation and Reform Act of 1996, inmates do not have to exhaust administrative remedies prior to bringing a suit in state or federal court.

T F 18. About 15% of prison inmates are released after serving their entire maximum sentence without any time excused or forgiven.

T F 19. The decision to parole is always determined by statutory requirement.

T F 20. Illegally-obtained evidence cannot be used in parole revocation hearings.

T F 21. Before the 1960s, it was the norm for convicted criminals to forfeit all rights and be declared civilly dead in the eyes of the state.

Multiple Choice Questions

1. More than _____ of all inmates are being held in large, maximum-security prisons.
   a. one-fourth
   b. one-third
   c. half
   d. three-fourths

2. Which of the following is **not** a characteristic of a total institution?
   a. individuals are segregated from the outside world
   b. individuals are forced to obey strict rules
   c. human functions are curtailed severely
   d. all of the above

3.	The _____ inmates are the ones who report that they have more difficulty with correctional officers.
	a.	younger
	b.	older
	c.	male
	d.	female

4.	The predominant emotion that male inmates must confront in in the early part of their prison term is:
	a.	depression
	b.	loneliness
	c.	hate
	d.	boredom

5.	What is the name given to an inmate that cannot defend himself from victimization?
	a.	snitch
	b.	punk
	c.	easy time
	d.	right guy

6.	The inmate's assimilation into the existing prison culture through acceptance of its language, sexual code, and norms of behavior is called _____.
	a.	social code.
	b.	argot.
	c.	prisonization.
	d.	inmate subculture.

7.	The _____ is the inmate who uses the inmate social code as his personal behavior guide.
	a.	right guy
	b.	punk
	c.	snitch
	d.	guider

8	Which of these is considered to be a white prison gang?
	a.	the Aryan Brotherhood
	b.	the Michigan Militia
	c.	the Vice Lords
	d.	the Caucasian Rangers

9.	The change from the "old inmate" culture to the "new inmate" culture seems to have been precipitated by the _____ in the 1960s and 1970s.
	a.	get tough policy
	b.	flower power movement
	c.	move to the hands-on doctrine
	d.	Black Power movement

10. What was the predominant societal view of female inmates at the turn of the 20th century?
    a. depraved people who flaunted conventional rules of female behavior
    b. hardened criminals similar to their male counterparts
    c. sinners in need of religion
    d. witches who should be burned at the stake

11. What factor is most responsible for the harsh treatment that women now receive from the courts?
    a. mandatory and determinate sentencing statutes
    b. the women's liberation movement
    c. the construction of new female institutions
    d. the increasing number of female judges

12. Prison administrators have been found to have a _____ concern for special-needs inmates.
    a. little
    b. great
    c. genuine
    d. no

13. Most inmates with AIDS are in the _____ population.
    a. general inmate
    b. administrative segregation
    c. inmate hospital
    d. special AIDS

14. Approximately _____ female correctional officers are assigned to all male institutions.
    a. 1,000
    b. 3,000
    c. 5,000
    d. 9,000

15. The Supreme Court, in _____, upheld Alabama's refusal to hire female correctional officers on the grounds that it would put them in significant danger from the male inmates.
    a. *Cooper v. Pate*
    b. *Dothard v. Rawlinson*
    c. *DeMallory v. Cullen*
    d. *Lindquist v. Idaho Board of Corrections*

16. In _____, the Supreme Court ruled that inmates who were being denied the right to practice their religion were entitled to legal redress under 42 U.S.C. 1983.
    a. *Cooper v. Pate*
    b. *Dothard v. Rawlinson*
    c. *DeMallory v. Cullen*
    d. *Lindquist v. Idaho Board of Corrections*

17. What is the term for a drug treatment program that relies on positive peer pressure?
    a. behavior modification
    b. milieu therapy
    c. therapeutic community
    d. transactional analysis

18. The Supreme Court held in _____ that seven inmate law clerks for a prison population of 950 were sufficient legal representation since they had a great deal of experience.
    a. *Cooper v. Pate*
    b. *Dothard v. Rawlinson*
    c. *DeMallory v. Cullen*
    d. *Lindquist v. Idaho Board of Corrections*

19. The _____ opinion of the Supreme Court ruled that state correctional systems are obligated to provide inmates with either adequate law libraries or the help of people trained in the law.
    a. *Bounds v. Smith*
    b. *Ramos v. Lamm*
    c. *Smith v. Wade*
    d. *Turner v. Safley*

20. The Supreme Court's opinion in _____ held that prisoners do not have a right to receive mail from one another because inmate-to-inmate mail can be banned if the reason is "related to legitimate penological interests."
    a. *Bounds v. Smith*
    b. *Ramos v. Lamm*
    c. *Smith v. Wade*
    d. *Turner v. Safley*

21. The Supreme Court decided in _____ that the institutional policy of refusing to deliver mail in a language other than English is unconstitutional.
    a. *Bounds v. Smith*
    b. *Ramos v. Lamm*
    c. *Smith v. Wade*
    d. *Turner v. Safley*

22 . Allowing inmates to have private overnight meetings with their spouse or family is what type of visit?
    a. long term
    b. conjugal
    c. sexual
    d. psychological

23. Withholding medical treatment is a violation of which Constitutional amendment?
    a. the First
    b. the Fourth
    c. the Eighth
    d. the Fourteenth

24. Approximately how many inmates escape from prison each year?
    a.   500
    b.   1,200
    c.   4,500
    d.   7,000

25. What model of early release sets an inmate's release date at the beginning of the term of confinement based on a percentage of the inmate's sentence to be served?
    a.   discretionary parole release
    b.   mandatory parole release
    c.   time served release
    d.   truth-in-sentencing model

26. Which of the following types of offenders have the lowest recidivism rates?
    a.   burglars
    b.   robbers
    c.   motor vehicle thieves
    d.   rapists

Essay Questions

1.   Discuss the reasons for the female offender population rising so rapidly.

2.   Describe the structure and process of a therapeutic community.

3. Discuss the benefits and weaknesses of work release and furlough programs.

4. Explain the private prison enterprise, focusing on the Percy Amendment and the "state-use model."

5. Compare and contrast the inmate balance and administrative control theories on prison riots.

6. Discuss the principles of the hands-off doctrine and how it shaped prisoners' rights prior to 1960.

7. Describe the three models of prison management.

8. Describe the criteria used by the Courts in determining whether a punishment constitutes cruel and unusual conduct.

9. List the four primary functions of a parole board.

10. Explain why many released inmates have a difficult time adjusting to general society.

CHAPTER 16 ANSWER KEY

FILL-IN-THE-BLANK QUESTIONS

1. social code, prisonization
2. segregated, scrutiny, surveillance, formal
3. liberty, heterosexual, security
4. attitude, behavior changes
5. hustling
6. argot, punk, snitch
7. smaller, nonsecure
8. little difference, life span
9. make, believe, fathers, mothers, children
10. deprivation, importation
11. maintenance, laundry, agriculture
12. self, help
13. duality, maintainers, advocates
14. *Estelle v. Ruiz*
15. parole agent

TRUE/FALSE QUESTIONS

1.	F	12.	F
2.	T	13.	F
3.	T	14.	T
4.	T	15.	T
5.	F	16.	T
6.	T	17.	F
7.	F	18.	T
8.	T	19.	T
9.	F	20.	F
10.	F	21.	F
11.	T		

MULTIPLE CHOICE QUESTIONS

1.	C	14.	C
2.	D	15.	B
3.	A	16.	A
4.	D	17.	C
5.	B	18.	D
6.	C	19.	A
7.	A	20.	D
8.	A	21.	B
9.	D	22.	B
10.	A	23.	D
11.	A	24.	D
12.	C	25.	B
13.	A	26.	D

Chapter 17

The Juvenile Justice System

Learning Objectives

At the conclusion of this chapter the student should possess sufficient knowledge to achieve the following learning objectives:

1.   Provide an historical review of the evolution of juvenile justice in England and the United States.

2.   Discuss the differences between delinquents and status offenders.

3.   Discuss the problems that faced the child-saving movement.

4.   Describe the development of the juvenile court and the arguments against its continuation.

5.   Discuss the differences between the juvenile and adult justice process.

6.   Describe the legal rights of children.

7.   Describe the various stages of the juvenile justice process.

8.   Describe the typical juvenile institution and proved a profile of the typical juvenile inmate.

9.   Discuss the concept of deinstitutionalization.

10. Describe the various juvenile institutions.

Keywords and Definitions

Juvenile Justice System: A system of agencies and organizations that deal with youths who commit acts of juvenile delinquency (crimes under a given age) and acts of non-criminal behavior (truancy and incorrigibility).

***Parens Patriae*:** The Latin term for "parent of his country;" refers to the power of the state to act on behalf of the child and provide care and protection equivalent to that of a parent.

Balanced and Restorative Justice Model: A new model of juvenile justice focusing on victim restoration, improving offender abilities, and protecting the public. Offenders, victims, and the community are all active partners.

Poor Laws: Seventeenth-century laws in England that bound out vagrants and abandoned and neglected children to masters as indentured servants.

Chancery Courts: Those English courts founded on the proposition that children and other incompetents were under the protective control of the king.

***Wellesley v. Wellesley*:** The famous English case in which a duke's children were taken from him in the name of *parens patriae* because of his scandalous behavior.

Child Savers: Late nineteenth century reformers in America who developed programs for troubled youths and influenced legislation creating the juvenile justice system.

Children's Aid Society: A nineteenth century civic group formed by New York philanthropist Charles Loring Brace to place indigent city children with farm families.

Juvenile Court: Courts that have original jurisdiction over persons defined by statute as juveniles and alleged to be delinquents or status offenders.

Juvenile Delinquency: The term used by the government for the participation in illegal behavior by a minor who falls under a statutory age limit.

Status Offender: A juvenile who has been adjudicated by a judge of a juvenile court as having committed a status offense (running away, truancy, incorrigibility).

Reform School: Facilities used to house juvenile delinquents in the early 20th century. Intended as state training schools, in reality they subject kids to hard work and punishment.

Illinois Juvenile Court Act of 1899: Established the first independent juvenile court to handle criminal law violations by persons under the age of 16 as well as cases of neglect and wayward youth.

Juvenile Justice and Delinquency Prevention Act of 1974: Federal statute creating the Office of Juvenile Justice and Delinquency Prevention (OJJDP) to identify needs of youth and fund programs in the area of juvenile justice. The principle goal was to separate juvenile offenders from the adult criminal justice system.

***Fare v. Michael C.*:** Supreme Court ruling that extended Miranda protections for police questioning and interrogation practices to juvenile offenders.

***New Jersey v. T.L.O.*:** The Supreme Court held that a school official had the authority to search the purse of a student, even though no warrant was issued and there was no probable cause that a crime had been committed.

Intake: The process during which a juvenile referral is received and a decision is made to file a petition in the juvenile court, release the juvenile, or refer the juvenile elsewhere.

Detention: Temporary care of a child alleged to be a delinquent or status offender who requires a secure custody pending court disposition.

Schall v. Martin: The Supreme Court upheld the right of the states to detain a child before trial to protect his or her welfare and the public safety.

Waiver: The voluntary relinquishing of a known right; the term also refers to waiver of a juvenile to the adult court.

Transfer: The process of sending a case from the juvenile to adult courts.

Kent v. United States: The Supreme Court decision that the waiver to adult court proceeding is a critically important stage in the juvenile justice process, and that juveniles must be afforded minimum requirements of due process of law at such proceedings.

Breed v. Jones: The Supreme Court concluded that jeopardy attaches when the juvenile court begins to hear evidence at the adjudicatory hearing; this requires that the waiver hearing take place prior to any adjudication.

Concurrent Jurisdiction: The prosecutor has the discretion of filing charges for certain offenses in either juvenile or criminal court.

Excluded Offenses: Legislature excludes certain offenses are either very minor or very serious.

Judicial Waiver: The juvenile court waives its jurisdiction and transfers the case to the criminal court.

Reverse Waiver: A judge overrules a state law that mandate that certain offenses be tried in adult court and rules that the case shall be tried in juvenile court.

Initial Appearance: The first hearing in the juvenile court process at which time the youth is informed of the charges, attorneys are appointed, bail is considered, and consideration of pretrial diversion options are considered. Similar to the arraignment in the adult court process.

Adjudication: The juvenile court decision terminating a hearing in which the juvenile is declared a delinquent or status offender or where no finding of fact is made against the youth.

Fact-Finding Hearing: Term for the trial in the juvenile justice system in which the judge hears evidence and presents a disposition.

In re Gault: The Supreme Court held that juveniles at trial faced with incarceration were entitled to many of the rights granted adult offenders; this included counsel, notice of charges, cross-examination of witnesses, and protection against self-incrimination. This case mandated a more formalized juvenile court system.

Due Process: The constitutional principle guaranteed by the Fifth, Sixth, and Fourteenth Amendments, which embodies the legal rights for children and adults in judicial proceedings.

In re Winship: The Supreme Court held that the standard of proof beyond a reasonable doubt, which is required for criminal prosecution, is also required in the adjudication of a delinquency petition.

McKeiver v. Pennsylvania: The Supreme Court decided that a trial by jury in a juvenile court's adjudicative stage is not a constitutional requirement.

Dispositional Hearing: For juvenile offenders, the disposition is the equivalent of sentencing for adult offenders. This ruling is set forth in a hearing conducted by a juvenile court judge.

Probation: A sentence entailing the conditional release of a convicted juvenile into the community under the supervision of the court subject to certain conditions.

Commitment: The decision of a judge ordering an adjudicated and sentenced juvenile offender to be placed in a correctional facility.

Deinstitutionalization: Movement to replace punishment and terms of incarceration with rehabilitation in the juvenile justice system.

Delinquency Prevention: Efforts to intervene in a young person's life to before delinquency manifests itself, thus averting problems in advance.

Chapter Outline

I. Introduction
   A. Responsibilities
      1. handle youth and juvenile crime
      2. incorrigible and truant children
      3. runaways
   B. Emphasis
      1. independent yet interrelated to the adult system
      2. originally based on surrogate parent (*parens patriae)* philosophy
      3. theme changed to legal rights in the 1960s
      4. modern focus on control of chronic delinquents
   C. Lacks comprehensive goals and purposes
      1. social welfare treatment organization
      2. crime control orientation
      3. impartial justice and due process rights
      4. balanced and restorative justice model?

II. History of juvenile justice
   A. Foundations of the juvenile court
      1. poor laws
         a. overseers indenture destitute or neglect children to train as servants
         b. Elizabethan poor laws of 1601 create added system of church wardens
         c. placed kids in poorhouses or workhouses or into apprenticeships
      2. chancery courts
         a. protection of property rights and child welfare of more affluent kids
         b. protective control of the king – guardianship and property use
         c. origin of the *parens patriae* doctrine to protect best interest of child
         d. *Wellesley v. Wellesley* - the court removes children under the doctrine of *parens patriae*
         e. major influence on development of American juvenile justice
      3. These two developments allowed the state to take control of troubled youth

B. Care of children in early America
   1. force apprenticeship and poor laws transplanted to the American colonies for wayward or destitute children
   2. serious child criminals were tried as adults
   3. middle-class intervention became the basis for the child-saving movement
   4. net widening of interventions into drinking, vagrancy, idleness and delinquency
C. The child-saving movement
   1. created programs for indigent youth
   2. youth reformatories provide family environment for street kids
      a. House of Refuge, New York (1825)
      b. Boston follows suit in 1826 with the House of Reformation
      c. state institutions open in Massachusetts and New York
   3. Children's Aid Society
      a. developed in 1853 by Charles Brace as an alternative to the harsh treatment in other juvenile institutions
      b. similar to foster care home
D. Establishment of juvenile court
   1. overwhelmed private charities and other organizations lobby for court entity
   2. Illinois Juvenile Court Act of 1899
      a. handled criminal law violations by wayward juveniles
      b. care for neglected and wayward youths
      c. created probation department
   3. most states had developed juvenile courts by 1925
   4. different rules and organization
      a. quasi-legal entity
      b. quasi-therapeutic focus
      c. personalized justice
      d. operated in "the best interests of the child"
      e. paternalistic
      f.. attorneys not required
      g. hearsay evidence admissible
      h.. verdict based on a preponderance of evidence
      i.. relaxed approach to the Fifth Amendment
E. Criticisms of the child-saving movement
   1. reforms expressed the vested interests of a particular social group
   2. continuance of middle- and upper-class values
   3. furtherance of child labor system
F. The development of the juvenile justice system
   1. reform schools
      a. billed as training schools, they were punitive in nature
      b. in the second half of the eighteenth century there was a shift from massive industrial schools to cottage system
      c. introduction of psychological treatment in 1950s
   2. Legal and legislative changes
      a. starting in 1960s, Supreme Court begins to extend due process of adults to juveniles
         i. right to trial
         ii. right to confront witnesses
         iii. right to counsel

        b.   Juvenile Justice and Delinquency Prevention Act of 1974 (JJDP)
            i..   Office of Juvenile Justice and Delinquency Prevention
            ii.   identify juvenile needs
            iii. funding for juvenile programs
            iv. separate wayward youth from delinquents and adults from kids
        c.   recent reforms rolled back allowing juvenile waiver to adult system

III.   Juvenile justice today
    A.   Two categories of offenders
        1.   delinquents
            a.   commit criminal acts
            b.   under a jurisdictional age limit
        2.   status offenders
            a.   truants
            b.   habitually disobedient children
            c.   ungovernable children
            d.   known as PINS or CHINS
    B.   Juvenile courts
        1.   jurisdiction over conduct directed at children
            a.   parental neglect
            b.   deprivation
            c.   abandonment
            d.   abuse
        2.   different maximum age statutes exist
        3.   some states exclude certain classes of offenses and offenders from juvenile courts
            a.   serious violent offenses
            b.   untreatable repeat offenders
        4.   evolved into an independent but parallel entity to adult court
        5.   similarities and differences listed
            a.   different case processing procedure vary
            b.   different terminology
        6.   courts with juvenile jurisdiction process 2 million cases annually

IV.   Police processing of the juvenile offender
    A.   1.6 million juvenile arrests per year (on the decline)
    B.   most large departments have juvenile detectives
        1.   investigate cases
        2.   take control of the case after arrest
    C.   Most jurisdictions don't have special arrest provisions for juveniles
    D.   Use of discretion (to release or detain)
        1.   type and seriousness of offense
        2.   parental ability to discipline
        3.   past contact with police
        4.   cooperation from child and parents
        5.   if child denies allegations and insists upon court hearing
    E.   Legal rights
        1.   same Fourth Amendment rights as adults
        2.   more rights than adults once taken into custody
            a.   access to parent or guardian during questioning
            b.   must be clear on youth's understanding

3. school searches
    a.   school officials may search students
    b.   school officials may search school lockers
    c.   school officials may question students
    d.   *New Jersey v. T.L.O.* - upheld warrantless search of student's purse by school official based on reasonable suspicion
    e.   use of breathalysers, drug-sniffing dogs, hidden video cameras, routine searches of students, lockers and cars permissible
    f.   *Veronia School District v. Acton* - public school athletes required to submit to random drug testing
    g.   reasonable suspicion standard applied to warrantless searches

V.   The juvenile court process
   A.   Juvenile courts process 1.7 million cases annually
      1.   delinquency cases on the rise
      2.   violent cases on the rise
      3.   drug cases on the rise
      4.   males comprise ¾ of defendants but females on the rise
   B.   The intake process
      1.   screening of the case by the juvenile court
      2.   done by intake probation officers
      3.   screen out cases not within court jurisdiction and cases not serious enough to warrant court's attention are handled informally
      4.   half of all court referrals end here
   C.   Detention
      1.   prosecutor decides to release youth to parents or hold until trial
      2.   modern emphasis on reduced use of detention but caseloads increase
      3.   most states require a hearing on the appropriateness of detention
      4.   legal criteria used in the detention hearing
         a.   protection of child
         b.   dangerousness of juvenile
         c.   likelihood of absconding
         d.   *Schall v. Martin* Supreme Court upheld right of states to detain a child to protect his or her welfare
      5.   reforming juvenile detention
         a.   separation of status offenders and delinquents
         b.   removing youths from adult jails
         c.   removal of juveniles from adult facilities
   D.   Bail
      1.   Court has not ruled on juvenile bail
      2.   most states emphasize release to parents as acceptable bail alternative
   E.   Plea bargaining
      1.   juvenile court terms: "agree to a finding" or "deny the petition"
      2.   procedural safeguards
         a.   know of right to a trial
         b.   plea made voluntarily
         c.   understand charges and consequences
      3.   little plea bargaining exists in juvenile court
   F.   The waiver of jurisdiction
      1.   transfer hearing determines if case gets sent to adult criminal court

2. statutory provision guides what cases can be transferred
   a. age
   b. nature of offense
   c. offense history
3. *Kent v. United States* - juveniles must be afforded minimum requirements of due process in waiver proceeding
4. *Breed v. Jones* - adjudication in juvenile courts followed by prosecution as an adult is double jeopardy
5. juveniles tried in adult courts in one of four ways
   a. concurrent jurisdiction
   b. excluded offences
   c. judicial waiver
   d. reverse waiver
6. less than 1% of all cases are waive into adult court
   a. 8 in every 1,000 cases
   b. waivers peaked in 1994
   c. equal numbers of property and violent offenses
7. criticisms of waivers
   a. sentences not always fair or equitable
   b. ineffective, inefficient, and out of step philosophically
8. support for waivers
   a. get the most serious offenders off the streets for longer
   b. most waived juveniles are not placed in adult facilities until age of 18

G. Juvenile trial
1. initial appearance similar to an arraignment precedes trial
   a. informed of rights
   b. appointed counsel
   c. bail
   d. sometimes case is settled with admission of facts and sentence
   e. bound over to trial
2. trial or fact-finding hearing
   a.. traditional hearing
      i. used to diagnosis and rehabilitate children
      ii. nonadversarial and informal in nature
      iii. criticized as punishment under the guise of treatment
3. post *In re Gault* (1967) hearing
   a. due process orientation adopted
   b. notice of charges, right to legal representation, right to confront and cross-exam witnesses and privilege against self-incrimination implemented
   c. *In re Winship* requires proof beyond a reasonable doubt
   d. *McKeiver v. Pennsylvania* - trial by a jury of peers is not guaranteed
   e. court enters judgement against child after hearing concludes
   f. dispositions imposed

H. Alternatives to trial – teen courts
1. supplement the traditional juvenile adjudication process
2. 300 in existence nationwide
3. handle cases of 10-15 year old with no prior record and minor charge
4. youth volunteer to have case heard in teen court
5. youth serve as court workgroup members
6. innovative dispositions

7. use peer approval and peer pressure on youth
8. four potential benefits
    a. accountability
    b. timeliness
    c. cost savings
    d. community cohesion
9. lower recidivism rates

I. Disposition and treatment
    1. Use of two-part hearing
        a. the fact-finding section
        b. the disposition or sentencing section
        c. preferred option because it allows use of different evidentiary standards
    2. Disposition is geared toward individualized treatment with numerous options

J. Juvenile sentencing reform
    1. traditional use of indeterminate sentence in order to achieve rehabilitation
    2. modern conservative reforms include waiver into adult court, determinate sentences, mandatory prison terms, and the death penalty
    3. status offender reforms
        a. use of diversion and community programs
        b. avoid institutionalization
    4. shift to just deserts model
        a. Washington state and the determinate sentencing law
        b. many jurisdictions continue to emphasize rehabilitation

VI. The juvenile correctional process
  A. More than 100,00 youth in secure facilities
  B. Juvenile probation
    1. the most commonly used formal sentence
    2. supervision carried out by juvenile probation department
    3. use of community treatment and reliance on conditions of probation
    4. modern use of a balanced probation approach
  C. Institutionalization
    1. commitment
        a. training school
        b. private residential facility
        c. length of sentence varies
    2. 95% of incarcerated youth are serving time for delinquency offenses
    3. Profile of incarcerated youth
        a. 70% in public facilities, 30% in private
        b. typical inmates is 15 year old white male
        c. mostly property, person or drug offenders
        d. minority youth incarcerated at higher rate than whites
  D. Deinstitutionalisation
    1. large facilities are costly and produce more sophisticated criminals
    2. replace with smaller, community-based facilities
    3. the DSO movement based on treatment and normalization
    4. impact of Juvenile Justice and Delinquency Prevention Act of 1974
  E. Aftercare
    1. final stage in juvenile justice process
    2. help with transition to free society
    3. supervision and support programs

                        4.   parole is popular

VII.   Preventing delinquency
        A.   Shift from control to advanced prevention
        B.   Community strategies
                1.   diverse options and agencies
                2.   comprehensive planning model
                3.   Children at Risk
                4.   Communities That Care (CTC)
                5.   Safe Futures Initiative
                        a.   targets youth providers and participants
                        b.   Juvenile Mentoring Program (JUMP)
        C.   Enforcement strategies
                1.   combining treatment with enforcement
                2.   targeting teen gun use
        D.   Should the juvenile court be abolished?
                1.   questions over effectiveness have been raised recently
                2.   Barry Feld argues that court should be discontinued and replaced by
                        alternative
                        a.   dual welfare and enforcement roles doom it to failure
                        b.   enforcement role subordinates the rehabilitation
                        c.   proposes civil liability vs. adult court alternative based on age
                3.   John Johnson Kerbs supports status quo and disputes Feld's assertions

Chapter Summary

The **juvenile justice system** deals with two categories of juvenile offenders: **delinquents** and **status offenders**. Early juvenile courts were based on the philosophy of *parens patriae*; that is, the idea that the state was to act on behalf of the parent in the interest of the child. This philosophy and the separation of juvenile and adult justice have their roots in the English **poor laws** and the **chancery courts**. Although the chancery courts were primarily concerned with protecting property rights, their authority extended to the welfare of children in general. The forced apprenticeship of the poor laws came to colonial America, but a **child-saver** movement influenced state and local governments to create a system designed to eliminate harsh discipline and poor quality physical care from the lives of destitute and neglected children. The child-saver movement also emphasized the need for a court system separate from that of the adult system to deal with children. This was followed in the early 20th century by the **Children's Aid Society** that sought to place troubled city children with rural families. Children were also placed in repressive **reform schools** that stressed punishment and hard work.

The first comprehensive juvenile court was established in Illinois in 1899. In its early form, the juvenile court was considered paternalistic and provided youth with quasi-legal, personalized justice. In the 1960's and 1970's, the Supreme Court radically altered the juvenile justice system by ruling on a series of cases which established due process rights for juveniles. Supreme Court cases such as *Kent v. United States*, *In re Gault*, and *In re Winship* made the juvenile justice process more similar to its adult counterpart. Juveniles have not, however, been granted a constitutional right to a jury trial. Today, the juvenile court seeks to promote the rehabilitation of the child within a framework of procedural **due process**.

During the investigation and arrest stages of the juvenile process, the police generally have more discretion than they do when dealing with adult offenders. School officials also have a great deal of discretion in dealing with children. This is especially true in school searches, where a child does not have the protections against unwarranted searches. Once taken into custody, however, the juvenile is protected by most of the procedural safeguards awarded to adults -- including the cases such as *Fare v. Michael C*. and *New Jersey v. T.L.O.* have extended the substantive rights such as the right to counsel and the privilege against self-incrimination to juvenile offenders. Juveniles have not, however, been granted a constitutional right to a jury trial.

After arrest and before trial, the juvenile defendant is processed through a number of stages which may include **intake, detention, bail, waiver hearing** and **diversion** programs. As a further distinction from the adult justice system, the Supreme Court, in the case of *Schall v. Martin*, upheld the right of the states to detain a child before trial in order to protect their welfare and the public safety. There are, however, serious issues in juvenile detention including the problems related to youths being detained in adult jails. Another important issue in the juvenile justice system is the waiver process which **transfers** juvenile offenders to adult criminal courts. There are four main forms of waivers (**concurrent jurisdiction, excluded offenses, judicial waiver, and reverse waiver**) that can be used when issues of transfer arise. Cases such as *Kent v. United States* and *Breed v. Jones* have defined the proper constitutional use of juvenile transfer.

Juvenile court proceedings begin with the **initial appearance**, which mirrors the arraignment in the adult system. Next comes the **adjudication** stage in which a **fact-finding hearing** replaces the adult trial. The judge presides over this hearing. Juvenile court judges have broad discretionary power in the sentencing of juveniles with **dispositions** ranging from dismissal to probation to institutional commitment. Recent trends in sentencing include the "get tough" approach with dangerous offenders, the removal of status and minor offenders from the system, and a shift in philosophy to the concept of "just deserts." Despite these trends, most jurisdictions continue to focus on rehabilitation as a primary dispositional goal. This is evident in recent federal court decisions which have indicated that youth who are committed to a juvenile institution have a "right" to receive treatment.

Fill-in-the-Blank Questions

1. Under the philosophy of _____ _____, the state is to act on behalf of the parents in the interests of the child.

2. The balanced and restorative justice model calls for _____, program _____, and _____ _____.

3. The modern practice of legally separating adult and juvenile offenders can be traced to two developments in English customs and law: the development of the _____ _____ and the _____ _____.

4. The _____ _____ were middle-class reformers who influenced state and local governments to create institutions called reform schools to take care of vagrant and criminal youths.

333

5. The juvenile courts are normally established by state legislation and exercise jurisdiction over two distinct categories of juvenile offenders – _____ and _____ offenders.

6. In the juvenile court process, the _____ _____ is the term for first hearing similar to the arraignment in adult court and the _____ - _____ hearing follows that resembles the trial in adult court.

7. The screening of cases by the juvenile court system is called the _____ stage.

8. The _____ hearing is the proceeding in which the court decides on the most appropriate treatment for a delinquent.

9. _____ is the most commonly used formal sentence for juvenile offenders.

10. Probation involves placing the child under the supervision of the juvenile _____ _____ for the purpose of _____ _____.

11. The case _____ v. _____ upheld the constitutional right to treatment for institutionalized youth.

12. The most severe of the statutory dispositions available to the juvenile court involves _____ of the child to an _____.

13. The disproportionate number of minority youths incarcerated may mean that African-Americans, Hispanics, and other minorities are more likely to be _____ and _____ with _____ crimes than are white youths.

14. _____ means removing non-criminal youths convicted on status offenses from institutions housing delinquents.

15. Although community-based programs are no panaceas, many experts still recommend more _____ and less _____ for juvenile offenders.

True/False Questions

T F 1. The juvenile justice system is primarily responsible for dealing with juvenile and youth crime, not incorrigible or truant children.

T F 2. Reform schools were not racially and sexually segregated.

T F 3. A delinquent refers to participation in criminal acts by children under a certain age.

T F 4. Juvenile court jurisdiction is established by state statute.

T F 5. The first juvenile court was established in Boston in 1911.

T F 6.   The *Miranda* warning is not required for the interrogation of juveniles.

T F 7.   Experts believe that one reason for the increase use of detention for juveniles may be the involvement of younger children in the juvenile justice system.

T F 8.   The Supreme Court has ruled that juvenile offenders have a constitutional right to bail.

T F 9.   The decision of whether to waive a juvenile to the adult or criminal court is made in an adult court waiver hearing.

T F 10.   Concurrent jurisdiction means that the prosecutor has the discretion of filing charges for certain offenses in either juvenile or criminal court.

T F 11.   The fact-finding hearing in juvenile court is the same as a trial in criminal court.

T F 12.   The judge has broad discretionary powers in the disposition stage in juvenile court.

T F 13.   Teen courts are run by teenagers instead of adults.

T F 14.   Today, most states do not require a youth to fail on probation before being sent to an institution (unless the criminal act is serious).

T F 15.   Most incarcerated juvenile offenders are held for status offenses.

T F 16.   State statutes do not vary much when determining the length of the child's commitment to an institution.

T F 17.   The typical juvenile inmate is a white male.

T F 18.   Despite the daily rhetoric on crime control, public support for community-based programs for juveniles still exists.

T F 19.   Chronic juvenile offenders are youths who are most likely to continue their law-violating behavior.

T F 20.   Juvenile parolees have a right to the same due process requirements for revocation of parole as do adults.

Multiple Choice Questions

1.   The _____ were the laws that provided for the appointment of overseers to indenture destitute or neglected children as servants.
     a.   indenture laws
     b.   neglected laws
     c.   chancery laws
     d.   poor laws

2. The _____ were the courts concerned primarily with protecting property rights, although their authority extended to the welfare of children in general.
   a. chancery courts
   b. common courts
   c. courts of appeals
   d. magistrate courts

3. _____ is the famous English case where a duke's children were taken from him in the name of *parens patriae* because of his scandalous behavior.
   a. *Smithe v. Smithe*
   b. *Breed v. Jones*
   c. *Wellesley v. Wellesley*
   d. *Morales v. Turman*

4. The forced apprenticeship system and the poor laws were brought from _____ to colonial America.
   a. Australia
   b. England
   c. France
   d. Germany

5. In the mid 1800s, a _____ was used to house vagrant, criminal, and neglected children.
   a. reform school
   b. house of refuge
   c. jail
   d. a and b

6. Which of the following nineteenth century programs were similar to modern foster home programs?
   a. the house of refuge
   b. the Children's Aid Society
   c. the Child Savers United Agency
   d. the typical house of reformation

7. When the juvenile court movement spread across the United States, _____ became the main concern of the new juvenile courts.
   a. constitutional rights
   `b. due process of law
   c. best interests of the child
   d. strict adherence to legal doctrine

8. _____ is the standard for verdicts in the juvenile courts.
   a. proof beyond a reasonable doubt
   b. preponderance of the evidence
   c. clear and convincing proof
   d. moral certainty

9. The legal category _____ includes truants, incorrigibles, and runaways.
    a. delinquents
    b. status offenders
    c. youth offenders
    d. youth criminals

10. The Supreme Court held in _____ that a school official had the authority to search the purse of a student, even though no warrant was issued and there was no probable cause that a crime had been committed; there was only suspicion that the student had violated school rules.
    a. *Veronia School District v. Acton*
    b. *Smith v. Massachusetts Teachers' Union*
    c. *Jones v. Davis*
    d. *New Jersey v. T.L.O.*

11. In _____, the Supreme Court said that urine testing of student athletes is constitutional even though the student does not engage in suspicious behavior.
    a. *Veronia School District v. Acton*
    b. *Smith v. Massachusetts Teachers' Union*
    c. *Jones v. Davis*
    d. *New Jersey v. T.L.O.*

12. The intake process is critically important because more than _____ the referrals to the juvenile courts never go beyond this stage.
    a. one-fourth
    b. one-third
    c. one-half
    d. two-thirds

13. The Supreme Court in _____ said that the waiver proceeding is a critically important stage in the juvenile justice process, and that juveniles must be afforded minimum requirements of due process of law at such proceedings.
    a. *Kent v. United States*
    b. *In re Winship*
    c. *In re Gault*
    d. *Breed v. Jones*

14. What is considered to be the centerpiece of the juvenile justice system?
    a. the police
    b. the delinquent
    c. the juvenile probation department
    d. the juvenile court

15. The Supreme Court in _____ ruled that the concept of fundamental fairness is applicable to juvenile delinquency proceedings.
    a. *Kent v. United States*
    b. *In re Winship*
    c. *In re Gault*
    d. *Breed v. Jones*

16. The juvenile court retains jurisdiction over a child until when?
    a. until the child completes the rehabilitation plan
    b. until the child reaches the age of majority
    c. until the child turns seventeen
    d. until the child successfully petitions for waiver into adult court

17. In the _____ decision, the Supreme Court said that trial by jury in a juvenile court's adjudicative stage is not a constitutional requirement.
    a. *Martarella v. Kelly*
    b. *Inmates v Affleck*
    c. *Morales v. Turman*
    d. *McKeiver v. Pennsylvania*

18. The rate of incarceration for non-Hispanic black inmates is almost _____ times higher than the white incarceration rate.
    a. 3
    b. 5
    c. 7
    d. 10

19. Approximately, _____ percent of incarcerated juveniles are held for delinquent offenses – offenses that would be crimes if committed by adults.
    a. 65
    b. 75
    c. 85
    d. 95

20. About how many juvenile arrests occur each year?
    a. 1.6 million
    b. 2 million
    c. 3.4 million
    d. 12 million

21. _____ are those who commit a disproportionate amount of juvenile crime.
    a. delinquents
    b. status offenders
    c. chronic offenders
    d. repeat offenders

22. Which stage in the juvenile justice process is considered to be critically important because more than half of all cases never go beyond this stage?
    a. bail
    b. intake
    c. detention
    d. trial

23. Programs such as the SafeFutures Initiative and Children at Risk are examples of what strategy?
    a. early prevention
    b. aftercare
    c. enforcement
    d. crime control

24. Recent programs that seek to control the spread of teenage gun use fall under the heading of:
    a. early prevention
    b. aftercare
    c. community strategies
    d. enforcement strategies

25. Deinstitutionalization efforts are principally focused on what type of offenses?
    a. drug offenses
    b. property offenses
    c. delinquency offenses
    d. status offenses

26. For how long must a gun-carrying student be expelled under The Gun-Free Schools Act of 1994?
    a. one week
    b. one month
    c. six months
    d. one year

Essay Questions

1. Compare and contrast the efforts of the child savers with those of the Children's Aid Society.

2. Discuss the shifts in US juvenile justice philosophy that have occurred since the 19th century.

3. Discuss the factors that are believed to be significant in police decision making regarding juvenile offenders.

4. Compare and contrast the juvenile justice system and the adult criminal justice system.

5. List the criteria most state juvenile courts provide to support the decision to detain a child.

6. Discuss the legal right of school personnel to search a student's locker.

7. Explain the four ways states allow juveniles to be tried as adults in the criminal courts.

8. Compare and contrast the structure and function of juvenile and teen court.

9. Discuss the three reform efforts that have been undertaken in the area of juvenile sentencing.

10. Describe the Juvenile Mentoring Program (JUMP) in terms of its structure and goals.

CHAPTER 17 ANSWER KEY

FILL-IN-THE-BLANK QUESTIONS

1. *parens patriae*
2. accountability, development, community protection
3. poor laws, chancery court
4. child savers
5. delinquents, status
6. initial appearance, fact finding
7. intake
8. dispositional
9. probation
10. probation department, community treatment
11. Nelson, Heyne
12. commitment, institution
13. arrested, charged, serious
14. deinstitutionalization
15. treatment, incarceration

TRUE/FALSE QUESTIONS

1.	F	11.	T
2.	F	12.	T
3.	T	13.	T
4.	T	14.	F
5.	F	15.	F
6.	F	16.	F
7.	T	17.	T
8.	F	18.	T
9.	F	19.	T
10.	T	20.	F

MULTIPLE CHOICE QUESTIONS

1.	D	14.	D
2.	A	15.	C
3.	C	16.	B
4.	B	17.	D
5.	D	18.	B
6.	B	19.	D
7.	C	20.	B
8.	B	21.	C
9.	B	22.	B
10.	D	23.	A
11.	A	24.	D
12.	C	25.	D
13.	A	26.	D